Sabine Lichtenfels

TEMPLE OF LOVE

A Journey into the Age of Sensual Fulfilment

About the book: An adventurous journey from the stone circle of Almendres in Portugal to the temples of Malta becomes a journey through a new hologram of history. Every event, every temple visit and also every difficulty is guided and thereby unexpected and unpredictable. Sabine Lichtenfels – with her mediumistic talent – shows simply and modestly what it means to travel in full trust under divine guidance. The temples of Malta act as antennae to the past for her and transmit descriptions and pictures of the culture that had once erected these buildings. This information gives a breathtaking view into a highly developed fulfilling and sensual life – at a time where we once thought that primitive people were running around with axes!

For the author, this view into the past is simultaneously a beginning of a humane future. The Temple of Love is to be recreated in the light of modern knowledge, in practical life between men and women in model communities for a future without war.

First edition
© 2011 Verlag Meiga GbR
Monika Berghoff • Saskia Breithardt
Waldsiedlung 15 • D-14806 Belzig
Tel. +49 (0) 33841 30538 • Fax: +49 (0) 33841 38550
info@verlag-meiga.org • **www.verlag-meiga.org**

Translated from the German
by Anna Bandini and Douglas Baillie

Original Title: *Tempel der Liebe*

ISBN: 978-3-927266-44-5
Cover Photo: Nigel Dickinson
Layout: Nadine Eberle, Juliane Paul
Printed by Lightning Source Ltd. UK/USA

Contents

Foreword

All knowledge is remembering
Plato

Everyone has the past that he deserves
Graffiti on a house in Berlin

What if the history that we learn from our history books is rather incomplete? What if our past was not just a series of wars and conquests? What if it turns out that our view of the past was so far highly one-sided? And what if our perception has been greatly influenced by patterns of interpretation that belong to a cruel but transitory age?

Those who work wholeheartedly for a positive peaceful future look for and need a different interpretation of history. If the human being were always an "intelligent monster" whose violent drives could only be restrained by threats of punishment, how would he then be able to live peacefully in the future?

But maybe everything was completely different. Historians are starting to admit that the present age of violence and fear is a barbaric but short period of only a few thousand years that interrupted a much longer time of peaceful development of high cultures. It is possible that human beings were originally able to live in peace. The last few peaceful tribes still in existence could be the dispersed remnants of a former global peace-culture. If this is really true, as archaeological finds seem to show, then part of the peace work of the future is to remember our past correctly.

Sabine Lichtenfels undertook an adventurous journey to do exactly that. Equipped with a talent for intuition and perception by means of inner resonance, with an unorthodox way of thinking and with discipline for the tasks of her inner voice, with decades of experience in creating community, in peace work and in conflict research, she followed the traces of the ancient culture on Malta. She had used these skills previously in her research into the stone circle culture of Portugal[1].

About six thousand years ago, a temple culture existed on the island of Malta. Megaliths and a variety of overground and underground temples and small female figurines are still to be found there. It was clearly a society without weapons or defensive fortifications, a culture which suddenly disappeared about 2500 years before Christ without any signs of violence, and a culture which still provides riddles for today's researchers.

What Sabine Lichtenfels discovered – through her dreams, her intuition, in her daily experiences and through her mediumistic research into the ancient temples – she describes here. Her story reveals itself before our eyes as excitingly as a thriller. As if searching for the right radio channel, she looks within herself for the frequency which is in resonance with a possible peaceful past. And she asks how we today, in the midst of our modern world, can create this resonance with a culture in which Eros was sacred. A culture in which there was no fight between the genders and in which women protected the innermost knowledge, a culture in which the Goddess was always present and every being and every thing was sacred.

Sabine Lichtenfels persistently overcomes, step by step, the confusion, doubts, habits and morals of today's culture. She succeeds in this to the extent to which she entrusts herself to her inner guidance.

From the very beginning she encounters a historical power which outlasted the ages, a personification of everything in the female soul that could not be controlled: Lilith.

Lilith is the name of a female knowledge which knows most intimately the destiny of every woman – the fire of first love, the lust of female desire, the pain of abandonment and the tears of every mother. She has herself experienced social exclusion and the fight against all that is female. She knows stamina beyond all hope, and everlasting new beginning. She has also been seducer and avenging angel; she knows anger, malice and fight. Lilith went through all of these, embraced them within herself and transformed them into deeply humane knowledge and deeply humane power.

Taken by her hand, we discover a culture which had sensual female knowledge and grace at its core. In this culture, that which is today forbidden and proscribed was the most sacred and deserved the greatest attention: lust, the power of Eros and the mutual joy of the genders. The knowledge of creation of true joy of life and joy in the body was the basis for living fearlessly and non-violently over the millennia.

This is the actual core of this book: the connection of the sacred and the sexual as a secret of a peaceful and fulfilled life. This is also the message for all those who try to build a new peaceful culture today: end the exclusion of Eros. Discover it and give it new life as a sacred source of joy and power. Discover its humane core, disconnected from entanglement with violence, commercialisation and false morals. Work together, men and women, youngsters and adults: end envy and competition and the war of the genders. Put healing Eros on the altar of your hearts and of the communities which must be built.

I wish for readers of this book to allow themselves to be touched by the power of Lilith and by the vision of a sensually knowing way of life, just as I was, and from this to draw consequences for their own life.

For the children of the future.

Leila Dregger, journalist
Berlin, May 2009

INTRODUCTION

The foundations of this book were laid at the time when I finished writing the book *Traumsteine* ("Dreamstones")[14]. I had already been living for some years in Portugal, where I had founded *Tamera** with Dieter Duhm and others. The founding of Tamera and the choice of its location were intimately connected with the Almendres stone circle, close to Évora in Portugal, which I had found while looking for land. Since then I had visited Almendres regularly and had undertaken various investigations and spiritual experiments.

During one of my visits to Almendres, I received the call from my inner voice to also follow the historical trail of the stone circle to Malta.

I decided to finish the book *Traumsteine* on the island of Malta. There I received such new and comprehensive information that it was impossible to integrate everything into one book. Also the way in which I received information on Malta was very different from how I had received information in Almendres. In Almendres I received information from single stones, usually verbally, almost as if I was talking to a single person. On Malta I usually saw the information playing in front of my eyes like a film.

Also, the unusual events in my everyday life on the island accumulated in such a way that I could not ignore them in my report. Many experiences that intensified towards the end of my journey gave clear evidence that I was under guidance.

In the beginning there was much confusion. I almost had the impression that opposing powers did not want to allow me to access the original information. Later this perception was dispelled by unusually precise experiences of inner guidance. Whether full contact with this cosmic guidance could be created or not and whether opposing powers could disturb me or not, was ultimately determined by how fully

---

* See 'Projects of Sabine Lichtenfels' p. 272 (publisher's note)

I was ready to leave fear behind and to trust. This attitude of trust was also the reason that it was not possible for me to distrustfully check the historical validity of all the new information that I had received through trances or intuition.

The Central Issue of Love and Sexuality

The issue of love and sexuality was so central to the journey and to the information that I received that I did not publish this manuscript for a long time as I had the feeling that the information was too intimate and too personal for a wider public. But my inner voice repeatedly admonished me not to forget the Malta manuscript. Several years have now passed. For a long time I have known that I am on earth to make a special contribution to the issue of love and sexuality from a female perspective. The insight that love is not a private matter but a political issue of the highest importance had already been the guiding motif for my actions even before I knew much about the political and historical connections.

In school we had read Sophocles's drama about Antigone. I had admired the power with which she rebelled against the tyrant Creon and shouted "It is my nature to join in love, not hate!" King Creon sentenced her to death with the justification "I am not the man, not now: she is the man if this victory goes to her and she goes free."

This is how I already understood at an early age the central role of the fight between the genders in many political decisions that lead to war and destruction.

During my theology studies I had to accept that the core of the history of Western religion consisted of a fight against women and against all that is female. It was based on violence and extermination of others. I only got to know much later that there had been cultures in which the female had been honoured and held sacrosanct.

The suppression of the female did not succeed despite all efforts. In many cultures the sacred Virgin Mother receives more attention than her son Jesus Christ. But even then, she is still only a distorted representation of this original sacred female elementary power.

How could a culture develop which perceives a large part of humankind – women – as inferior beings? Why have humans so far been unable to unite the two poles, male and female, in creative symbiosis and mutual completion?

Charity might be accorded high importance in the Christian religion but in reality society works against it. For a long time I have searched for the background of our historical dilemma. Eventually I had to accept that the cause was false axioms in love, especially in the area of sexual love.

Sensual and sexual love were degraded early in history to become the root of all evil. But how should charity be possible while we are fighting against the innermost core of love, the sensual and physical basis of life? Humankind has trapped itself for thousands of years in a cage of hostile morals, conventions and prohibitions.

The books of Karlheinz Deschner gave me the power to finish my theology studies despite the many disappointments. Through spirits like him I found the courage and power for truth. He wrote, "But the truth is, from Saint Paul to Saint Augustine, from the scholastics to the notorious Pius Popes of the fascist era, the leading spirits of the Catholic Church have bred an eternal fear of sex, sexual disorders and a unique atmosphere of sexual prudery and hypocritical suppression, aggression and guilt complexes. They have surrounded the entire life of the human being, his joy of existence and sensuality, his biological lust-processes and his access to passion, from childhood until old-age, with moral taboos, systematically created shame, fear and inner crises and then exploited him – out of pure greed for domination or because they themselves were suppressing their sexual drives. As they had been tortured themselves, so they tortured others, literally and figuratively."[2]

How can one really love one's neighbour, whether a man or a woman, if the biological base of mutual sensual recognition is excluded from the outset? Did the human being have so little trust in creation that he considered his original loving impulses so wicked that he encaged and forbade them? If he already denies the truth of life on a biological level, how should he then honour creation and become able to love?

Karlheinz Deschner: "Eaten away by envy and at the same time cleverly calculating, they perverted for their followers the most harmless and the most joyful: the feeling or perception of lust and the practice of love. The church has perverted almost all values of sexual life, has labelled the good bad, and bad good, degraded what is moral to immoral and twisted the positive into negative. It prevented or hindered the fulfilment of natural desires but elevated the fulfilment of unnatural commandments into a duty, on pain of loss of eternal life and highly barbaric punishments here on Earth."[2]

I specifically want to emphasise here that with these words I do not intend to judge those who authentically serve the world and serve love within the Church and within religious structures. They all have my deep respect.

But in the context of this book I also want to point out the destructive aspect of the church and religion, as its fatal consequences have still not been seen clearly enough.

THE EARLY ANCIENT CULTURES AS A POSITIVE SOURCE FOR FEMALE LIFE

I was looking for positive sources for female life and I found the roots of early ancient cultures. It is becoming more widely recognised that religion bound to a Father God was preceded by a religion bound to a great Mother Goddess. In Sumer, Babylon, Mesopotamia, Egypt and on Crete: mother goddesses originally existed everywhere. And everywhere, patriarchy set in and male gods showed up.

The oldest social relationship is that between mother and child. The female body was considered to be analogous with earth and the fertility of life. All life comes out of the female body; this fact was celebrated in the earliest religions. We find statues of mother goddesses everywhere, striking in their impersonal but fully sexual character. The Great Mother who was honoured in nature sometimes shows up as a voluptuous woman, sometimes as a fish, pig, she-goat, toad, cow or mare. She is the caretaker of all life and the guardian of life and death; She is the embodiment of beauty and sensual love; She is the gate to sexual fulfilment; She stands guard over human beings, animals and plants, and embodies all elements. Before Christianity took over the fish as a symbol of the Eucharist, it was the symbol of fertility.

"She (the Goddess) reflects the circle of natural life, especially the generative powers. As She destroys, so She creates, and as She kills, so She reawakens. Night and day, birth and death, becoming and passing away, the horror of life and its joy all come from the same source, from the womb of the Great Mother. All beings proceed from and return to Her."[2]

But how did these cultures live? What kinds of relationships did they have with each other? As these times lie before written history, we know only little about them. And especially, how did the cultural historical change occur? When and why did the male god arrive on the scene? Was he a cruel god from the very beginning? Was the ceremony of the sacred marriage of early cultures a transition? In this ceremony and in the fertility rituals which extended into the culture of Dionysus, there was a time when male and female gods coexisted and united. But eventually the female was displaced.

When I came into contact with the stone circle and later with Malta, I received sophisticated information which gave me an insight into the sensual and sacred life of the early ancient cultures. The traces I found gave an impression of great joy and mutual recognition of the genders. But I also found traces which brought me to an understanding of the sexual background of the arrival of violence. Without the sexual-historical background, the cultural change which occurred everywhere can hardly be understood. Only with this background can it be understood why women allowed themselves to be displaced and why men enthroned male gods and equipped them at first with phallic symbols of potency while all that was female was transformed into evil and life-devouring. In my book "Dreamstones", in the story of Manu and Meret, I tried to describe this process of the soul which must have simultaneously occurred in a similar way in many other cultures. It is essential to the understanding of the temple culture on Malta. This is why this book also starts with this story.

Regarding Proof of Historical Validity

As I receive most of this information mediumistically, I have only little evidence that these cultures actually existed in the form I describe here. Many scientists currently agree that cultures directed by women did exist, but leave open the question of non-violence.

On Malta, no signs of a violent intervention in the ancient culture are to be found. And yet, the people there must have disappeared suddenly. This is a riddle for the scientists. How and why did this legendary culture which erected these huge temples disappear as noiselessly as it appeared?

If I concentrate in my work too much on the question of whether my statements are in line with historians' reality, my mediumistic ability is usually immediately diminished.

On the one hand, I found much in the traces I saw that is consistent with history and on the other hand, my intuition contradicts conventional written history. Finally I decided to follow my intuition fully without asking too early about its objectivity. The dream I saw is anchored deeply and objectively enough in the longing of the human soul to bring it into the light of recollection for many people.

I also did not aim for scientific precision concerning dates. My aim is to present a cultural concept which was able to create peace for many millennia. From my perspective it seems as if violence did not have any significant role on earth before the appearance of patriarchy. In this, I substantially contradict statements of written history.

When I write about countries or areas, I usually use the names that are used today to avoid confusion, even if I am quoting a priestess of ancient Malta. Only when I received clear information about names, which was especially the case concerning people, did I use them. Of course, I researched these names after my journey, to see if they have shown up sometime in history. And I found some surprises; the results are in the appendix*. Some things remain in the dark. For example I do not know if there is a connection between the Nammu I mention here and the Nammu who was worshipped as a Great Mother in Sumer. I had already received the name clearly in a trance in Almendres and again on Malta even though I had never heard it before.

Yet I am sure, due to many experiences and through confirmations in books, that my vision is based on historical reality. I want to follow the beautiful image of Alfons Rosenberg which he describes in his work *Die Christliche Bildmeditation*: "One could compare the historical core of the legend with the grain of sand which enters an oyster and is surrounded by the oyster, as a defence against the unknown source of pain, by the finest layers of lime until a shining ball, a pearl, develops from the rough grain. An analogy of complete beauty. Such a pearl is the legend, in which the time, place and circumstances have united with the causal personality. The basic historical event is then surrounded by stories and interpretations within which the facts remain inherent. This is why a legend says more about the character of a human being or an event than the bare historical report

* See 'Some Remarks about Names, Places and Symbols', p. 259 (publisher's note)

which can be important to archive facts. The legend puts the sense of these facts into words or into an image."[20]

My pressing question regarding the objectivity of my intuition was answered in a completely different way. I was continually amazed how precisely inner guidance functioned and how closely the dreams in which I had seen Malta corresponded with reality. Later I was asked in the stone circle Almendres to visit the Toda tribe living in India, so I visited them, in the Nilgiri mountains and was astounded how much of their daily life is still living evidence that they have their roots in a completely humane and female form of culture that is similar to the one described in this book.

THE WAY THIS BOOK IS STRUCTURED

I report here not only about my discoveries but also about the many experiences which enabled me to fathom the depths of the secrets of the temple. I report on the experiences of guidance and coincidence through my cosmic companions, about the confusions and the first temple visits. It is important to me that readers obtain an impression of the way I live and work, as I entered the frequency I needed for insight into the ancient cultures only by following the intuition and information of my inner guidance very precisely in the present. Elements of the prehistoric past continually extended physically into my present reality. Sexual experiences were part of that.

Some readers may be surprised that I describe in detail spiritual situations with which they have never in their life had contact. Others may be disturbed by the sexual experiences and think that they lower the spiritual character of the book. But this is a specific main purpose of the book: to bring these two aspects together, to be understood once more in one context. Those who can bear the tension might make a new discovery.

16

I tell in narrative form of the visions and trances which showed me the historical life of the ancient cultures.

For example we get to know the young priestess-to-be Nudime who leads us through the temples of ancient Malta. Almost all names mentioned here I received in dreams and trances. Only a few I added later.

Consequences for My Own Life

The experiences described here led to consequences in my personal life. Together with Dieter Duhm, my long-term life partner, I had created a contemporary peace school in Tamera where the foundations for a humane life practice can be studied. This vision has been further nourished through my experiences on Malta.

It is also surely no coincidence that Dieter Duhm and I, while dealing with completely different issues at completely different locations, found exactly the same name for this school. While I was on Malta I had a telephone conversation with him while he was in Portugal in which he told me that he thought about naming the developing peace school in Tamera, *Mirja**. He couldn't give a specific reason except that he liked the sound of the word. I was very surprised because I had received the first information about the temples of love on Malta during a trance on the same day, and I got to know that the female servants of love were called *Mirja*, here and also in the stone circle. Maybe there is often a positive past extending into our present action without us being aware of it.

May the matrix of our positive origin provide our present actions with high power and effectiveness – for lived peace and for the generations which will come after us. May the future find a wiser and more peaceful human being on planet earth than is found in our time.

* *Pronounced 'Mirya' (translator's note)*

LILITH

Lilith is continually mentioned in this book. For me, Lilith embodies female knowledge throughout history, which has now reached a higher level of insight. Together with Lilith, I want to say that the many cultural-historical experiences of fear, hatred, anger, revenge, of victim- and perpetrator-hood, of dawn and dusk of various cultures, religious obsession, megalomania and intrigue, heroism and martyrdom may have made us more intelligent. It is as if the first human beings awaken from a long nightmare and realise their original connection and affinity which lies beyond all religions. The last great pain will be the pain of insight. Maybe the human being as a species is now ready to manifest a dream of life which has been the great longing of their heart, their cells and their higher consciousness since ancient times and which will not rest until it has found fulfilment. This dream of life cannot be achieved through conquests or preaching. Only an authentic experience is able to open our hearts again and enable them to see the universal love which radiates with a new light through the whole of existence. May this book help many people to rediscover and walk the path of their own heart.

THE STORY OF MANU AND MERET

The 96 stones of the Almendres stone circle are distributed over a hill close to Évora, in the landscape of the Portuguese Alentejo. My investigations into this stone circle became for me both an inner and an outer adventure. I discovered deep connections in cultural history. I found that I could access information that seemed to be stored within the stones. In this way, a culture and a story from prehistory revealed itself to me. My book *Traumsteine* describes this[14].

Long ago in this area there lived a tribe: a peace culture of high standing. I could see it ever more clearly with my inner eye. Thus I came to know more about the connection between birth, death and rebirth. I also received information about the possibilities of telepathic communication. The members of the tribe communicated telepathically with each other and also with plants, animals, other tribes and extra-terrestrial beings. I came into contact with a non-violent culture. I researched these connections especially deeply as they are also relevant to the present and to the life we live today. It was as if I had come into contact with a generalisable version of a universal culture of peace. I also learned that looking into distant pasts can demand a complete revolution of our present conditions of life.

I was repeatedly touched by the question of why this peaceful culture ended. As an answer I eventually received the story of Manu and Meret. According to my trances, it happened in this and similar ways simultaneously at many places on Earth. It is a love story; it is also the story of the start of a way of thinking against the Goddess that brought new cultural ideas to Earth. With the story of Manu and Meret, the age of violence started. I summarise here what I learned at the Almendres stone circle. The complete story is written in my book *Traumsteine*[14] and is available in English as a brochure[16].

Welcome to the campfire – to a time long before Christianity. The priestess Newar has returned. She had been sent on a journey to find information about the danger threatening the tribe. For a long time the priestesses have been receiving forewarnings of an approaching catastrophe which will soon threaten the last remaining peaceful tribes. Newar relates events which have occurred far away. Let us listen to the voice of the priestess.

She had met a tribe which called itself Narwan. The Narwan had been travelling for a long time looking for food. The Narwan are much more physically dependent on food than the tribe in the surroundings of the stone circle and had started to hunt animals to feed themselves and their children. They lived in an area where the winter was cold and the earth was often covered with snow and ice. It was mostly the men who went hunting and as a consequence their powers grew. Because the Narwan ate meat, their bodies developed faster than the bodies of the people in their surroundings who were vegetarian. Their way of life meant that they took in the power of the animals without being fully aware of their consciousness. A group of young men had been travelling for several days to look for food. They had left the women behind at a fire so that they and the children would keep warm. On their way the men arrived at the tribe of the Wsalagi, a tribe who were very similar in their way of life and thinking to the tribe at the stone circle with whom they also had telepathic contact: they too were guardians of peace. Manu was a man from the Narwan. He and his people had been expected. Their coming had already been announced to the priestess of the temple, who knew that a sensual marriage between a woman of the Wsalagi and a man of the Narwan should take place as it was the wish of the Goddess that their forces might unite and serve continuing peace.

It was at the time when the first love celebrations were taking place, with the aim of driving away the winter and welcoming the coming spring. The foreseen encounter was to be celebrated at the beginning of the festivities.

Manu was the chosen one; he was very beautiful and tall. As a representative of his tribe, he experienced a sensual encounter with a Mirja: a temple-servant and love-priestess to be.

Meret, who was in education as a love priestess, was happy to give herself to him in the service of love. She liked Manu at first sight and enjoyed his masculine power. For Manu it was a huge experience. For the first time he was touched by the bright fire of elementary feminine power. He experienced something entirely new during the sensual encounter with this beautiful woman. All of a sudden, during the sexual act, he felt a power rising within himself – a very manly power. Ignited by the inner fire of Meret, he felt strengthened; it made him feel full of joy and it uplifted him in a way he had not known before. As he held her in his arms he suddenly knew only one desire: he wanted to keep her with him. He knew that she was a Mirja, a woman whose sacred service to the Goddess was to introduce men to sensual love. She had been chosen as such by Nammu and the elders of the tribe. He also knew that she was only allowed to give her service at specific times when the moon invited her to do so and the whole tribe agreed that it was the right time. Meret had offered him the possibility to be close to her for several days. He had to receive permission from the council of the elders and follow the instructions of the oracle priestess of the tribe.

Meret was also touched in an unusually deep way by the strength and sensitivity of this man's body and by his beautiful and sensual language. He seemed to have learned and practised the art of love songs in distant lands, and the rolling sound of his dark voice made Meret shiver with desire even before they had met each other sensually. Manu embodied a male archetype which touched in Meret a great dream of longing: the dream of personal love.

Her whole tribe lived in a free form of love: men and women could freely choose in which form they wanted to come together. During the last centuries an additional picture of love with a very intimate and personal character had been preparing itself here. It was said that this personal dream of love was a dream of creation which was wished for by the Goddess, but which would require great maturity from men and women. The dream had to be introduced and prepared for carefully in coherence with the whole until their bodies and spirits would be ready to fully manifest it.

Every woman planted a tree of life as a child. The time would come when this tree would bear fruit for the first time, and the time would come when the fruit of this tree would reach such ripeness that the woman could give it to a man that she had chosen as a personal lover and partner. The right time was decided in communication with the priestesses, Nammu and the tree of life. The dream of personal love had grown so strong in Meret that her whole body was filled with it like a firm bud. It seemed as if she was ready at any time to open in splendour and beauty. One male touch could make her whole body shiver. But she knew that her fruits on the tree of life where not yet ripe. She had been insistently warned by the priestesses not to become impatient now. They told her:

Wait until the time is ripe. Otherwise you will bring great suffering to yourself, your lover and the whole tribe. Your lover will feel his phallus to be excited by your burning fullness but find no equal to it in himself. He will be magically attracted by your fullness. However, when he comes in touch with your shining ball*, there will be at first a growing new force inside of him – rather like a force borrowed – and he will not want to lose it again. He will seize it, want to own it and not notice that by doing so he will destroy the seed of young love. You will be inflamed by his passion and his growing strength. Your yearning will flare up so strongly that you will not be able to cope with it. You will not be able to hold the shining ball. Instead, you will lose it by handing it over to the man. Against better judgement you will betray your standing with the whole tribe; you will reinforce in yourself and in him the belief in the "strong male". You will prematurely encourage his loving force by feigning something to make him believe that he is something

* Shining ball or blue ball: Symbol of self awareness, identity (publisher's note)

which he is not yet. When this happens, Creation will fall out of balance and Nammu will be disturbed in Her sleep of Creation. The entire relationship with Earth and nature will change. As you kindle the restless desire of this man you will at the same time awaken his fiery anger. Humanity will take centuries to win back the shining ball. The dream of personal love is not yet fully prepared.

But in Meret as well as in Manu, the fire of love was already burning too strongly.

Manu was sent away. And although he tried to follow the advice of the priestesses, a strong desire and impatience took hold of him. He wanted this woman so much more intimately to himself than had been possible so far by following the customs of the tribe. He saw the Shamanu, the higher temple priests, who were able to come together with Meret much more easily and more often. Why should he fit in? Did he not have a special affection for Meret? Why should he obey the dreams of Creation of the great Nammu when it was now that he felt the burning urge for fulfilment. Hadn't Nammu herself endowed him with the spirit, strength and freedom to fulfil the dream of love out of his own intelligence, particularly as he felt such great strength and an independent momentum within himself? Was this not also Nammu calling? Was not every human being a creator and as such able to dream his own personal dream of creation? Why wait? Why share this Mirja with many others when thanks to his own strength he could win her fully for himself?

The concept of wanting to have someone fully for oneself was entirely new and most dangerous. The idea of owning Meret gave him the feeling of being totally potent. What advantages did he have over the high Shamanu, the servants of love at the temple who were maybe foreseen to be Meret's companions and lovers, if not his physical strength and his great talent for creating intimacy?

He felt his strength and he felt the growing revolutionary thoughts rising up against the principle of Nammu, the Mater, and against the never ending patience and communication that was asked of him with regard to everything around him. He felt his strength in his arms. What if he used his growing strength to oppose?

This was the starting principle of revolution: a revolution against that which had given birth to him and all humans, and that he despite this now wanted to change. Manu experienced it as a premonition of great force and of great freedom. He anticipated huge new masculine works of creation. Strangely, it was accompanied by a dark feeling of somehow wanting to seize matter in order to disconnect oneself from it, be independent of it and thus to be able to win it over to be at his own disposal. For the first time the latent thought of possessing the woman and thus possessing the whole of Creation emerged. He forgot that he himself was a part of Nammu, which he now wanted to own. He forgot that his desire for fulfilled personal love was wanted by and in full accordance with matter, with Nammu herself, but could only find loving fulfilment when in harmony with the greater whole, meaning at the right time. For the first time, dark thoughts of power arose in Manu. While he was seemingly obeying the priestesses, he followed very different inner plans.

One day, while looking for food with a group of young men, they met a group of members of the Wsalagi tribe. Manu had eaten fermented fruits and the meat of a buffalo that had just died. Normally that was not allowed as the buffalo was a sacred animal.

A young Shamanu of the Wsalagi tribe reminded him of this prohibition and asked him to return the bones of the animal to their resting place where the animal had died*.

Something happened in Manu that had never happened to him before. It was as if he was following an entirely new inner magic. He lifted up a bone as a cudgel and ran, arms over his head and without any further explanation, towards

---

* It is especially interesting to read the complete story at this point!
See point 16 under 'References', p. 269 (publisher's note)

the other group. Something unbelievable happened, something incalculable, an event that nobody had known up to now. Manu, with the cudgel held high, looked so strong and powerful that the group that surrounded him drew back baffled with an expression of fear in their eyes. This further increased his new feeling of power and strength, as he was already drunk from the berries. The power now became independent. He ran towards the young man who looked at him touched by fear, but who still did not move. Manu struck him dead with his cudgel.

Black clouds drew up at his deed, followed by a heavy rainfall as if he was to be drenched by the tremendous sadness of Nammu that what She had feared all along had now happened. And by now, Manu too was moved by sadness as he slowly started to realise what had taken place. His growing revolutionary thoughts had led him to act in a way which he would have been unable to even dream of not long ago.

Through Manu's actions, something terrible had occurred: he had killed a part of his own memory, a part of his inner compassion for the love-laws of Creation. He had killed the animal consciousness in himself, and without being aware of it had internalised only its compulsive strength. Something in his spirit had died at that moment. Without knowing what had happened he fell into numb mourning. In the place where previously a young and curious heart had been beating inside him, a new callousness and the first signs of cruelty set in. This happened unnoticed and unconsciously. He was overwhelmed by the completely new processes within himself.

What was new in this was that he had experienced this unusual power fully as his own power: he had conquered it himself without being in contact or in harmony with anything or anyone else. He had not had to ask anyone nor be considerate to anyone. It was the feeling of total independence and of power over others. It set him on fire as it brought him emotionally nearer to his aim of seizing Meret.

This is how it happened. Meret ignored the warnings of the priestesses, handed over her still unripe fruit to Manu and left the tribe with him. Together they looked for new possibilities for their future.

This also happened at other places on Earth. Over the centuries a completely different form of culture developed from this and spread as a field, based on the male concept of Creation. Men invented a god of war. They created their own altars. They created the archetype of the angry and punishing Father God. Together with him they wanted to conquer peace-loving peoples. A new concept, and thus a new way of acting, came into existence. Fear of death emerged, together with the concept of being able to decide upon the death of others and thus have power over them. This was the birth of a new and independent human cultural history.

Anything that still held the slightest reminiscence of the old culture of love and the adoration of the Great Mother and of woman per se was persecuted, destroyed and forever banished. Man could only fulfil the sexual dream of strength by replacing the potency of love – which he had not yet come to know – with thoughts of power, conquest, contempt and violence. And the woman in her infinite longing to redeem the dream of love let this happen by passing on the fruit of the tree of insight to man too early. No longer was she the pole of love, kindness, protection and of care for all that was alive. Instead, by following her desire she subjugated herself to the man. She had but one thought left: to win a man for herself. Wherever beauty and wildness and her connection to the Goddess still flared up, and wherever she was not willing to submit to this cultural step of subjugation, she was forced to maintain her silence during the centuries and millennia to come by the most brutal of means.

Hunting became the symbol of power. People killed animals for the pure lust of hunting. In this way a new state was established: the state of fear, which spread everywhere like a virus. Animals were killed without being asked first, and died in fear. Fear creates loss of memory. More and more human beings and animals on Earth forgot paradise and did not remember their true origins. Even plants returned with a spine *of poison which they used against animals and human beings in order to survive.*

Because the consciousness of human beings had been numbed by forgetfulness, life on Earth became bare of joy for them. Full of envy they began to take for themselves what others had created. They visited tribes who had developed writing in Nammu's honour, killed them and robbed them of their knowledge. To the same extent that humans learned writing and arts, they lost their memory.

Outwardly this may have looked like progress. Mankind was forced to make inventions since the contact to nature had been broken. One had to protect oneself. Towns grew to enormous size. Mankind forged ever more artful weapons using metals ripped from the Earth. They did not notice that the Earth needed these materials for her balance. Matter appeared alien to them and threatening as they no longer understood its language.

The fears of the priestesses of the stone circle became true to a much greater extent than they had expected. They understood during the course of the years that the human being even had the liberty and possibility to kill the Mater, Nammu, if he forgot his origin completely.

By so doing they would also destroy themselves and the whole of Creation's dream of paradise on Earth. The elements became more and more alien to them. They had to build houses to protect themselves against the cold. They had to eat more in order to take in enough energy. Since man had fallen out of the state of trust he was no longer able to hear and understand the singing of the stones, brooks, rivers, plants and animals; all of them shedding tears about the lost dream of Creation. Man had lost the contact to his own dreams and his own inner nature and to all the beings in the universe.

As he had rebelled against the principle of eternal return, and as he had independently taken action, he forgot his own origin and he therefore no longer knew of the possibility of communication with the whole of Creation. Human beings had learned to misuse their power of insight. Time changed into a mere linear thought of progress, and space was reduced to a vessel without soul. All matter became representational, reduced to lifeless objects, there to be used. All awareness of the union and simultaneity of all things had passed away. Man stayed in his self-made cage, no longer knowing where the roots of the ever-present force of love were to be found. This was Newar's story at the campfire.

Centuries passed. The tribe of Almendres in the south of Portugal continued at first to live peacefully after the episode of Manu and Meret. The members refined their knowledge during this time and learned more in order to protect themselves against the coming disruption. The Mirjas in training deepened their knowledge in the art of love as they knew of their high responsibility towards the men.

After this incident occurred on Earth, they had to become much more careful in their work of guarding information and memory. They started to build substantial graves, which had not previously been usual for them. They perceived it as their task to safeguard memory over many ages and cultures. For this reason they worked for more than a thousand years with the stone circle, to continually refine its structure of information. They knew that it had to carry, channel and protect a stable body of information through the millennia. It was most important for them to bequeath a fearless message of community knowledge which would remain effective and accessible for many future generations. Eventually the dream of Nammu would be sufficiently ripe that other guardians of peace could use it to introduce a new culture of peace.

The story of Manu and Meret also became known on the island of Malta. Everything possible was undertaken there to develop and deepen the knowledge of peace. They were prepared, if their location became threatened, to move on and continue to develop the culture of universal sensual love and there to introduce a culture based on partnership.

ON THE TRACK OF MY DREAMS

After several years of deep research in the stone circle I was sent on further voyages of discovery. One day I received the following task:

This winter you must start a new book. Write about the inner experiences which the stone circle triggered for you. Describe your journey through history and the changes it has brought about in your present life. Go to Malta. Visit the place of the sleeping priestess. Find the stone circle there and the temples of which you have often dreamt. Discover and understand the connections between Malta and this stone circle. Open yourself to the information you will find there. Rediscover the trail leading you from Malta to Crete and to Egypt, Nubia and Eritrea, to India and Tibet and to the most diverse corners of this Earth. Follow the symbol of the fish which you will find in these places and try to understand it. Understand its mythological content. Perceive how the humane impulse has survived, even through times of oppression and is still present today. The silent signs are now waiting to be heard and articulated once again. Learn to understand and interpret anew the logical threads behind everything that you encounter. You will soon have to undertake the first journey of this task. It is important that it will happen soon, as this country here is being destroyed. Many lines of power and circles of information are being cut, and prehistoric information will soon be even harder to access.

This call was so clear and direct that I had to accept it. I had also been told that a peace school from which we can still learn today had existed on Malta during the time of the prehistoric culture. Getting to know more about the school was a pivotal reason to travel to Malta. I wanted to start my journey in February. It took some time until inner voice and vision came together with reality. As I almost always live in community I knew that it would be an important experience for me to be on the road alone again.

My flight went from Lisbon via Cologne to Malta. The first thing I saw in Cologne was a huge advertisement for "Him and Her" – an exhibition about power and domination. That fitted perfectly with my topic for the journey and I took it as a hint to visit the exhibition. I was impressed by all the information which had been assembled from various times and various nations. At the same time, the one-sided nature of the information was disheartening. Even though it was seemingly a women-friendly exhibition, the main focus was always on the suppression of women. All the forms of life which were presented were already conditioned by violence. In most of the cultures, cruel rituals were held to suppress sexuality. Female circumcision and concision seemed to be normal everywhere.

I was looking for very different content: information about societies in which women had not been suppressed, or hints from history about societies organised by women. But Çatalhöyük – now Sumeria – and Malta, Crete and early ancient Egypt were not mentioned. There was also no word of still-existing societies which bear witness to non-violent cultural forms shaped by women. Thousands of people attended this exhibition and had their existing views confirmed that the woman has always been the weak, suppressed victim of history, for whose protection marriage and other social frameworks were created. Even up to the present, all traces of female power and authenticity are denied and destroyed by all possible means. The rare established material that does exist is accepted by very few scientists. This is the last bastion of our present society in its defence against the soft female power which is now emerging and which has its origins in prehistoric cultures. Through this exhibition I became aware anew that I was travelling to Malta with the task of bringing new information about original forms of society to light, so that women – but also men – could find the courage to gain different perspectives of life. Some basic sentences from the *Tamera Manifesto*[4] show the *geistig** background with which I started the journey:

Today we are approaching the greatest revolution since the Neolithic era. It is the transition from the patriarchal era to a new form of human civilisation. The global structures of violence and fear, fight between the genders and male dominance, racism and genocide, exploitation of the Third World and exploitation of nature have historical origins and can therefore be changed historically. The personal issues, for which millions of people see therapists today, have historical origins and therefore require a societal and political answer in addition to individual treatment. The environmental crisis and the inner crisis are two aspects of the same overall disease. They can only be understood and overcome if they are seen in their totality.

I perceived myself as a pioneer searching for the basic matrix of an original intact form of culture. It was like a new version of the search for the Holy Grail. It is generally accepted now that women should be less oppressed. The next challenge we face is to rediscover women in their elementary sensual freedom, their femininity and original source. If women rediscover their positive roots, they will reach a new power to shape history whose source lies hidden in prehistoric cultures. Whether it is found, seen and understood or not will determine whether there will be war or peace between the genders, and whether the powers of life can flow or whether they will have to continue to be suppressed.

I was searching in order to rediscover a vast primal power which we have all forgotten: the female source, sexuality. Its suppression is an important cause of war and violence. Both the source itself and the fact that it is suppressed are so

---

* *The German noun Geist (adj. geistig) is used throughout this book, as there is no simple adequate English equivalent for the concept "intellect, spirit, mind and soul" that the term expresses (translator's note).*

hidden from our consciousness that the entire subject is now rarely perceived in its depth.

In the afternoon I went to the train station to meet my daughter Delia. Blond, young and slim, she came towards me with a swing in her step. What a beautiful creature! How beautifully all these beings would walk through the world if they were no longer forced to doubt their native sensual beauty – if they would no longer be forced to domesticate exactly this wild and elementary nature. If instead they were respected precisely for this!

We had an intimate women's talk. Delia was facing the same questions as many young women: how can sexual adventure in love and in life be connected with the longing for lasting friendship and intimacy? What makes truth in love possible? And what about jealousy? Where do I find a space in which I can talk about all of these issues without having to fear indoctrination?

Wouldn't it be great if we had places where young people could learn about love? There is so much to learn and to ask in this area but it is exactly here that society remains most silent. We have made love, the most universal, highest and holiest gift of nature, into a private matter. Like lemmings, we all leap off the same cliff. I took this talk as an additional motivation to dive deeper into the following questions: how were humans introduced into the questions of love and sexuality in early prehistoric culture? Did they already know the same longings as we do? What places did they have in which to learn love? I felt compelled to get to know more about this, in order to build such places in their contemporary form. My dream is that in this way, an international movement for a free Earth will be founded. One major task that we are facing is to undertake meaningful actions for the healing of the environment. The other focus that is necessary for a well-founded movement is the development of models for a meaningful way of living together. I am determined to make *Tamera* into an international meeting point for a new peace movement. I will do this mainly for the generation coming after us: for young people who are searching for a perspective worth living.

The next morning I was driving to the airport. *Be aware,* my inner voice told me. *You can already book a hotel here and you will save a lot of money.* I am always grateful when my inner voice and impulses of guidance extend into the simple things of everyday life. I collected my ticket and asked the blond woman at the counter whether I could still book a hotel. She shrugged and said grumpily "Too late."

But my inner voice remained firm and led me directly to another counter. The young employee sitting there attracted me magically. I asked her for a hotel.

"Actually, I am not allowed to do that," she said, "but I can have a look what I still have on my computer."

"I would love to have a calm, simple and cheap place with a space to cook," I said, "so that I can be independent."

Accurate information attracts the corresponding reality. I test this spiritual principle again and again in simple, small actions. The more precise the information, the more likely is its manifestation. I tried to imagine a hotel room full of light, with a beautiful view, large windows and available for a good price. She was searching in her computer. "Seems to be difficult," she murmured. "Ah, there is something, the only thing I find with a place to cook. The price is ..." she paused, "eighty Euros per week! That's nothing!" I immediately knew that I was under guidance and that I had to accept this offer.

After a flight of several hours I finally arrived on Malta. From above one could see a single blue-grey ocean of houses and meagre cliffs. It looked as if the whole island was littered with houses. So this was the island of the stone monuments, this was the place of which I had continually dreamt in the stone circle. A high culture had blossomed here, a culture of non-violent tribes with highly developed communication structures, a culture which was able to communicate tele-pathically with other tribes. Here was where my stone friends from Portugal had sent me.

In Mistra village a real palace awaited me. Here I would continue my book. Two sliding doors reached to the ground, just as I had wished for in my most beautiful images. They led onto a terrace with a gorgeous view over the bay. On the far coast, modern skyscrapers crowded against each other and from this distance they were picturesque. Between me and them rested the turquoise-blue ocean to inspire my spirit and give the eye calmness for visionary dreaming.

I thanked my inner guidance and immediately started to arrange my new living space. I carried the little desk close to the window, put my computer there and my books onto the shelf, decorated the room with pictures of the stone circle and the temples of Malta and finally went exhausted to bed.

MIGRATION TO MALTA

Before I describe what I found on Malta, I want to reflect on my perceptions from the stone circle in Portugal about the connections between the prehistoric tribe that was once there and the Maltese culture.

For many centuries, wandering semi-nomadic people had lived in the surroundings of the stone circle. They lived in the fertile forests, ate the berries and fruits and, despite their simple life had a highly developed spiritual culture. They had built the stone circle over many centuries. It was an important meeting point where the whole tribe would gather for special occasions.

In their culture the stone circle was much more than only a sacred site and a meeting point. It had also been built as a repository for knowledge of Mother Earth. As such it was intended to safeguard peace-information for the coming generations and peoples and was also a geomantic place of protection through which the effect of the sacred treasures of Mother Earth, such as uranium, should be strengthened and supported. The tribe at that time was aware that a wave of destruction would crash over Europe and other parts of the Earth. They saw themselves as guardians of peace with the task of keeping the knowledge of peace safe for coming generations. Nammu, Mother Earth, was sacred to them. They were in permanent communication with Her. The Earth spoke to them through the whole of life on the planet. The members of the tribe knew how to communicate with the plants, animals, stones and all that lived here and they were able to receive important information from Mother Earth at any time. In this way they were also in telepathic communication with other tribes and cultures.

About six thousand years before our time, the oracle priestess – who according to the tradition of the tribe was called Bechet – gathered the whole tribe together. She had received an important dream which had urgently warned her to take action. At first she had only called the three young oracle priestesses Newar, Tamara and Vatsala. They had also felt a coming danger, so they gathered the council of the elders. Bechet had dreamt that the warmongering tribes which are today called the Kurgans were approaching to destroy the stone circle and kill all who lived there. Bechet gave the others the information that she had received:

We have to protect the Earth. We are threatened by an immense danger. A wave of murder will break over our region and over other parts of the Earth. It will intensify the great amnesia. New religions will arise. If it continues like this, soon nobody will want to know about Nammu and her ancestors. Some humans have already fallen out of the dream of Creation to the extent that men have started to condemn Nammu. They have created gods of war. They have started to scorn women and their secret of Creation. They know about our tradition of dreaming and try to influence our dreams with dark powers.

The whole tribe withdrew together for three days to receive guidance and intuition. Then they met at midnight for council. They knew that long-predicted events were now unfolding; they must start their long journey. Their tribe would separate and start to walk north, east, south and west, to unite with those tribes they had long known from their dreams and telepathic communications. On the journey they would follow their intuitions.

From other befriended tribes they had heard that the Kurgan used the most brutal methods to draw secrets from the guardians of knowledge before they died. They wanted to avoid this at all costs. None of them should make the transition to the kingdom of death in a state of fear. To remain untouched by fear was a precondition for the protection of the peace knowledge. Each member of the tribe received certain instructions which together made a meaningful whole.

One group of young women and men should walk overland and let themselves be guided to Africa, to the inhabitants of Eritrea and to the Nubians with whom they had been in intimate telepathic connection for centuries. These tribes were also threatened and needed protection and reinforcement. In Europe and other areas, the wars would spread, and they had the task of guarding and further developing the culture of peace.

A different group of twelve young men and women should take to the ocean. The stars, their dreams and the fish in the water would guide them on their way. Nun, the goddess of the waters, would accompany them. They had been told to first walk to the ocean and there build a great ship. They worked for many days and months to build the ship. It became their greatest work of craftsmanship. After having worked continuously for many days and nights and having skilfully arranged cloths for sails to speed them over the ocean, they were finally ready. They were to sail to a centrally positioned island which they already knew from their dreams. It was the island that we today call Malta.

There they should support the founding of a school for guardians of peace. At the core of their work would stand the school of the Mirjas. The Mirjas protected the healing knowledge of love. Related tribes from the most varied regions would arrive during the next centuries to take this knowledge further. It had been announced to them that Malta would become a flower of their loving culture for some centuries and that here they would further develop the knowledge of dreams, telepathy, arts, and especially the knowledge of love.

Finally the groups, which each had to manifest a different aspect and a different task of healing for the world, set off. They did not know whether they would meet again in this life. In this way, a group of twelve young men and women travelled to Malta. The goddess Nun was with them. They had a calm sea and the winds were favourable. They easily navigated the Strait of Gibraltar, passed by the coasts of Morocco and Algeria and once they had left the tip of Tunisia they knew that they would hug the coast of Sicily to Malta. After one more day and one more night, they arrived, close to the place that is called Bugibba today, where a temple with a stone tablet showing three fish still commemorates their journey and arrival on Malta.

They met a peace-loving tribe which already lived on that island, having arrived from Sicily some centuries earlier. They lived from fishing, plants and occasionally from hunting and they worshipped the Goddess in Her various forms. Small sculptures of a female goddess still remind us of this early stage of the blossoming culture.

Besides the few humans already living on the island, they encountered fertile flora and rich stone. Also here on Malta the stones were honoured as special guardians of earthly memory. There were many animals, the largest of which was a particular species of elephant which they soon befriended and which accompanied them on many of their ways. The humans who lived there had already started to breed animals and so they were surrounded by pigs, sheep and goats which they later celebrated in pictures on the stone tablets. They created pictures of animals to worship the Goddess in Her animal form.

The inhabitants of the island were already expecting the new arrivals and it was easy to create a way of living together that corresponded with everyone's needs. During the next centuries ever more people came to the island.

Through the group which had come from Portugal to 'Malta, soon everyone on the island knew the story of Manu and Meret intimately. Each Mirja was told of the historical background and it was explained to each Shamanu. The meaning of the word Shamanu is "He who serves the Goddess". A Shamanu was a priest of love. He was educated in the temple to be in the service of love for women and to be the messenger of the Goddess in the fertility rituals. The Shamanu had the task of tending sexual power as a cosmic power and of ensuring that the sexual balance of the whole tribe was cared for and respected. For fertility and to honour sensual love, the sacred marriage with Nammu was celebrated at least once a year.

The tradition developed that members of the tribe who were particularly dealing with the issue of personal love were called Manu or Meret. They had the task of making a historical contribution to healing through their lives and of dealing with the issue of love differently, in a more healing way, than Manu and Meret who had ended up so unhappy.

THE FIRST NIGHT: MEETING LILITH

The first evening on Malta, before I fell asleep I focused again on the purpose of my journey. I asked to find a way in. I asked for dreams in which I would encounter an elementary female power: a guardian of the historical knowledge of Malta. I wanted to create a personal connection with this historical background, and I wanted to get to know more about my spiritual task here on Malta. I soon fell asleep and dreamt at first of many temples.

I walk from stone to stone, examining each one and observing everything carefully. But the images are constantly changing. My dream changes from images of prehistoric times to the present. I wander streets full of traffic, between honking cars, looking for something which I can't remember. Then the image changes abruptly again. It feels as if I am shaken by a peculiar movement of energy, basically like a spiralling vortex. Then I see the spiral inscribed on a stone. I am a student, sitting in front of the stone and I have to concentrate on this spiral.

I awoke, surprised by this clear image of the spiral. Then I fell asleep once more and dreamt again of the temples. One picture I clearly remembered:

In one area of the temple I see a little girl who has just started to crawl. It is my task to take care of her. Next to me stands my lover Pierre, who says "See what I am doing. I do nothing more than observe this being. Through that I seem to understand her more and more. I do not intervene in any way. This is exactly what seems to give her protection. Her name is Lilith."

With these words I awoke again. Lilith? How did that name come into my dream now? Wasn't she the aspect of the female who was condemned in the Bible as evil personified? Eve was the one who was married to Adam and who was driven from the Garden of Eden by God. But Lilith was the aspect of the female that could never be trapped. She was the wild aspect of the female, who despite all attempts could not be tamed and who remained active in the background throughout the millennia. Wherever she was denied freedom, she caused destruction.

And now, was I taking care of this female aspect in the form of Lilith at an age where she was just starting to crawl? I interpreted the young Lilith as a symbol of a new cultural impulse, which now wanted to be nurtured and perceived. It seems to be our task as women to rediscover this female aspect within us and to take care of it without interacting or commenting. Lilith seemed to be an embryonic aspect of female creation, a proclamation of a new cultural impulse. I fell asleep again.

I am again in the temple. There are tiers of seats carved into the stone, like an outdoor theatre. I have been rehearsing a theatre piece with young people, which is intended to bring the different human archetypes on stage. We have been rehearsing for two days and today is our opening performance. The last preparations are being made.

I woke up, surprised at how many places my soul had wandered, and I was grateful for the first hints. I felt that here on Malta I was facing more than ever the task of connecting images from the past in a meaningful way with the present. The sun was rising and while I was writing my dreams into my diary I noticed how many hints I had already received in the first night.

I thought about my dream and looked for a connection to the cosmic female source of knowledge. I tried to hear within myself the voice which led me here. "Why do I dream of you? Do you have hints for me about my being here?" I asked, listened to my inner voice and very quickly received answers.

You are here to reawaken female knowledge which has developed over millennia and has been fought against for many centuries. Support it to find a new form and support its concentration to a new field-building power.

"Who are you, Lilith?" I wrote down the answers.

I LOVE BEING A WOMAN

I am the power you find, not yet integrated, in many women: in their wishes and fears, their misery and their deeper longings. I am a historical primal power who cannot be killed. I have been through a long history of transformation. I am the female historical archetype who is able to initiate a field-building process of societal healing connected with the universal processes of healing and the prehistoric culture of peace.

Connect as deeply as you possibly can with my guiding principle so that you are led along the path of the Mother of All Life, where you will meet my wild and untameable power for a historic new beginning. The principle is:

I am a woman. I am grateful for that because I love being a woman.

This statement initiates a complete revolution of the present culture's conditions of life. It is your path to a feminine knowledge of peace. This statement, spoken in full truth, requires a profound change in the world-view of the woman and a return to her true and most beautiful sources. It requires steps of liberation from the corset of society in which ways of behaviour which do not correspond to my true universal source of life were forced upon me for thousands of years. In the history of religion, the rupture when my original female sources of knowledge were stolen is represented as the fall of mankind through original sin. As all women are descendants of Eve, the whole female gender sinned with her. What has been forgotten is that far older myths of creation existed around Eve. Originally Eve meant "Mother of All That Lives". Before she was called Eve, she was called Nammu.

I, Lilith, am Nammu's wild daughter who could never be caught. I was Adam's wild bride and I ran away before Eve – the original mother – was changed into his bride, supposedly created from his rib. But I have never submitted to a man. I was condemned by a god whom I have never accepted as divine. This is why he could never destroy my wild nature.

Many ancient peoples perceived the Goddess and the snake as their ancestors. Religious pictures show how Eve gives the man life while the snake winds itself around the apple tree, the tree of life. These are pictures of the original religion of creation, while Eve was still the mother of all that lives. The human being was driven from paradise by cultural changes in history. I too was driven from paradise, as the idea of revenge awoke inside me through the infinite pain I experienced when I saw what they did to Eve and to all women. This idea brought me a lot of power, but it also drove me from my original paradise and destroyed it.

According to the Kabbalah, paradise can only be regained on Earth through the reunion of the genders. Even God, it says, has to be reunited with his female counterpart Shechina – also called the heavenly Eve.

What has to be achieved now is what I call a culture based on partnership. An essential step on this path is to reconnect with the female original sources. Here on Malta you will find all of the essential information, still intact, about the tree of life, the snake, the original mother and the historical dream of life and love of a female power which gives birth to itself.

"What happened to the original dream of the Earth, to the personal dream of love which Manu and Meret had dreamt; what happened to the wish for a culture of peace based on partnership? What has to be done for the healing and manifestation of this original dream?" I asked, and already started to write the answer.

This dream bears within itself a picture of partnership which is no longer bound to conditions, but which takes place on the path of two freely-loving humans who on their path of love can include many other men and women. This kind of faithfulness develops from a free and compassionate attitude towards the world and from deep communication about this compassion.

43

In early history the stove was the social focal point and the sacred place of a community. The woman was the heart, not only for one man and her children but for the whole tribe. There is an archaic and elementary longing inside me calling for community. It calls for forms of life which are again integrated into a greater context. The memory of this is stored in my cells. It is a memory of an old form of matriarchal living together in which the stove was the centre of the community and therefore also the social and religious centre for the blossoming of the whole community.

I want to live in a community with men and women, with children, animals and plants so that I am not continually forced to hide my actual being from the others. Perception and contact are forces of life that are as elementary as breathing. If these are possible, then I love being a woman, because I can then be a woman to my full extent. My fulfilment as a woman has always taken place within community. This almost biological longing still lives in my cells.

Under present societal conditions I am forced to confine this longing for contact, continuity and faithfulness to forms which are far too small. To make it possible for love and Eros to unfold in a way that corresponds to my actual femininity, community is needed: a larger love-community based on trust. The new human peace culture depends on our ability to build functioning communities. It is strange that humans can live at all without community. In the patriarchal culture, they have been separated from their natural universal tribal context. Communities nowadays always fail because of the issue of love. They always fail because of the unresolved issue of competition and jealousy.

"What was healing and special about the early peace cultures?" I wanted to know now.

In the early cultures, we were all connected with Mother Earth and our life was in her service. This state of being connected with Creation, we called love. Together we formed one big interconnected family. All love relationships were in connection with the greater whole. Private love relationships did not exist. And here I come to the essential point of my being a woman, the point which has been oppressed and denied the most: it is the point of sexuality.

I am a woman. And as I am a woman, I am a sexual being. And I love being a sexual being. A woman who makes this statement today in the 21st century needs revolutionary courage, which so far is only rudimentarily present in only a few women, even though we seem to live in the age of so-called sexual liberation. This statement means:

Letting go of shame.
Letting go of the fear of violence.
Letting go of the fear of suppression and punishment.
Letting go of false morals.
Letting go of the fear of the envy of rivals.
Letting go of the norms of the beauty industry.
Letting go of the religions of the patriarchal culture.
Letting go of the old picture of love.
Letting go of powerlessness towards men.
Letting go of sexual comparison and pressure to perform.

There is hardly anything that women do not have to let go of in order to be able to say this statement freely without a secret feeling of guilt. A historical fear of sexuality has been lying in the cells of the female since the development of patriarchy. The intensity of this fear increases immediately when the woman does not bind her "yes" to sexuality to only one man. Pictures of violence, of demolition and destruction of all elements of the female, and the sexual atrocities of a history that went wrong between men and women lie today as a sediment of fear in the cells of the woman as soon as she approaches the issue of sexuality. But the cruelty and the fear of cruelty are not part of sexuality itself, rather a result of sexuality that has been misdirected and suppressed for thousands of years.

What a start! It was the first morning on Malta and before I had seen anything of the island, I had already been taken to these depths of the issues. My dream had not only led me into the past, but had also awakened thoughts of the future. What was the meaning of the spiral? Why did it appear in the dream of this first night? And then Lilith's words: they created a direct connection between past and present. Lilith had been quite unknown to me so far. Even though I knew that many women from the modern women's movements referred to her, I had not previously given her serious attention. I got up, deep in thought.

Now it was time to take care of my physical well-being. In a supermarket close-by, I bought food for a small breakfast, arranged it as a celebration and enjoyed eating in peace on my little terrace. I thought about my first experiences here and tried to find a structure for the start of my time on Malta. I was in surroundings that, except for what I had seen in my dreams, were completely unknown to me.

Our culture has restricted Eros to the private sphere of two individuals and has thus prevented us from experiencing the deeper zones of sexual magic. But these zones will not let themselves be ignored, as sure as we are human beings. They continue to live underground in secret fantasies, they serve the advertising industry as subconscious seduction, they vibrate in the bodies of whores and saints, they plentifully supply literature with its imagination, they forcefully break out in sexual excesses which are then reported in the press. Society has relegated the explosive power of Eros to the domains of crime and pornography. Today it is this sin which is bringing about the downfall of society, because we are no longer prepared to lead this false existence.
Dieter Duhm[3]

Female Sexuality and Religiosity

After I received this comprehensive introduction I started to work with the notes that I had made on the tragic love story of Manu and Meret at the Almendres stone circle. I asked myself why Lilith had suddenly appeared now. "Why had Eve been brought into the game? Why wasn't she just called Nammu as she was when she appeared to me in the stone circle? Was it possible that excessive longing for love was also the historical background of the biblical story of Eve who seduced Adam to eat too early from the tree of insight?"

I took my voice recorder and left the hotel to take a short walk, hoping for further insights. Directly behind the house was wild macchia scrub, with small trees, bushes, flowering rock-gardens and bright shining stones. I was grateful to have this wild piece of nature so close to me. This was not to be expected on this densely populated island. I walked a few hundred metres up a little hill, sat down at a beautiful shady

47

spot under a tree with a view of the coast, and listened into myself again. I inhaled deeply of the scented air and listened to the distant sounds of the harbour. Lilith's introductory words from this morning were still in my mind. I thought of the small group from the tribe of the builders of the Almendres stone circle who had sailed from Portugal to Malta. Where exactly did they land? Would I be able to find their traces?

I am looking for a connection to prehistory: for a connection to the tribe of the stone circle in Portugal. A small group left Portugal to find a new home. They crossed the sea and were led to Malta. On Malta they founded a school for peace, in which the knowledge of peace was protected and passed on. "Why am I now receiving the name Lilith? Why is the name Eve appearing? Is this in any way connected to the prehistory for which I am looking?" I did not have to wait a long time for an answer. The dream of last night had given me easy access to my intuition.

The original female sources have been given different names during history but actually the powers are the same everywhere. Malta has a rich cultural history. There are many layers of information here. One line will lead you to prehistory, to the temples of love, to Manu and Meret, to the dream priestesses and the oracle priestesses. If you are patient, you will come into contact with this information.

To come into that contact, you will probably have to work through many different layers of culture. You should also expect a lot of resistance. Priests came early to Malta, bringing the religion of the Old Testament here. The Phoenicians lived on Malta. The apostle Paul was stranded here and bitten by the snake. The early Christians settled here. Many other spiritual movements were resident here. In addition to the knowledge of peace, you will find the first signs of decline and the signs of the arising of destructive forces and concepts of power over others.

Lilith has her roots in prehistory. But the Lilith you met in your dream, and who speaks to you now as an adult, is a person who unites past and present inside herself. She paves the way to a new future. You will find in her the seed of a culture based on partnership, which fully affirms feminine knowledge. Lilith knows separation; she knows the pain and the state of being disconnected; she was mistreated and hunted. Lilith was wild and indomitable. She knew revenge; she resisted the forced patriarchal forms of motherliness. She took care of the pure and elementary sensual dream that could not be squeezed into any patterns, and to do this she seemingly stood up even against Nammu, who was called Eve in later cultures. But particularly because she has been through all of this, she has comprehensive knowledge and comprehensive experience of female history. She is now in a greater and deeper connection with the knowledge of healing. Nobody knows the cultural historical false turns as intimately as she does and nobody is as deeply connected with the new growth of healing knowledge.

She could never be domesticated and she knows the dream of personal love of Manu and Meret, in its clear and undistorted form. She is Meret's wild sister; but Lilith could never be seduced by the offers of a Manu. Whoever follows Lilith's traces connects with the voice of a female power of revolution and is simultaneously led to the roots of prehistory from which Lilith comes. Here you will be led more powerfully than at other places to sexual healing knowledge, as the essential point where peace knowledge was destroyed and wounded lies in the area of sexuality.

I spoke these words into my voice recorder and once more consciously felt into the sound of the statement:

I am a woman and I am grateful for that as I love being a woman.

I felt that more explanation was needed than the introduction from the early morning had given and so, on the spur of the moment, I listened to Lilith again.

I am a woman and I love being a woman. I am a woman and therefore a sexual being and as this sexual being, I am a woman who relates in loving and sensual connection to more than one man and wants to unite with them on a geistig, sensual and sexual level. Sometimes it is difficult to understand how much courage for truth such a statement needs today. A woman needs to overcome her fear of men. She will attract the enmity of many women and the contempt of many men.

Many women become angry as they see a repetition of dependence on the man in the positive affirmation for heterosexuality. Now she does not only want to be there for the one, but she even wants to sacrifice herself for many. This creates an even bigger dependency. They perceive in this statement a boycott against the freedom and independence which they are seeking. The disappointment about men and the hatred of men that have arisen from this have become so strong that many women no longer want to get involved with the erotic attraction between men and women. And for them it is certainly not about peace between the genders. Revenge has a much stronger power for them than the wish to serve peace between the genders. All this is understandable from a historical viewpoint. Interestingly you will notice that particularly those women who strongly stand for independence follow images of submission to the man in their sexual fantasies. The lust for sexual submission has unconsciously grown so strong that they are shocked because they cannot bring this into a meaningful connection with a self-image of a free and independent woman.

They do not yet know that it is fulfilled sexuality that changes the pictures of submission and violence to pictures of real compassion and contact. Fulfilling sexual contacts give rise to genuinely free women.

Only a few women can positively affirm this in the sense of real female emancipation. Only a few can imagine that a free and independent woman wishes for full erotic contact with the man. It is the free wish of a woman to enter into partnership with a man. As truly as I am a sexual being, I say as a woman: I need the man. But I need him neither as a tyrant nor as a hen-pecked husband, nor as a dominator, nor in his old role as a preacher. I want him as a genuinely potent lover who knows sensual love. I will neither submit to him nor place myself above him and mother him, as neither answers my true sensual longing. And I will also not falsely bind him to me, as I have experienced through the last centuries that blackmail in love destroys exactly that which we had originally loved about each other. I will take care that the genuine free and lustful encounters with men for which I have wished for millennia become possible. Eros in its nature is free and cannot be directed artificially. The enlightenment that I am seeking does not occur in the world beyond. It takes place in my cells, earthly and elementarily. Its nature is absolutely sexual. Here I refer to ancient female mystery knowledge which is slowly returning to the light of consciousness and which causes a natural shift in these times. But this shift cannot be made until we once again honour our natural sexual source as a source of knowledge and universal love.

The friendship and faithfulness which I also wish for from the man arise from a different power than blackmail and false laws. I will support men in their development by showing them what I love and desire about them and what I do not. Real surrender to the man which is also lived sexually does not create dependence, but freedom. It was only a result of my resignation that I seemed to withdraw for so long. I followed the path of revenge because of my wild despair that the erotic world for which I was longing could not be created. It was because of my resignation that I seemingly entered restricted and exclusive relationships and made personal demands in love. But nobody can keep me imprisoned for long. Eros demands an opening and participation in the sensual world that exceeds all borders of marriage.

The picture of a sensual, lustful and lasting love contact is an anarchistic picture because the laws of Eros have an anarchistic *power which exceeds all false norms. A deeper faithfulness and permanence which is no longer based on prohibitions and restrictions arises from the sensual recognition of the other gender and the acknowledgement of erotic reality. An ever-more comprehensive revelation to the other opens this path of insight, leading to faithfulness that is deeper than was possible in the system of marriage and exclusion of others.*

The people of Malta already knew this thousands of years ago. Without the patience and infinite bounteousness of Nammu we would never have prevailed. Nammu embodies eternal bounteousness. But my pain was much too strong for patience. Now, however, the time may have come to bring this ancient mystery knowledge for a sensual culture of peace to light once again as a supporting power.

"What happened? Why do all women and men feel that the longing for intimacy and partnership contradicts a free love-life? How was this in the early cultures?" I asked.

Living with a false picture of love made us women change our natural concepts of love into concepts of possession and exclusion. That made it impossible to continue living the natural matriarchal sexual reality which would truly correspond to my actual original nature as a woman. Sexuality is a universal form of encounter. It can definitely be wanted outside relationship. In the existing society, however, it is only allowed in relationships.

There is an aspect of sexuality which we created in former cultures through our intimate connection to nature and to the Goddess. In sexual fertility rituals we honoured Eros itself as a cosmic celebration and a cosmic thanksgiving to Mother Earth. Fertility rituals were held publicly, in which we women could naturally reveal our sensual lust. This was not private sensual revelation in front of an individual man. It was a temple celebration in which we thanked Mother Earth by giving our sensuality. The men also did not perform the sexual act with us personally but in service of the Goddess. A woman who tried to attach a man to herself personally in the temple of love had failed in her service of the Goddess.

This kind of elementary, simple, sexual but also immense encounter between man and woman has been suppressed in our present culture. It is the lack of understanding of the immensity of Eros itself which has led to the suppression of women and through that to violence. Love and sexuality were separated. This is why historically, the romantic troubador and admirer of women developed, who wanted to idolise her and made her unreachable, while on the other hand rapists developed, who follow the power of forbidden Eros. The prohibition of the simultaneously sacred and lustful aspect led to forms of sadism and masochism and to real violence, which runs as a trail of blood, of unspeakable cruelty, through the whole history of patriarchy.

"What can we do today to fulfil the sexual aspect of our existence again? How can a woman who positively affirms Eros live in our present times?"

The longed-for manifestation of love in all its aspects needs the integration of the sacred aspect of sexuality. And we need natural forms of community once more, where this truth can be lived. What kind of historical cultural change could take place if we invested our caring power in the creation of community based on trust, rather than disguise, so that we could live according to erotic reality? How much fuel is used in cars in the search for erotic contacts? How much substitute consumption is needed to silence the erotic longing? There will be no peace on Earth as long as there is war in love. An awakening is demanded of us here. As I am a woman, I unite the sexual and the sacred realities within myself. How could we allow sexuality to be separated from the religions for so long? I want to be able to worship the sacred and holy character of life itself with all my lust for surrender. Of course I also want to love and worship the male powers. What fulfilment I experience when I am allowed to surrender truly and in full trust to the man, knowing that he will no longer abuse this surrender!

My female religious longing does not need churches or altars. Patriarchal religions and their exercise of power developed from the suppression of erotic and sexual reality. They were an instrument of power against the erotic authority of female cultures. The symbols of that are Eve and the snake, who were banished from paradise and recast as evil by the male God. But there is a sacred component of life itself which cannot be banished and which prevailed through thousands of years of destruction and oppression.

It is this ancient sexual knowledge that now makes itself heard once again. It is to do with the fact that matter also contains a sacred energy. The term matter comes from 'mater', Latin for mother, and means much more than objective lifeless mass. Matter carries consciousness with which we, as surely as we have cellular knowledge and the cellular ability to remember, can communicate.

I as a woman will develop to become a powerful organ for the care of Mother Earth. I will take care that a geistig field and a consciousness for these contexts can develop. You should support this by placing yourself in the service of your higher femininity. The Earth is as much a body as we are. We can regain access to a knowledge of the body, a cellular knowledge, through the correct form of awareness, the correct perception and awareness of each other and through entering a sensual presence for this Earth. A completely new concept of ecology develops out of this awareness.

An ancient power of trust which we had long forgotten emerges once again. It is the original trust in the elementary powers of nature herself. Through this trust it is possible to connect with these powers in such a way that they protect us. A great possibility of fulfilment lies in connection with these powers.

"Which path are you following? How do we trust in the birth of a new culture in which it is possible once again to freely and joyfully be a woman?"

The longing exists. Within the longing also lies latent the information for its fulfilment and the path to reach it. The longing exists because the possibility of fulfilment exists, just as thirst only exists because there is also water. This way of perception leads every woman who comes into touch with her female source to a theology of decision. It is the decision for reconnection and re-entry to greater contexts of information and communication. Then your actions are no longer arbitrary. Your life has become a prayer. This decision requires surrender to matter itself and to the peace knowledge which lives accessible in matter itself. You must put yourself into the service of the Earth and all its co-creatures. And this, despite the huge powers of destruction which are increasing at the end of the fading patriarchal age.

In this sense you will joyfully trust in the biblical sentence: "Follow me as I am with you always, until the end of the world." In this case you do not follow a guru, but give yourself, full of trust, to the Goddess: to the living aspects of the Earth. Imagine what sensual trust enters our cells if we can follow this biblical sentence in such a way that no fear can arise, as we perceive the protective powers of growth of ensouled nature and can connect with them consciously and in bodily perception.

From this perspective there arises a spirit of research, through which each woman who has come into contact with me feels challenged to develop and build conditions of life in which this biological trust can once again flourish. This is when we finally start to become political in a truly female way.

This is of course only possible if you include and positively affirm sexual reality. As long as the woman has to deny sexual reality because of fear, she will work against material reality in general and she will experience the elementary power of life as a threat against which she has to protect herself.

But if we are allowed to follow that track fully, then we reach a basic knowledge in our female cells. They carry the information needed for our fulfilment. It is as if we remember an archaic dream, a prehistoric state that holds the dream of a culture of peace.

On the basis of this new reflection I am on the way to find a new relationship to myself as a woman and as a historical being. Let yourself be guided, but this time no longer by leaders, no longer by laws made by patriarchy. Be guided instead by the universal powers of growth and guidance which are inherent in the original dream of paradise of the Earth and of matter itself. In this sense my freedom is to place myself in the service of Mother Earth.

Follow these tracks on Malta. Discover that the traces of the female original source can be found everywhere here. It will not be easy as many opposing powers have gathered during the centuries and made me silent, but if you go through the resistances you will find a way to me and through that also to the Goddess. You will understand Her language and make that possible for others too. Now take time to get to know this island.

I was now feeling fully confronted at the very beginning of my journey with my female nature. Already I had a feeling that the sexual issue would be more central here on Malta than it was in the stone circle. My impression was that I had come into contact with the female manifesto of lust and genuine religiosity beyond time. I felt challenged to visit and examine the temples with this aspect in mind. Now I was ready to get started and to dive deeper into the secrets of prehistory.

THE FIRST TEMPLE VISIT

I had rented a car. The next morning my first visit to a temple brought me to Ggantija on Gozo, a small neighbouring island which belongs to the archipelago of Malta. Although the villages, streets and the alleys between the numerous houses were completely unknown to me, I immediately felt secure and protected at the temple. It felt as if I was arriving home. Deeply moved, I walked through the circular rooms, which had been there for thousands of years. Their forms reminded me of a womb. The bright walls reflected the sunlight and gave a friendly impression. Inside, I let out a gasp of astonishment. This place was thoroughly familiar to me. I had once dreamt of a young priestess, and the surroundings I had seen in the dream were here, in these walls. In the dream, I had also visited a stone circle in the surroundings of the temples. Could it be possible that the stone circle still existed? On the maps of Gozo, at least, no stone circle was shown.

My attention returned to the sunlit walls. Many of the stones had fist-sized holes and cavities, giving them an individual character. Immediately beside the entrance my attention was drawn to a circular hole at about eye-level. I looked through, imagining that previous visitors to the temple had also looked through this hole with high expectations. As if they were looking through a magnifying glass, my eyes were pulled towards another stone just behind. This stone also had a hole, which seemed to me like a mouthpiece from the depths of the Earth. I felt a strong bodily reaction as if a direct warm breeze came from the stones, but inside me all was calm.

Certain stones had a personal character similar to that which I knew from the Almendres stone circle. I also had the impression that I was being scanned by an energetic sonar: a feeling which I knew deeply from the dolphin stone in the stone circle. But here only a few of the stones had this personal character. Most of them seemed to have been placed for practical considerations to create the circular form of the temple. I had the feeling that some stones were from a different era. My intuition told me that the original form of the temple had not been so tightly limited by walls as the present form, and that this outline had been constructed later. The form of the whole temple was reminiscent of a female body. The left front wall was about six metres high. The impression that all this gave was gigantic, but friendly. Strikingly, there were large holes bored everywhere into the stones. Some of them seemed to me to be intended for practical use, for example to support beams, which I later found confirmed in books. Others seemed to symbolise certain chakras of the body. It seemed to me that they were to help visitors, students and people who came seeking advice, to focus energy on the parts of the body represented by the stones, and thereby receive information about these parts of the body.

The large holes which were directed towards the centre of the Earth had a magnetic power of attraction over me. It was easy to imagine that the open mouth of the Goddess of the Earth gave direct messages here to those who came seeking advice. These holes immediately created awe in me and strengthened my feeling of connection with the Earth. It seemed to me that they were symbols of the mouthpiece of the Great Goddess from whom all life comes and to whom all life returns.

I paused with one of the stones which stood in a corridor leading directly to a large horizontal altar stone. I considered it to be an oracle stone. It was full of large circular cavities. "Cavities for sacrificial offerings to the Great Mother, or cavities which served as a mouthpiece to communicate one's wishes and hopes to the Great Mother," I thought. In front of it stood a very similar stone. When I moved towards it I felt clear reactions in my body. Something connected me very strongly with the Earth, almost as if I was being pulled downwards. A warm breeze repeatedly energised my whole body. But I did not receive any pictures or intuitions. It was like a friendly welcome: *First take time to arrive.*

The only other clear information I received was: *You will often be confronted with death and rebirth here. Pay attention to the labyrinth and the spiral.*

At the entrance I had already noticed a spiral carved into the stones. It had immediately reminded me of my dream from the previous night. In many cultures the spiral symbolises the power of infinity, the source of life and female powers of creation. It is a sign of change and transformation. It is the energy form for the development of all life and the energy movement that signifies inner transformation processes.

Even though I was very touched by the beauty of this temple and by the information that I was perceiving, it was still difficult for me to enter into a deeper mediumistic state. People were continually coming in to the temple. One couple seemed to be permanently beside me. I was continually running away from them to have space for a calm meditation. But they seemed to be attracted to the same places as I was. How difficult it was for me to enter the state of trust and opening when unknown people were around! The state of trust is the basic precondition for mediumistic work. How many people know religious experiences and the experience of happiness only when they are alone in nature! Almost everyone can tell of such experiences, but who knows the same opening of trust amongst humans? One immediately, and probably for good reasons, closes. Even with familiar people it is difficult to allow the depth of experience which one knows when one is alone. Probably some time will pass until people choose trust amongst each other, until the old game of hide and seek ends and we develop more beautiful and more universal ways of interacting with each other which correspond to our actual nature and joy of communication.

As I was leaving the temple, the couple approached me and asked me what I know about the places, why I was here and what I still wanted to visit. A small talk developed and I saw that they had a very interesting book about the temples with them. I had an intuition that meeting these people was in a way meaningful to me. After a short talk I said goodbye. "We will for sure meet again!" the man shouted after me.

I arrived back in my already familiar room at sunset. I went into prayer and asked for clearer guidance to find the spiritual entrance gate here on Malta more easily. I received the direction to relax, to be slow and to switch on the television. As it happened, at exactly the moment when I switched it on, a picture of a labyrinth was showing. It was a movie which mainly circled around the issue of death. As I had been told to pay attention to the labyrinth in the only mediumistic information I had consciously received in the temple, I was of course very interested in this scene in the film. The labyrinth kept appearing, particularly a picture of a labyrinth on Crete, and I remembered that one of my next journeys was supposed to lead me to Crete. Often the main actor was sitting for hours alone in his studio painting spirals as a threshold and transition into the kingdom of death. He said, "The soul reaches the end of its long journey and approaches, naked and alone, the divine light."

I was puzzled by this unusual film. Why did spirals and labyrinths show up on the television right now? After my dream of the spiral and the information in the temple: *You will often be confronted with death and rebirth here. Pay attention to the labyrinth and the spiral.*

The main theme of the film was the experience of a state beyond fear. A man had survived a plane crash and had stood at the threshold of death, and through this experience he came into direct contact with the "It-forces" of life. These are elementary powers which naturally act without us having to contribute anything. One encounters these forces through a direct surrender to the powers of Creation when one has forgotten one's own concepts and efforts. The man had saved many victims of the plane crash and had then left the location as if in a trance. Since this experience he had no more fear of death. He visited a woman who had also survived the plane crash and helped her to deal with the death of her child through a series of most unusual experiences. They found a happiness in love that lay beyond their marriages, from having stood together at the threshold of death. Despite his unusual freedom from fear he could no longer live in normal culture as he noticed that he could no longer lie. Everyone wanted to get him back into the normal world. A psychotherapist, a lawyer, his wife; for reasons that one can understand, they all called him back into the societal cage in which everything should return to its normal and seemingly free state.

For me it was no coincidence that I had switched on the television right now. Beyond our everyday world of experiences and logic, very different contexts interweave our lives. If we are aware, they shine directly at us, sudden and elementary in their cosmic context, and combine into a meaningful whole. Such chains of "coincidences" which together take on meaning appear everywhere, but we do not usually consciously perceive them. These threads trace through our inner world, our experiences; even extending into the movies we "accidentally" watch. Or we perceive them in radio programmes or an advertisement on the wall of a house. Here there is a connection of context which simply cannot be explained with normal logic. Of course it was not me who caused the television to show a film right now about death, rebirth, the spiral and the labyrinth. And still it was no coincidence that I had switched it on at exactly the moment when the labyrinth was shown. These threads of significant synchronicities stand beyond logic and combine the events of our life in a way that might be different but which can still be experienced and understood. If we have the necessary patience to feel into them then we enter new contexts of experiences. Our ancestors probably lived mainly in such contexts and made most of their decisions dependent on the lines of meaning showing themselves on their inner horizons. They permanently followed this track.

The mythological world of the distant past and the modern information that we receive from chaos theory probably circle around the same riddle. This riddle can probably only be solved from a holographic world-view.

I wrote down my thoughts from this day and finally went to bed. I hoped for messages in my dreams which I could understand. But something different happened. This night I had nightmares of a kind that I had not experienced for a long time. Because of my long research into dreams I am quite experienced in transforming nightmares into dreams with a positive power from within the dream itself. I am used to using research into dreams as a training field for my everyday life. This night I was sorely tested.

DREAM OF ANDA CÁ

I have just solved a task whose exact content I have forgotten. And now I am sitting in an unknown apartment. One door is open and moving slightly. Through the open door I see in a mirror on the wall that someone is standing in the next room practising frightening grimaces in front of the mirror. He comes out of the room directly towards me. He makes horrible sounds, makes faces which are no longer similar to a human face, and wants to grab me. "You don't get me that easily," I tell him. "I have too much before me in the future for that. And I am protected by my kindness." He approaches my face determinedly, laughing horribly. "Anda cá!" I shout loudly and clearly – a saying I probably unconsciously heard from the Portuguese who often say this to their dogs. "Go away!" I want to say with this, and my loud and clear voice awakens me.

As I wake up, I realise that "Anda cá!" means the opposite of what I wanted to say. It means "Come here!" Astonished, I thought about the dream. Why was my start here so confusing? I switched on the light and tried to find my bearings. I had imagined the start of the time on Malta would be a little easier. Had I paid too little attention to the details and sub-contexts in my visions and dreams? Why had I said in my dream "Come here!" in Portuguese, convinced that I send the monster away with this? Did this mean that I myself was in the process of opening for the powers of fear and danger instead of for the powers of peace and protection?

The next morning was dark with heavy rain. I stayed at home and worked. It became a calm workday on which I read a lot about the history of the island. I found a very interesting detail in an illustrated book on archaeology. There was a report dating from the end of the eighteenth century from an Italian antiquarian, in which he mentions that he examined a labyrinth close to the temples. So far nobody has found it. Archaeologists are still searching for it and hope to have more success using new methods. Another piece of information about the labyrinth!

Later I found out that the text referred to the subterranean labyrinth beneath the stone circle of Gozo, of which I had dreamt and where new discoveries had very recently been made. But I still had to take some detours before I would know that.

IN THE TEMPLE OF TARXIEN

I had received my first clear directions, but I then found some avenues closed at first. For example I learned that the famous Hypogeum, one of the main destinations of my journey, was closed. Several of my dreams had led me directly from the stone circle to the Hypogeum, and I did not want to accept that this particular gate was closed to me. Despite such obstacles, I travelled the next day to Valletta, the capital of Malta, to visit the temple of Tarxien and to find out if there was a possibility that I could visit the Hypogeum anyway.

It became a chaotic odyssey through dense traffic. I found hardly any direction signs. There were no traffic lights, and a lot of honking cars. After many manoeuvres and despite the lack of signposts, I finally arrived at the temple of Tarxien. It lies in the centre of the city. On one side it is bordered by the walls of a modern and unfortunately ugly church resembling a bunker. I tried to tune in fully to the direct surroundings of the temple which silently told me of the millennia before our time. I could clearly feel that this temple had been built later than Ggantija temple which I had visited before. Again I was surrounded by this sublime power and again I immediately felt reactions in my body. For a short moment it felt as if the ground swayed. I checked it and I repeatedly felt the same reaction at the same point as if something was wanting to draw my attention to the fact that here was a very special energy in the depths of the Earth. I would have loved to have had a geomancer at my side then: someone with whom I could confer.

Deep in thought, I wandered on. At one point I felt a similar déjà vu to that which I had felt in the temple on Gozo: I was standing in front of exactly the steps which I had closely examined in a recent dream. I remembered them so clearly because I had looked at them for a strikingly long time in the dream. Again and again I saw the same picture, as if a secret was hidden here. A little further along the corridor should be a big stone on which, according to my dream, former oracle priestesses gave prophecies for the common people. And indeed, my searching glance fell upon such a stone. How I would have loved to lie down there on it to research it!

But around me raged the noise of a city and many people. Noisy school-classes, Japanese people taking pictures, old English people who repeatedly shouted "How wonderful! How lovely!" I had not imagined Malta like this! In my picture of Malta I had just erased modern life. In my vision I had dived into the ancient world and I had almost forgotten that meanwhile millennia had passed. Malta had developed into a thoroughly Catholic island. With great effort, churches had been built here in the last centuries. One could imagine that this was the attempt to build an independent Papal base. The oversized cupolas which many churches carry here also seemed intended to compete with the Dome of Saint Peter, which is extremely strange on such a small island.

It is said that there are 365 churches on Malta. They bear witness to the Christian cultural history through which this island has passed. Two different and incompatible cultural impulses collide heavily here.

How should I now start my mediumistic research, for which I had travelled so far? One would have to be a goddess to tune-in here! I tried to calm myself, sat down on a large stone lying in the surroundings of the temple and started to write my impressions.

The temple was in good condition and led me, whenever I managed to concentrate, directly into images of former times. In one of the rooms stood a figure which must have originally been about two and a half metres high. One could clearly see the folds of her skirt. Below the skirt were two fat legs on which the feet were carved almost naturalistically. From slightly above knee height the rest of the figure was missing.

This figure left a strange impression in me. She did not at all fit with the impressions I had gathered in the temples so far. While the sleeping priestess that had been found in the Hypogeum was tiny, this figure felt disproportionately large. Through that she had something dark, as if certain persons had tried to restyle the temples with the stamp of a different power.

Did the first break from the old culture happen here? Was I already seeing the first influences of the priest-cultures? I almost felt the blowing of the first winds of an early spirit of the Old Testament. At first I just noticed this impression without questioning it and remembered the first words of Lilith that I had received at the beginning of my journey:

Malta has a rich cultural history. There are many layers of information here. One line will lead you to prehistory, to the temples of love, to Manu and Meret, to the dream priestesses and the oracle priestesses. If you are patient, you will come into contact with this information. To come into that contact, you will probably have to work through many different layers of culture. You should also expect resistance. Priests came early to Malta, bringing the religion of the Old Testament here.

I was surprised that a simple figure carved from stone could evoke such an uncomfortable association in me. Similar dark feelings often overcome me in churches in which the violence of the history of the church which was connected with this architecture can be clearly sensed.

In addition to these dark impressions there were also many different ones which connected me to bright pictures of a peaceful culture. Everywhere I saw stones carved with spirals. Pigs and rams were lovingly depicted on stone tablets. As they are depicted in the temples, it is a likely assumption that they were worshipped. Probably they were also seen as a form of the Goddess.

Between the walls of the temples are large individual megaliths. I was quite sure that most of the things I saw here originated from a later time than the stone circle in Portugal. This is certainly true of the altars which were supposedly for the sacrifice of animals. In this temple there are impressions of violence and dependency which are unusually strongly mixed in with the older influences which still radiate something of the sublime peaceful culture which honoured life itself as its only religion. At this time the stone settings served the people living here only for contemplation and orientation to connect with the powers of creation of the Goddess: of Life. These were impressions and elements I already knew from the stone circle in Portugal and on the tracks of which I felt I was travelling.

While I was writing I was sitting on a large stone outside the temple, which was probably part of the remains of a dwelling. But as soon as I had found some calm, a school-class of babbling teenagers passed by. I couldn't maintain my concentration against their laughing and babbling and I became impatient with myself and my surroundings.

Be slow. Gather impressions. Practice the art of waiting. You will enter more deeply into the contexts soon enough, said my inner voice. Then just as I was writing down some impressions in my diary, I saw the couple that I had met on Gozo the day before. That was no coincidence! At this point my inner guidance seemed to require awareness and presence rather than contemplation and deeper entry into the past. I noticed these two as they reached me and started to talk to me. While I was listening I asked myself why I met them again now. *The book,* shot sharply through my mind. I could have noticed that earlier! The book that the man had been carrying in his hand on Gozo was one that I had not seen in any shop so far. I asked him about it. He took it from his pocket and offered to sell it to me. I immediately saw that it was a special book in which I could find information about the less well-known places. I joyfully agreed, also told them my name and started on my way home.

ODYSSEY ACROSS THE ISLAND

The visit to Tarxien left me exhausted. I had reached a point where I started to silently question the purpose of my journey. What was I actually doing here? Hunting stones? Looking for the idyll of the ancient past in the noise of the big city?

I was driving over the bumpy roads in chaotic traffic. After about twenty minutes I arrived back at the place from which I had started. The traffic signs were misleading. Did I now have to find my way out of a modern form of the labyrinth? Stinking exhausts, crossing after crossing, honking cars, and every now and then illogical hidden little traffic signs which usually only pointed to the place directly next to them.

Through my slight over-fatigue, I suddenly saw the grimace of a grinning priest in front of me. It was the face I had seen last night in my dream. "Go away!" I mumbled, annoyed at the tangle in my head. Behind me a woman was honking, gesticulating wildly and pointing at something on my car. I stopped and saw that I had a flat tyre. My God! I felt as if I was in the middle of a Castaneda nightmare, and I really do not like this kind of spirituality where a new danger lurks behind every bush. "Isn't there any supporting protective power here? I am not looking for war-like fantasies and adventures. I want to get to know something about a culture of peace." I was swearing. Immediately something inside me gave me a warning: *It is difficult to find peace within oneself but it is impossible to find it anywhere else!*

I knew that I had to be careful not to attract further misfortune through my inner attitude, and thought of the spiritual teaching never to react immediately. If one is capable of this art, life provides a solution in every situation and help will come. Immediately I made an inner shift.

I ignored the tyre and decided to drive on carefully. I hoped I would soon find a petrol station. I turned right and saw a petrol station directly in front of me! So there was a helping hand! I let them inflate the flat tyre and then drove on. In one hour it would start to get dark and I did not at all want to still be driving on these streets by then. That meant I first had to find a way out of this city congestion. The superstition arose in me that someone deliberately wanted to mislead me.

Only those who allow themselves to be misled are misled, countered something inside. I had to agree sheepishly. My distraction seemed to lie deeper.

The temples here had a very different character to the megaliths in Portugal. Here there were no stones representing the different archetypes with which one could connect. Here one could not walk from stone to stone asking questions to each. Here I had to approach the secret completely differently. I also felt that I had to let go even more deeply of the question whether or not my perception was scientifically correct. Nobody can say for sure whether violence had dominated here or whether a peaceful culture had erected the temples. Everyone can interpret the stones however he wants. I was looking for evidence that could confirm my inner image of peace. But in order to find it, I had to first allow this vision to develop in peace at a calm place, rather than immediately looking at every stone and altar in search of evidence for or against my thesis. Was this a sign of a peaceful culture or did bloodthirsty savages live here? Basically it was the inner uncertainty that exhausted me so much and made me drive disorientated through the streets.

After a long odyssey – I had somehow left the city but still did not know where I was on the island – I saw several signposts leading to temples. When it was already almost dark I passed directly by the temple of Hagar Qim.

Slightly surprised that my odyssey had led me directly to the next temple, I stopped the car. Hagar Qim lies in beautiful surroundings overlooking the ocean. Soon the sun would set. It was clear to me that it was not the right time to visit another temple now. But I was grateful to know that a temple in such a beautiful location awaited my next visit.

Now I knew at least more or less where this temple was. I saw on the map that Hagar Qim was on the south coast of the island. My hotel was on the opposite side, in a north-western bay. My inner compass seemed to have abandoned me for a while.

The view was breathtaking. The road wound its way along the cliffs. Only the cliffs and the ocean were visible. I drove on, passed by Rabat and Zebbieh, and in Mgarr I saw another sign, this time pointing towards the oldest temple on the island.

Later I found out that my odyssey had led me directly to all the important temples of the island. Had I been un-consciously led by a leyline of the island connecting the temples?

I arrived at home in the dark. I sat down on my couch and tried first to find inner calm, to find somewhere in the tangle of my thoughts and feelings, my "on-board computer", my inner voice.

Your search touches the hottest issue of history. It doesn't work here as simply and softly as it might work in the world of visions, which do not have to rub against material reality. This is a place of great power. But it has also been occupied by powers of suppression for millennia. Even in the times when it was used, it was also misused and wrongly channelled. You have to protect your spirit well, as everyone who wants to access the inner secret will also be attacked by opposing powers. You have not yet arrived in the promised land. You are here as a pioneer. Practise spiritual meditations of protection. Take care of your body. It needs special awareness now. Take care with what you allow to reach you and what you do not. Go to bed awake and prepared. Orient yourself with the directions of the compass. What you do now and how you do it are very important. Your headache is because all these deep and healing places have experienced a terrible injury. Whenever you open mediumistically you come into contact with this. This is why it is so important that you continually cleanse yourself energetically.

Now let yourself be well and accept all the presents that you have received today.

Grateful for this message, I first prepared myself a good meal. Then I leafed curiously through the book *Temples of Malta and Gozo*[25] that I had bought from the couple. I wondered what it was that had felt so familiar to me during the temple visits so far and what had felt so strange. This mixture of things intimately known with vast strangeness was something I had rarely experienced so strongly. Again I thought about my dream. It seemed to be important that I had become aware of the present danger before I could research the deeper background of this place. I had repeatedly seen sleeping priestesses on Malta and dreamt of them. In the dream, clear and impressive pictures of the steps and walls had come to me and dreaming, I had studied the stones although I had never been to this place before. Now I had already seen two places which were very similar to my dream pictures: the first on Gozo and the second in Tarxien on Malta. The very first priestess in my dreams had lain in a temple like the one on Gozo. But very close to this temple I had seen another place which was similar to the stone circle in Portugal, only smaller and embedded in the earth. Steps led down, and under the earth was a kind of natural labyrinth with various corridors and caves. I had expected to find a stone circle here on Malta. But I found no mention of any stone circle, dolmen or menhir in my guide book or in the illustrated book even though I had been certain that I would find such monuments. I felt how much I was trying to find these places through objective means. I couldn't avoid my disappointment that my dreams corresponded only distantly with reality and that I had instead arrived in a big sprawling city with a few great temple ruins.

I leafed thoughtfully through my new book and after a while I found an astonishing hint. I saw a watercolour that was remarkably similar to my original dream picture. It had been painted by Charles Brochtorff in 1829 to document an excavation. It showed a stone circle: a large horizontal stone surrounded by other megaliths. The stone circle was slightly sunken into the earth. I was immediately filled with a wave of joy and read on, transfixed. The former stone circle had been very close to the temple on Gozo. I also found mention of many menhirs that had been found in former times and which were now largely lost. So my dream of the stone circle and of megaliths on Malta was close to a former reality. Researchers had been seeking the stone circle, today called the Brochtorff circle, during the last years. And they had recently found the original site. A farmer who had felt disturbed by the many large rocks in his field had removed them. The whole site was located – as I had thought – a few hundred metres away from Ggantija. I was thrilled about this discovery and I knew that I would visit this place again.

Lilith Says: Stop Being a Victim

I fell asleep early and awoke in the middle of the night knowing that something special had just happened. I had easily and naturally moved into the world of the early temples and had continued my dream of their story. When I awoke I felt disturbed and slightly feverish. I wanted to remember what had excited me so much and I could remember that it had been about a snake-like fish which had been found engraved into a stone at Ggantija on Gozo. I also remembered that I had been on ships. I had found myself in prehistoric times. The first priests had arrived on the island. We had been told to hide our knowledge from them. I dimly remembered that they had invited me to a ship for a meeting. Then my memory refused to go any further. I tossed and turned in my bed. Troubling and disturbing things had happened there but I could no longer catch their content. Even today there are still memories which my subconscious censors: *So far but no further.*

Then something like a prohibition on thinking and remembering sets in: *If you think further here, danger threatens: inquisition, banishment, persecution. There is a danger that your body would be poisoned by thoughts of identification and fear. These would suffuse your insights of paradise with the poison that has destroyed whole centuries. Identification with evil and fear blocks insight.*

I was shaken by doubts which had probably been triggered by my dream. How could you be so insane as to write such a story? You will be branded a witch; women will revile you and men will fight you as the one who tries to usurp their territory. The Church will condemn you. The women will denounce you. There will be a few who will find a possible truth in the core of this story and see consequences for their own lives and go on a search for their true friends: these people will not have an easy time as they will meet one border after another

73

which society and the dominant world-view will create for them. In such moments I would rather that none of this had ever happened. And I want to keep all these experiences to myself like a fish in the depths of the ocean which silently lives its life. This is why some women have remained silent for millennia despite their knowledge.

Don't make the mistake of speaking something out too early while it is not yet ripe. Don't take on the burden of the anger of people who do not think like you. But bring your dream in silence to its fulfilment, the doubting voice said.

But another voice felt like an order, clear and insistent. It came out of me like an inner necessity which tore me away from my doubts. It was this voice which brought me fully awake, made me get up to bring some fruits and a glass of water and led me to my desk. I wrote down my dream and went into prayer. After a short while the voice started speaking again. I recognised that it was Lilith by her unflinching and awakening spirit. She knew the many pains of history and had now become my companion who led me carefully but clearly out of the confusion of doubts. I listened to her words.

Stop Being a Victim!

A revolutionary is a person who draws her attention to those points where other people are suddenly afraid. Doubt is always doubt in one's own willingness. Behind every doubt there is an insight waiting.

The only reason that you cannot be truly insightful is that you perceive yourself as a victim. Leave the fear of being a victim. Now it is time to speak things out. This is your very personal dream but it is also a historical dream which has meaning for many and which you have to speak out. Nobody else can do this for you; you have to speak about what you have seen and experienced. Dare to go further into the land of memory, into the land of forbidden fruits. Take care that you do not fall for the thoughts of anger and revenge, and neither for the thoughts

74

of identification and fear. Whenever pain and fear set in, you cannot access the decisive insight. But this is exactly what is so urgently needed today. To put it into old pictures: Nammu demands from you the sacred rage which can give you the power to fully perceive these things. For thousands of years this side of all of you has slept. For millennia Nammu could only pass on Her knowledge in secret. She had to continue giving birth to Her dream of Creation. She had to find pictures which would be able to withstand violence. She has prepared a dream of rage which gives you power but which does not connect to hatred. You will not seek and worship a goddess outside of you again, but Nammu will start to speak again in many women. With sacred rage She will stand up for Her altar of love and will no longer allow it to be persecuted, forbidden or destroyed. This rage is awakening powerfully. It will arise in many in the course of time. It will reconnect with the power of love and of kindness. Support the growth of a new seedling of sensual love between the concrete walls of false morals. Despite the field of power and domination, despite the dirty thoughts of perverse loveless sexuality, this seedling, at first maybe unnoticed but then more and more powerfully, will unfold its true blossoms of culture. Plant this little plant and provide it with the power to survive through the courage of your language and thoughts. May this seed grow. Just as many plants grow on rubbish dumps to bring healing to the soil, a new cultural concept can arise from the ruins of the present culture. This is one of the few chances for survival which still exist today. The knowledge will be sought and found by its original guardians. It will cause memories in other people, memories which come into the light from the still unconscious layers of their eternal soul to nourish the courage for a new life which no longer follows the old patterns but instead aims towards new shores. It will reawaken the power of the higher self and will remind us that the knowledge of creation is anchored in every individual and wants to be taken care of. To do that you do not have to worship any gods outside yourself; you also do not have to follow the power of over-rational thinking which removes the sacred from life and treats it with disrespect.

Today a holiday is celebrated on this island: the day of Saint Paul who was stranded here on Malta. He brought the authority of writing here. Many other people also landed their ships and left their knowledge here. Over the millennia Malta was a place to which knowledge was carried from different sources and in different forms. Here it has been refined and further developed. As well as writing, very different signs exist which we can read and interpret. Today when many of you awaken from thousands of years of amnesia with a new dream of creation, a new age could be introduced. Since ancient times a comprehensive vision of peace has been resting in the human memory. Fear has separated you from this vision. Accept the worlds of transformation which are connected with the rediscovery of this information. The historical pain which you have experienced separates you from a higher, more healing and more comprehensive possibility of peace which can reconnect you with the power of a lived life. This pain which has left in your cells a historical tubercle of fear, is no longer necessary. Now it is about no longer following the fear. Follow the higher frequencies of your soul so that a new possibility of existence on this planet becomes possible, to a place where a comprehensive vision of peace awaits you.

The Dream of the Spiral

It was the middle of the night. After Lilith's words I felt stronger again, and yet a dark and strange veil still rested over everything. The dream of the past had not yet opened to me. I decided to go back to bed. Following the instructions of my inner voice I had practised orientation and had first found out how my apartment was aligned with the directions of the compass. I had also checked the position of my bed. After deeply preparing myself spiritually for the continuation of the night I asked for empowering signs. I dreamed of various temples but it seemed that I was far too tired to dream with awareness. If I had not been awoken in a special way, I would have been unable to remember any insights.

It is as if I am shaken by an energy movement, which again works itself like a spiral through my body. I see the spiral carved into a stone in front of me: the same form as I had seen in a previous dream. I sit in front of it as a student and I have to concentrate on this spiral.

I spoke into my voice recorder.

This is an important aspect of the art of dreaming. All oracle priestesses had to be highly practised in this so that they would not be distracted by unconscious pictures arising from the soul into digesting events of the day. They had to learn to distinguish between dreams of seeing and processes of creation, and digestion dreams which their own psyche needed. The spiral was the ancient sign of all life-creating processes. It was the connection between the origin and new creation. It represented the connection with the nameless aspect of universal love in Creation. If the intention was only to focus on a question, as in your case now, they worked with a picture of the single spiral. If it was about a new creation or if they had the task of solving questions for the future and dreaming a dream of creation to an end themselves, then they connected with a double spiral. This allowed them the wished-for concentration. This process ensured that no pictures would arise inside them which were not connected to the whole. Concentrating on the spiral was also connected to a second process: the erection of an inner pillar of light aligned with the spine. They were thereby fully connected with the power of Creation. In this way they were able to become stronger and make themselves completely empty. All new information required this inner emptiness.

I spoke all these explanations directly out of my dream into my voice recorder. This is a method in which I only succeed when I bring myself into inner alignment very well before I go to sleep. I talked for some time before I was fully awake. My spine felt completely flooded with light. I remembered another dream picture. I saw myself as a young woman and student in the temples, where I had the task of observing what kind of disturbance was caused by thoughts which had not been thought through to an end.

Thoughts create reality, and you can become a witness of this process at any time, I still heard the voice of my teacher saying. I had had to make myself absolutely empty inside. After that I had walked around the temple, looked for a calm place and carved a spiral into a rock using a tool. This had made me completely calm.

Now I was completely awake. The spiral seemed to be the answer to my question for the night. It was the sign that I had asked for and to which I should connect when I wanted to go into spiritual contact with this ancient temple-school on Malta. I concentrated on further intuitions and without an image of anyone appearing to me, I received information which I can summarise as follows:

Nammu has no name. Even "Nammu" is only a helpful label, an artistic icon which represents a certain personal maternal aspect of Creation. She represents the fact that life here on this planet wants to manifest a strong female divine aspect. The female divine principle reveals itself to men and women to the same extent. It is represented by the ancient aspect of the original mother. But in the end, this aspect is also eternal change itself. The spiral is also always a reminder for you of the aspect of new creation, of the eternal present and of transformation. As human beings increasingly sought spiritual objectification, they brought the divine qualities to the outside by giving them a name. They sought these divine qualities outside themselves. This quickly led to a cult of religion. The divine source, however, in its most original and most authentic nature is that which is eternally nameless. The religious character of life can only be experienced inside and touches Creation from there. This process makes the world shine in its aspect of universal love.

An epoch completely free of occultism and religion has been prepared and will start. Your ancestors did not have a religion as you understand religion today. Existence lived in the name of universal love is the religion which is written by life itself. Life itself is permanently recreating the original patterns of Creation; you can find them everywhere. In every science – in physics, mathematics, astronomy, geology, technology and geomancy – you will meet the same original secrets of life everywhere. The question remains open whether humans as co-responsible carriers of Creation will continue to use them for destruction and self-destruction, or whether they will finally learn to read the inner secret of universal love. To be able to manifest this sacred aspect of life which can be found in everything that exists, you need the connection with the whole of Creation. Sacred artistic icons of the soul which are created by you and which support you to manifest your own eternal gestalt will help you to reach success. But never forget that these images and beings reflect and represent only a part of the whole. Emptiness is always the starting point. That is why it was so important that the oracle priestesses knew the art of making themselves empty like a stone and then connecting with the spiral.

When I woke up I thought about this secret. It is plausible that originally, life itself was the great divinity that contained all aspects. No Creator had to be sought behind Creation, no God behind existence. This life did not have to be condemned and another life sought beyond it. Life itself was divine enough and it contained the physical aspect as much as the metaphysical. It was reflected in the sources of life and death. The statues of the goddesses only made the sacred power of life visible, which made it easier for humans – for women and men – to come closer to the female and sacred secrets of Creation. The great challenge is to redevelop and research this art of life. The path which needs to be found and followed is the sacred track of life itself. Whoever is searching for the sacred secret of Creation treads a fine and delicate line. Whoever treads this path has to overcome many traps and deceptions. They have to find the path between occultism, old beliefs in gods and idolatry, and impenetrable atheism. Atheists usually run into the trap of no longer allowing any entrance for the secrets of life. They idolise signs and logic without realising that this excludes the sacred light of life. The atheist also no longer perceives how much his science and logic is conditioned by beliefs.

Occultists are caught in the web of symbolism. They seek God and the divine secret behind the objects and events of life. They celebrated rituals of cult and sacrifice. In the background there almost always stands fear of a punishing authority.

Through my dream the gateway on Malta seemed to have opened further. I had come closer to the secret of the spiral; I understood more deeply why Lilith had suddenly appeared to me, why Nammu had then come up again, and Eve, the original mother of all existence. I don't like religions which become a cult centred around a personality, and neither do I like the hullabaloo of the many female rituals, pseudo-witchery and menstruation cults. I perceive almost all of them as a substitute for life and a bulwark against the sexual original powers of life. And still I was seeking the origin of a female religiosity and was hoping to find it in an original elementary, true and female view of Creation.

This dream was a milestone on my path. I felt free and strengthened for whatever would come.

HAGAR QIM AND MNAJDRA

I awoke strengthened and refreshed from the night. *Wash your face in happiness and health by taking delight in joy.*

This sentence came up during my morning exercises while, with closed eyes, I moved my body back and forth like a snake. The morning meditation felt as if I was cleansing my soul by bathing in light. It was something like a kind of morning dance we used to do in Tamera. Often movements arose during the dance which reminded me of sculptures of dancers and priestesses of the ancient cultures. My hands were led naturally upwards in praying and blessing gestures or in crescent moon forms above my head, and my body demanded that I kneel down on the earth, with lower back arched and arms extended. I loved this position particularly, even as a small child. It leads to calmness: to connection with the universe. In a trance I learned that this was an ancient position of the Goddess. There is a "Toad-Goddess", a terracotta figure from Anatolya from 6000 BC, who rests in this position.

Wash your face in happiness and health by taking delight in joy. I knew that sentence well. It is an old Egyptian temple inscription from about 2700 BC. I had made a habit of finding a power-sentence every morning during my meditation, to give me orientation that I could connect to during the day.

I was called by Hagar Qim, a temple by the coast. I hoped to find a soul-connection with the secrets of the temple more easily there. This time I made a profound meditation before I left as I wanted to prepare well to protect myself from losing my orientation. The dream of the spiral helped me. It had become clear to me again: if you want to do peace-work, then you also have to start to bring light into the areas that you have so far completely avoided.

Suddenly I had an impulse to do an *I Ching* reading. I have often had interesting experiences with the *I Ching*, although I also have often felt irritated by the very male and warlike language that is used. It is a written historical oracle that has grown through the centuries and has therefore also been shaped by the patriarchal eastern culture. But behind it, a secret which lies beyond coincidence is acting. I have tested it often enough and I was able to use it as a source of wisdom. It is also no coincidence that the construction and structure of the *I Ching* corresponds to the mathematical structure of the genetic code, and the genetic code has the form of a double spiral. How many people have already thought about this secret!

I used the preparation for the reading of the oracle to focus on my question. An essential process in the art of oracle is to perceive one's actual questions. People in former times often went into silence for days before they consulted the oracle. The world is full of answers, but they can only be perceived as such if one rediscovers the deeper and conscious connection to one's own questions. Accessing knowledge can be compared to the Internet. Much knowledge is also stored there. But one has to know the right code or keyword to be able to access this knowledge. In a similar way, the *I Ching* is also a support. The message comes partly through the words in the book and partly through one's own source of wisdom.

First I asked how I could best find the entrance into my work on the book. An interesting direction which I adapted to my situation was:

Just as water flows without interruption, you shall pass through difficulties without losing your trust. Your attitude carries you successfully through by using firmness in a balanced way. Action is worthwhile. That means that through this undertaking something will be reached that is worth the effort.

Then I asked if it was the right time to leave for Hagar Qim. As an answer came the hexagram "Peace" and the changing line was:

Embrace those who are imperfect and also those who have been abandoned, trust those who know how to cross rivers and do not neglect those who are in the distance. When the companions have left you can understand the value of balanced action and this provides brilliance and glory.

I tried to commit these words to memory, and left. This time it was easy to find the way to the temple just by trusting my intuition and I soon arrived there after a short and inspiring ride. Unfortunately, there were also fairly many people walking around here. But unlike Tarxien, this temple is not so tightly squeezed between modern city buildings, so it did not disturb me so much. I paid my entrance fee. Next to an attendant stood a man of about forty who somehow felt known to me. I asked myself whether I had seen him already. He radiated a very male and sexual energy. There was something in his expressions and his movements that felt deeply familiar, but I did not know of whom he reminded me.

I was transfixed by the first sight of the temple. The stones blazed with sublime light! I was overwhelmed by sacred magic! Standing freely in the landscape like this, the temple filled the space with glory. The globigerina limestone was tuned harmoniously to the land. Despite their size – they were about four metres high – the stones felt in no way oppressive. At the north-eastern side was an approximately seven metre long and three metre high stone block. It was as if two huge faces were looking at me out of it: faces that I knew well from old stones in Portugal. At the north side was a single huge menhir which was larger than all of the others and towered like a guardian over them. I enjoyed the wind and the view over the deep blue sea to the small island of Filfla which lay close-by. I inhaled this picture greedily as if I wanted to anchor the impression deeply in my soul and never lose it again. Something deeply known, memory, awe and the feeling of permanence and greatness, touched me in a way that filled me with utter joy. It was one of these moments in which one feels the eternity of Creation, and at the same time the deep and elemental love for matter. I saw the stones of the temple before me as if they had just been erected yesterday.

"Every construction is an absolute beginning. Therefore it tends to recreate the beginning and the abundance of a present that does not contain any trace of history."

This quote from Mercea Eliade expresses in a few words what moved me in this moment[18].

I took a deep relieved breath; I had arrived again and I was reconnected to a world of inner trust and cosmic dimension. All stress fell away.

Suddenly I heard footsteps. The man who I had noticed at the entrance stood next to me.

"Do you want to come with me? I will show you where the entrances are and tell you what I know about the temples," he said in English, with a friendly and firm tone.

I did not really know what was happening to me. I came out of my rapture and looked at him closely. For a short moment I was irritated and felt disturbed from my calmness.

"What does he want from me: money or sex?" shot through my head.

But this only took a few seconds and before I could react in the typical way of an inaccessible woman, I stopped my inner dialogue of mistrust. I knew right away that I had to go with him and that a present awaited me if I remained aware enough. It felt as if I was pushed before I had time enough to really think about it. I felt as if I was in a dream where one has to decide within seconds if one faces a friend or an enemy. In this moment I felt that he was a friend.

In his company I was led through the temple for the first time, and I felt protected from the tourists. I could not do the meditation that I had hoped for, but I knew that I would find an opportunity for that later. He led me from corridor to corridor, from stone to stone, and everywhere he told stories as naturally as if he himself had lived there. He showed me faces in the large stones, and a reclining figure carved into the

85

stone. He showed me hidden spiral patterns and single stones which were full of little carved niches which shone in the light of the sun and felt to me like orgone. He showed me the altars, talked about animal sacrifices and pointed out a large horizontal stone which he interpreted as an altar on which animals had been sacrificed. Next to it was a basin which he thought had been used to hold the blood of the sacrificed animals. He also showed me a small shrine in which a knife made of stone had been found. So he knew an individual story for every stone.

I did not want to fully accept this information as it did not correspond with my picture of a peaceful culture. The tribe whose story had revealed itself to me in the stone circle had neither killed nor eaten animals, and had certainly not sacrificed them in cult rituals. They did not even have the concept of keeping pets. Whether his story was true or not, what I could feel for sure was the direct connection of this man with this place. And it was indeed likely that animal sacrifices had taken place here at a certain point. He told me that he had worked here for seven years. Then he mentioned an older temple not far away from Hagar Qim.

We climbed down a steep path to the temple, which is called Mnajdra today. Its appearance is very different to Hagar Qim. It is made from different stone: a rather hard bluish coral-like limestone. As one walks down the hill, one can also see in the landscape how the nature of the stones changes. So probably most of the stones for the construction were taken from the immediate surroundings.

Mnajdra consists of two temples and one additional circular building. These buildings are on different levels. Each temple consists of two elliptical rooms called apsides. When I entered these buildings I had the same experience as I had had on Gozo and at Tarxien: I had the feeling that I recognized the oracle room. A large horizontal stone – which people usually call an altar – seemed to be the place where originally oracle priestesses had slept their sacred sleep.

In the anteroom were two bigger horizontal stones which I thought were for students who were taught the sleep of the oracle priestesses here. I felt astonishingly few traces of violence here, also not of violence against animals. I was very curious what information the books would give me about this place but I decided not to read them until I had gathered sufficient impressions of my own that I would not be unduly influenced by their interpretation.

I asked Jo, my companion, his opinion of the purpose of these horizontal stones. He shrugged. "I don't know exactly. It's possible that visitors or guardians slept on them." An astonishingly similar association to mine! He seemed to be even more connected with this place than with Hagar Qim and he animatedly described everything to me.

"Look at this," he said, as we walked around the outer walls and saw a small circular room which was connected through an opening with the inner room. "Here the oracle priestesses stood and gave their messages in reply to the questions asked by the people in the temple."

"I think that it was rather the other way around," I said thoughtfully. "Those who had questions for the oracle came here. And they received their answers from the oracle priestesses on the inside."

"The books tell it differently," he insisted.

"Who knows?" I said, "Even the authors of the books do not know what it was really like. Actually we can only guess and take it for our own inspiration."

He saw that I was seriously interested in the temples and he seemed to be happy about it. He offered me the chance to wait until the temples were closed and then return with him to study everything in peace, as he had the key.

"Fewer people," he said, "That's better, isn't it?"

I had the impression that I was being offered an important opening to memories from the past. Being alone in a temple for a while and being able to fully connect with my mediumistic vision was certainly my biggest wish. Of course I agreed.

ADVENTURE WITH A FISHERMAN

For those who know the path
The cosmos opens –
Those who have lost it
See only chaos
Monica Sjöö [22]

Jo and I were standing at the entrance of the temple thinking about what to do now, as we still had a lot of time until the temple would close.

"If you want, I will show you the caves at the sea. It is one of the most beautiful places on the island. Yesterday I was there with a German woman. She immediately wanted to swim. You can even swim naked there. You will see. It is worth going there," he said, in that tone which transports wishes.

I felt the adrenaline shooting into my blood. An unknown man was offering to climb down to the sea with me and was talking about swimming naked. He didn't hide the fact that only yesterday he had been there with another woman. I liked him for that. The sexual energy which I had already felt a little, now started vibrating between us and filled my body with tension.

How different the worlds in one's fantasies can be depending on whether one follows fear and mistrust or images of trust, a fine censor inside me noticed immediately. Fear leads to images of violence: an unknown man with a dark expression who would force me while climbing, into sexual acts where no one could help me, who would use me for his pent-up unfulfilled sexuality, who would have enough strength to overpower me. And if I tried to defend myself he could throw me down into the sea. Nobody would miss me until after some days someone would notice that nobody answers the telephone in my apartment. When you follow fear, there is a vast choice of horrific pictures to choose from: film, TV, media, one's own fantasies and last but not least, reality, are full of such pictures.

The alternative is to choose trust.

Choose your thoughts in such a way that you can remain in the light, was the intuition which I now followed. In my imagination it led me down to the sea. I could enjoy the beauty and wildness of nature and was led to places which I would otherwise never have seen. I was at the side of an attractive and knowledgeable guide and I had the unique offer of the temple visit. While climbing down I could check if I felt like having a sexual adventure, and if so, I could invite the man at a beautiful place by the sea on a sun-warmed rock, for a mutual celebration of sensual love. That would certainly correspond more to the ancient world of original trust to which I was connecting through my research. I stood at an inner junction where I could choose my path, and I knew that I had to be precise.

I recalled the introductory words of Lilith. How would she act in her incorruptible love of truth? My thoughts were moving rapidly. I have a lot of experience with men and I know how to make their sexual tension disappear. But to Jo I felt attracted. I was not yet sure if I was also already sexually open to him as I knew what kind of desire a southern man has for a woman once she has opened the gate for him. But I trusted him. I liked his sober and simple way of speaking and I was really happy about his offer to visit the temple after it was officially closed.

Now I remembered the *I Ching* oracle from the morning.

Embrace those who are imperfect and also those who have been abandoned, trust those who know how to cross rivers and do not neglect those who are in the distance. When the companions have left you can understand the value of balanced action and this provides brilliance and glory.

I had to smile thinking that it could also be meant so direct-ly. I accepted. In the bright sun we climbed down the shim-mering bluish-pink rocks. He confidently led the way and I followed. At the more difficult points he turned and reached to help me. I did not feel a hint of fear. As we climbed down I looked at his bull-like neck and his sun-darkened skin which already showed some wrinkles. The traces of wind and weather were visible on his leathery skin. I saw how his strong black hair nuzzled into his neck. I liked him and I now had the feeling that I would – not right away, but probably soon – do it with him. We took a break at a wild canyon where the cliff dropped away directly to the sea. I estimated the drop that opened before us to be about thirty to forty metres. I caught my breath and stepped backwards as I don't have a head for heights at all. Fantasies of fear and violence briefly touched me then, but again I heard the voice of Lilith.

You cannot develop peace between humans as long as you are in resonance with the powers of violence.

I decisively ended this second attack of violent fantasies. Often it is our fantasies and fears which separate us from a much more beautiful reality.

We sat down two metres away from the cliff on a sun-warmed stone.

"Are you married?" he asked.

"No, but I live in a partnership," I answered. "And you?"

He shook his head. I started to ask him about himself and his life. He had worked in the temple for seven years and he loved this work. His salary was just enough to live on, and he earned additional money by fishing. He was the son of a fisherman and had grown up in a big family. If I understood him correctly, he lived in a very simple garage where he also stored his fishing nets.

"Do you also cook there?" I asked him.

"Yes," he said proudly. "When I visit my friends in Berlin I always cook for them."

He had never wanted to marry.

"Marrying – that's not good. There are so many difficulties in a relationship. The women on Malta are very jealous. When you are married you are not allowed to go to another woman ever again. And I don't want to lie. It is better like this," he said, and told about the women he had met recently.

He told me that he often met women who invited him sexually, or rather, whom he invited successfully. I was impressed by his simple honesty. He invited me on all kinds of possible adventures: a trip in his fishing boat to show me sea caves, a trip to Gozo. Again I had to smile when remembering the *I Ching*: *"Trust those who know how to cross the great water"*.

While we had been slowly getting to know each other we had been climbing further down and had arrived at the sea. Crystal-clear water played softly and peacefully around the bay. A large cave opened into the cliffs. Jo said that people lived here in the summers and that the people of former times must have lived in the caves, as hardly any houses had been found on Malta. He also mentioned that excavations had uncovered very diverse finds, including unusual animals from former times.

"Do you want to swim?" he asked.

"No."

At this moment I only wanted to sit on a rock in silence and enjoy the view of the great ocean. So, here they had lived thousands of years ago and had developed their own culture. They had been protected from the immensity of the ocean. They had trained their telepathic abilities to communicate with the people on the mainland. In my vision, Malta had been a central communication point. Some special treasure and special knowledge, valued and used all over the world, had been guarded here. But did the ancestors also have direct contact with the people on the mainland? Did ships already exist at that time? And how did people live on the island itself? Were they also nomadic? Did they live in caves, as Jo thought? Living a permanently nomadic life on such a small island didn't seem to make much sense. What did the vegetation look like? What kind of animals were here? The sculptures of Tarxien showed clearly that pets, sheep and pigs had already existed.

Even though the temple of Tarxien was younger than Hagar Qim, I was still surprised that the domestication of animals had started so early. It is said that the temples on Malta are older than the oldest pyramids in Egypt. Was there also a connection to Egypt here? The more I started to befriend this place, the more lively the questions became to me, and my hunger for knowledge increased. I would surely soon be able to gather things together through my own intuition and also through reading books. Again I had the strong impression that these temples originated from a slightly later culture than the stone circle in Portugal. Concerning my dreams, there must have also been stone circles and some megaliths here which came from an even earlier culture. So I was deep in thought and for a while had almost forgotten Jo, who was still sitting next to me in silence.

I was just wondering what the fish meant. Why had I received the direction in the stone circle to be aware of the symbol of the fish? What was the connection between the fish and Malta, Crete and Egypt? I should follow its traces to the early Christians. *Don't lose sight of those in the distance,* the *I Ching* had said. That was maybe a hint that I would now have the opportunity to get into deeper contact with the early Christian culture and to learn more about it.

Jo asked "Shall we go up again?"

"Yes," I said, grateful that he was not at all pushy. Again I had to smile, realising that here was a first, quite profane, connection to the fish. Jo was the son of a fisherman and a fisherman himself. He had opened the first gate to Malta for me. Encounters with fishermen are not normal for me.

He easily climbed back up the cliffs, although he was a smoker. I could barely follow. At the halfway point, we made the next break. I was completely out of breath.

"Do you want me to kiss you?" he asked.

"Not yet," I answered. Out of breath, I indeed did not feel

like kissing. But I enjoyed the erotic tension between us. It gave wings to my spirit and I knew now that I would do it with him soon. He had gained my full trust and I was only waiting for the right situation to create it in a way that I would like it.

He suggested eating something and then waiting until the temples closed.

"I once made love with a woman there. It was amazing. If you want, we can do it there," he suggested.

"Maybe. We will see," I answered, again surprised at his combination of directness and sensitivity. In a small harbour bar, close to the bay of Ghar Lapsi, I ate ravioli with Maltese cheese filling. Jo sat opposite me without eating anything. Often we sat in front of each other without talking. The erotic tension had increased immensely. I knew that we should not wait any longer. It would still take an hour until the temples would close, and much as I liked the idea of a sexual adventure in the temples, I wanted first to greet them in calm. Only when I had fully taken in the special and sacred power of this place would it seem appropriate to me to look for the right place there to honour the Goddess and the old temples of love. It was a beautiful picture to show my respect for the ancestors by offering my body in the sacred temple to a simple fisherman and to give him something of my knowledge of sensual love, to give him something in return for the opening to the temple that he had made possible. This was a continuation of the customs of the prehistoric culture. Those who had made peace with the body could also make peace with the world. This had been one of the great secrets of the early cultures, through which they ensured the peace of their tribe.

Now it would no longer be creative to wait. Jo suggested showing me his "garage". I accepted happily. I was curious about his "villa" at the sea. We took my car and he showed me the way. A steep street led us down to a bay. Directly above the sea was a long row of many garages built of stone. In front of one of the gates he asked me to stop. He opened the green, slightly weathered iron gate, and we stood in his "palace". In the back corner stood a simple bed. Around the bed and on the walls were many calendar pictures of naked and half-naked women. So they were his temple servants, at least in his fantasy. Judging by the pictures, he did not have the worst taste. In the middle of the room stood a table covered with tools. Everywhere – on the ceiling, above the bed, on a board, were fishing nets. In the corner on a chair stood a strange vessel with a small lamp which was blinking. When I went there I saw that the vessel contained many small eggs. He was breeding baby birds here. In another corner stood his stove on which he prepared his food. Impressed, I looked around his house. But there was not much time left for that. A hand came and touched my body. We kissed, and I softly put my hand on his lips when his kisses became a little too fast and intense.

"Slow down, we have time," I said. We undressed and went to his bed. He had a good firm grip and a velvet skin: exactly what I love about men. On his arms he had some tattoos. His belly was soft. For me this is more sensual than rigid, over-trained male bellies. With the surrender and lustful fascination of the very first time, he played with my breasts. Often in such moments, the small boy is still very alive in the man, the boy who is finally allowed to arrive at the breasts of the mother without being punished by her for that. He is allowed to act undisguised, elementarily, directly. What liberation for both genders! He already came once before the sexual act. He was a little ashamed about it. For me it was completely okay. Performance anxiety between the genders is one of the main obstacles which make a normal and undisguised encounter more difficult. Isn't it normal that a man who has not been with a woman for a long time ejaculates too early? It is actually a beautiful sign of desire and honour of the female gender. I did not have the feeling of having received too little attention. I do not like it at all when I feel that a man is mainly occupied with the question of how to satisfy me.

I was also not especially hungry or needy as I felt well-nourished by my men at home. He was hungry like a wolf. He didn't want to stop yet, and his directness further increased my lust. I held his beautifully formed, relatively big phallus in my hand and it did not take long before it was ready again in its full size and splendour. We put on the condom and now he had gained sufficient calm to enter me ever more deeply with his careful and powerful thrusts. It was a beautiful, simple, almost animal-like creative contact. Afterwards we rested for a while next to each other. We got up and he showed me some more pictures of a young pretty German woman who had been with him.

"Great that despite the general trend of sexual phobia, there are still other women who love sex and who also show it," I thought.

While I was standing there looking at the pictures and at the room in its natural tidiness, I suddenly remembered a dream from long ago on the *Chairos,* a sailing boat. We had been there for research into contact with dolphins. One night I had had a moving dream.

I am standing on a beach on an unknown island. A dolphin jumps out of the water directly into my arms. I stand there completely astonished and with the question what I should do with this dolphin on land. I ask myself how to save it. At that moment the dolphin changes into a fisherman who points towards a simple hut where he lives.

Now I remembered who Jo reminded me of. He was the man from this dream which I remembered so clearly. Now I remembered many things from that journey. The permanent high tone of the dolphins which we heard through the loudspeakers on board and which I could later also hear without loudspeakers. This tone had brought me after some days into a very particular track of perception and made me perceive the events of everyday life quite differently than I usually did. I had been almost permanently in a mythological space of experience. I remembered with what intensity I had perceived the fishermen at the harbour. At that moment they all represented a mythological message for me. One of them had continually spoken about Mary, who symbolised the archetypical mother for him. At that time I discovered a deep connection between Mary: the mother of God, and the fish. But all that had its own logic which I could not remember clearly, rather as if in a dream. It was the second time that my unconscious referred to the fish in the contact with Jo. At first I just perceived it without any further interpretation.

Today I would not visit the temples any more, but tomorrow afternoon I wanted to come back and visit the temples all on my own.

The matrilineal system of descent of the ancient times, in connection with the access to the sources of food and natural abundance which the women in the village-cultures of neolithic times, with their fruits and their clay vessels and Goddess figurines still had, guaranteed personal and erotic independence. But in the course of time (…) this natural participation in communitarian processes was taken away from the women, and they were suppressed into the privacy of marriage.

A system of snake-movements (…) in the mystery temples of the orient, was the most direct path to supranatural vision. The illusion of fixed forms disappears through appropriate stimulation.

Eluan Ghazal

NIGHT THOUGHTS ABOUT A FEMALE REVOLUTION

That evening, in the small hotel bar, I took out a book which I had received as a gift from a friend shortly before I left for Malta. It was the book *Schlangenkult und Tempelliebe. Sakrale Erotik in archaischen Gesellschaften* by Eluan Ghazal[6]. I ordered a Maltese beer and started to read, fascinated. I opened the book at a page which, to my surprise, fitted perfectly with the experience I had had today: it was about the sensual love of early priestesses and queens. Eluan Ghazal wrote about Celtic women who, in return for services of all kinds which were important to them, offered their bodies.

The author comments:

In both the East and West, priestesses used their "sacred body" to guide the community. Today this is different. Which women – western or eastern – would be able to do that! Lady Diana had to hide her affairs, and when they became public, she lost the throne.

I had to smile when I thought of today's adventure. Would the report about the experience with Jo the fisherman fit into the book? Was it by now acceptable to include these simple elementary experiences in our research journeys? A large proportion of humankind would perceive my experience as dishonouring the sacred. Because of such self-revelations they would question the sincerity of my work. But part of my work and what I stand for is overcoming privacy in these essential issues of the human being. My task in the service of a new femininity and of politics of the heart is specifically to liberate the concepts of love and especially the sexual concepts from the private ghettos. To talk about the things which one does not usually reveal, and to talk about them without artificial sentimentality in a way that sensual truths can return to the light: this is what the prehistoric culture, wild Lilith and with her many women, demand from me today. It was clear to me that I had to include these adventures which had occurred in the search for prehistory.

"The first women have found the path. They will open new doors and gates," I thought, grateful for this beautiful book, well-written by a woman who found words to express similar issues to mine. At this moment, this book was a friend at my side. My heart was full and longed to share. Soon I would tell Pierre about my experiences.

I have the exceptional possibility in my life that I can tell my lover Pierre openly about such intimate experiences. I know that a part of my revolutionary power originates in the fact that we have both remained faithful to the erotic issue in our lives and have tried in every way we can to stay truthful. A different kind of friendship would not be possible with Pierre. Like me, he is on the search for new ways of living and he is a revolutionary and a political thinker. We do not have many possibilities on such a path to withdraw together into false ideas of love. I know that he does not only accept my experiences because it is necessary, but that he joyfully participates in my adventures and that this increases our erotic attraction and anticipation. If women in important societal positions could and would act like this officially, if they did not have to hide it, what a different world would open up! Lady Diana became a public idol despite her affairs. Her funeral showed this clearly.

I continued reading, and to my surprise I noticed that Eluan Ghazal also wrote about Malta. Her touchingly sensual and female language, and also the pictures of the sleeping priestess and of other figures, fascinated me. I am always grateful when I meet women who are on their own path of emancipation and still, or possibly because of that, positively affirm sensual love in all of its aspects. If enough such women unite, who no longer submit to the man, but who also no longer fight against him, if they unite in a new and deeper kind of solidarity which does not end because of love issues, if women decide to research the secret of Eros in its depths again after all these many millennia, if we are ready to take on the social responsibility connected to that again, wouldn't it then become possible to introduce a transformation and revolution in love with worldwide consequences? Wouldn't that be an important new beginning for female politics in the third millennium? How else should the massacre, the eternal killing and the fight between the genders ever end?

I continually dream of such a revolution: of a non-violent revolution of soft power. Why should we continue to support something which creates despair in ourselves and others? I can see what will happen when mothers and young women, saints and prostitutes, wives and single women, unite in true female solidarity; when the prostitute is no longer a threat to the wife and the wife no longer a threat to the lover because they can communicate together on a deeper level, as they know that they all see and seek the same in the man. Now they can share the work and make men become the lovers they have hoped and longed for through the centuries. Mothers will no longer allow their sons to grow up in a system that makes them into soldiers or criminals, into secret or open murderers, or into robots without emotions and feelings, into CEOs of huge companies who have to compensate for what they lost of life and love with a false power.

Women will remember their true female power. Together they are able to stop the eternal cycle of massacre, the killing, torturing and death, and to recall the simple qualities of life, love and the Goddess. Isn't there a historical key hidden here that can end the power of a Hitler or a Putin, can end the war in the Middle East and ensure that the refugees in the Congo receive help? We would finally stop paying attention to the meaningless debates of vain politicians who perpetuate a system of violence and corruption. A new and deeper women's solidarity contains an overwhelming power and magic for every male heart. We have to fully regain this knowledge now, as until then women are far too ready to believe in their powerlessness instead of believing in their power.

During the next days I visited Hagar Qim and Mnajdra several more times. I had the opportunity to enjoy the temples in calm, alone. Jo played the guardian and I finally had the chance to follow my intuitions. What Jo was doing was in no way allowed. Of course one tries to protect the temples from strangers. One of the temples is already marked with ugly graffiti at several places. Even the guardians are not allowed to visit the temples with foreigners outside opening times. During my research, Jo was hiding behind a stone at the entrance gate and took care that nobody disturbed me. I thanked him and all good spirits for making this possible.

Twice I could visit these sacred places alone. I saw clear pictures of life as it was originally lived in the temples. Now I was looking forward to spending some days in the hotel writing down my intuitions and reading the many interesting books which I had brought with me. Although I had had hardly any literature to support my research into the stone circle in Almendres, I had found quite some material about Malta. Shortly before I had left for Malta, my publisher had given me a book about the island. In my world-view there are no coincidences. Coincidence is only a word for contexts which we have not yet investigated. Late in the afternoon after my second temple visit, I said goodbye to Jo, drove back to my hotel and spent the next two days there.

IN THE TEMPLE OF DREAM-POWER

I climbed onto a huge flat altar-stone which was magically attracting me in Mnajdra Temple. I assume that oracle priestesses slept here to receive their messages. It is conventionally estimated that the temple was built about three thousand years before Christ. But I feel that all this took place much earlier. Maybe later these stones were used for other purposes: for sacrifices, religious ceremonies, as an altar, as a place for harvest offerings and many other purposes. But originally, the oracle priestesses slept here. This thought stayed with me stubbornly.

Jo had left me alone, so I could listen to my intuitions in silence.

I felt my cellular system changing, and I was now close to opening myself to the resonance pattern and frequencies of inspiration. My images and intuition led me to the heart of an ancient culture.

In a side-room I see women guarding a fire that must never be allowed to die: the sacred fire of life. I seem to be in a temple-school for the education of female shamans. One could also call them priestesses. Here they learn the arts of prophesy and oracle.

In Mnajdra, three priestesses guarded the sacred grove in rotating service. They were in permanent contact with Raschnim, the head shaman in the caves of Hal Saflieni. The Hypogeum was there, about half a day's walk away from here. For some centuries the Hypogeum of Hal Saflieni had been the place where the oldest priestesses guarded the knowledge of Creation inside Mother Earth. They were in permanent contact with Mother Earth and received vital messages from Her. In Hal Saflieni, the stories of the cultural development of Malta from more than two thousand years ago were guarded and passed-on. This temple had been built as an underground cave so that contact with the powers of the Earth could remain undisturbed. The women felt protected here from the frequencies which had increasingly disturbed the oracle and the telepathic connections to the other tribes during the last years. Since tribes spreading the concepts of power and domination had been living on Earth, the development of the peaceful cultures had become endangered. The priestesses did everything to avoid disturbing the germinating powers of creative dreams of peace. The wise temple-priestesses who had given their service to Mother Earth for centuries were buried here in a specially created room. So the Hypogeum was both temple and sacred burial space. The dead were later honoured as sacred contact persons and consulted by the priestesses who followed after them. They had agreed certain signs with their successors, so that their messages could be recognised.

But let's return to Mnajdra, the temple and former dolmen power-place. And let us fathom this place.

The large altar on which I was sitting had been guarded by one of the priestesses at all important times. Around full moon and new moon, one of the priestesses always held her sacred temple-sleep here to receive special messages from Nammu, the Mother Goddess. The others prepared for three days and three nights for this special time, to then be ready for the divine answers from the mouths of those qualified to give them. They passed on the knowledge received from the Goddess and the newly-gained answers when the many inhabitants of the island came to the temple for the public oracle. Once a month, the oracle was open to all the inhabitants of the island. They came when they had questions in special situations in life.

The people I saw were rather small and delicate: very different to those I had seen in the surroundings of the Almendres stone circle. Thoughtfully, I looked around from my raised position. The entrance faced east. Two imposing stones separated this room from a bigger elliptical room. In front of the entrance to that room were two large ashlars which looked as if they were meant to provide seating for those who came for the oracle and for priestesses-to-be. Outside the protection wall stood three large stones which outshone everything. Where was I? What was the purpose of the elliptical anteroom? Why was the room in which I was sitting separated from the anteroom by a smaller altar? I closed my eyes again so that my intuitions and impressions could deepen ...

In the room to the south of me, two young priestesses are stoking a fire. They are servants of the temple and are being educated here in the art of oracle. The three large stones standing outside the protection walls radiate a very personal energy.

We represent the three sacred aspects of life: past, present and future. Depending on which state of presence you are in, you access different aspects of a possible future and past. This process is very important for the education of the young priestesses, as they have to learn to focus in such a way that they only let in the desired information which serves the healing and protection of the whole archipelago.

The other meaning of these three sacred stones is that they represent the female cycle of the trinity of the Goddess: the aspect of birth and youth, the aspect of maturity and sexual union, and the aspect of death and rebirth into a new form of existence. The priestesses have the task of balancing these three original powers of the Goddess for the whole tribe and of making them usable.

"What is the purpose of the outer room, which is called the oracle room? Did the oracle priestesses really stand there?" I asked. This conventional interpretation did not fit into my picture, as that would mean that those who came with questions were in the inner part of the temple, while the priestesses were standing outside in an extremely strange and uncomfortable position, giving their messages through holes in the wall.

No. This room will only be added later. Those who come for only one day to the oracle to seek advice remain in the outer area of the temple and ask their questions from there, came the immediate answer.

Those who have particularly existential questions prepare themselves accordingly. They stay for three days and three nights at places intended for that purpose, before they consult the oracle. Then they are assigned a certain place in the inner part of the temple, where they receive the answer. Before they receive their answer from the oracle priestess, they must first practise finding answers themselves, because every person is trained in discovering the aspect of the Goddess within themselves. After three days they are allowed to enter the fire room in front of the small altar, give their offering and then tell the oracle the answer that they have found during the previous days and nights. Then they are allowed to receive the message from the oracle, which is told either by the oracle herself, or by one of the young priestesses.

"Do you sacrifice animals?" I asked.

At first we did not. Later we did. The field evoked by the story of Manu, which occurred at a very different place on the mainland, is having an effect. Of course it is known here too. Guardians of peace have come to Malta from many directions for centuries. Tamara, Newar and Vatsala were co-founders of the Maltese culture, and their names are passed on according to their tradition. The language spoken here has developed over the centuries from the many languages of those who arrived here. What happened between Manu and Meret has not remained an isolated incident. In Eastern Europe and Northern Asia, but also at other places in the world, very individual patriarchal cultures have developed from this, worshipping a god or gods of war. Their information and actions cloud the telepathic ether. This leads to the concept of sacrifice as reparation. Especially in the upper temple, Hagar Qim, you find places where animals were sacrificed. It is not possible to understand this quickly. Come back to it. You will get to know more about this later.

"What is the purpose of the large room in the East? Why are there two temples here in the same shape? Between the two temples there is also a small strange room with a columnar altar. What is the purpose of this room?" I asked.

Walk around. Look around. Open your intuitive antennae. You will receive information in a frequency of images rather than words. Surrender to these images and you will get to know more about life on Malta many millennia ago.

I walked through the softly sunlit rooms of the temple. I visited every room and stayed in each for some time. First I went into a chamber between the two temples, which was connected to a cell. One could only reach the chamber from the centre of the temple, through a tiny gate. I sat down on a low stone which seemed to be inserted into the wall as a bench, and thoughtfully looked at the small altar with its slim columns, which seemed almost like a traditional fireplace. Pictures came to me immediately. I felt like a young student priestess from prehistory, waiting to be taken into the high service of an oracle-priestess in training.

NUDIME SPEAKS

In a small room stands a jar of water. There are also some dried berries and a few fruits for me. I have been sitting here for two days already. I have to hold out for one more day and one more night, with little water and the few fruits. At a given hour one of the priestesses will also give me some of the berries, which will enable me to clearly see the vision which I am to receive here with open eyes. The berries support the contact to the great Goddess Nammu, with whom I am to connect myself now, to initiate the next phase of my life – maturity.

The berries appeared to me in a dream as a support for the contact with the Goddess. In the next days it will be decided whether I will enter education as a dream-dancer, or whether my profession will be as a guardian of plants. I deeply long to be accepted into the circle of the temple priestesses. Mudima, the oldest priestess here, received me a week ago in the neighbouring temple, together with 27 other students, and held a speech of warning and introduction.

"Pay attention to your wishes. Your wishes are signposts to your true nature which waits for you in Nammu, your universal mother, and which is now germinating inside you. Sometimes wishes make you too impatient, and you become separated from the greater cosmic knowledge. You are then no longer able to hear the fine frequencies and nuances which make it possible for your wishes to be manifested at the right time. The story of Manu and Meret shows us what misery can overcome humans if they act too early and do not remain in contact with Nammu. Nammu, in whom we are all embedded securely and who lives in each of us, knows the right moment. Always stay centred. Do not follow impatient desire, but be aware where your desire leads you if you remain calmly in the centre of your body. True visions are always born of calm and inner fulfilment. This is how you can recognise them. There are inner movements and feelings which you experience as a great longing. They drive

Creation forward. They come from the original dream of the universal mother, of Creation and wisdom of which we are all part. Sometimes this longing wants to carry us away and seduce us to act too early. Everything comes at the right time. Longing needs the power of calm in order to manifest. The paradise for whose manifestation we are all here is born only from calm."

We all greatly love and admire Mudima. Mischief, grace and knowledge twinkle in her eyes. At the age of 85, she can still move her belly and hips and let the Goddess of the Moon talk from within her. We young women observe her performance with a mixture of deep seriousness, awe and serenity. She is able to tell the stories of our people's past in such shimmering colours that they become alive directly in front of our eyes. Mudima is my anchor and my role model. Later I want to become like her.

Every year, 28 young women from the island who have reached the age of maturity, and who have stayed for one revolution of the moon in the sacred women's temple on the neighbouring island of Gozo, are called here to receive a deeper introduction into the art of dreaming and of visions. We are here to learn to listen to the voice of Nammu, of original Creation, and to bring her secrets to fruition, as far as this is still possible after the first injuries which have taken place far away. We learned that many of our ancestors have already gone to different spheres to guard the secret of Creation there, which is damaged since the incident with Manu. The gifts of the Great Mother – recollection, the art of dreaming, intuition, memory – are threatened with destruction. We know about this. We were already told as children about the disruption of evolution and Creation. We are consciously on Earth and have the task of making a culture flourish and manifesting the dream of paradise, at least at some places on this planet, so that it can manifest in the cellular system and the bio-genetic memory. It is our task to take it further towards completion despite the dangers. If we are careful enough, we can manifest this dream. We hope that we can do so, despite the aggressive actions of the Kurgan tribes on the European mainland. The warlike tribes *from the north have increasingly spread in all directions. It is necessary to advance our culture to the point where the seedling of love protected by Nammu can grow. And in later centuries, when all humans will see the error of their ways, guardians of peace will be able to access our dream from the memory of the Earth. Then it can be brought to completion. We must manifest the dream of Nammu, of Mother Earth, which is unique in the whole of Creation. At the heart of this original dream is the realisation of sensual love between men and women, the manifestation and fulfilment of polarities. We must learn to deal consciously with the nature of space and time.*

Smell, taste, sight, hearing, sensing, touch, movement, talking, and making sounds are all qualities which exist in this form only on Earth. They carry an idyllic possibility of fulfilment. All spaces of existence are connected to and in relation with the universal whole and only find their purpose, authority and fulfilment in this connection.

Mudima the temple priestess came to us every morning last week. In the inner area of the second temple, she practised the dances which make it easier to cleanse the body for the messages of the Goddess with us. Then she asked about our dreams. We were all sleeping together in the neighbouring temple. We were awoken twice each night and asked about our dreams. Sometimes it happens that young women have very special dreams. Then they are called into the inner area of the temple. Sometimes it also happens that a woman is visited by the power of the Goddess during a dance. Women who are visited by the Goddess during a dance are sent to the upper temple, to Hagar Qim, for further preparation and education at the place of dances, studies and love.

The temple here is the temple of the art of dreaming. Further up is the temple of dances and the art of love. Both temples are guarded only by women, by the oracle priestesses. In the upper temple, men are also educated. Here in the temple of dreaming, nine of the twenty-eight young women are called into the inner temple during one revolution of the moon, for one cycle of dreaming and waking. Three of them are chosen to enter the temple education. All will eventually be directed to her task and place.

During last night, my sixth night in Mnajdra, I was suddenly shaken strongly in my dream. The eyes of a night owl were looking at me, and I recognised in them the eyes of Surnja, my grandmother, who died two years ago. As soon as I perceived the owl, it transformed into my grandmother, who gave me red berries. Because of the intense shaking of my body, the eyes of Surnja, and the red berries, I realised that this was my dream and the sign that would lead me into the temple.

I already knew that I would be called into the temple to receive initiation. Then Mudima called me to her.

"Is there a plant who recognised you in your dreams and who called you?" she asked.

"Yes. The red berry," I answered. The red berry is a plant which rarely grows in our area. There are many similar plants, but the red berry is a sacred plant which is dedicated to the Goddess of sexuality and healing.

"Then go to the mountain. You have twelve hours. If you find five red berries, bring them with you. They will grant you entrance into the temple."

I set off, and after I had walked for six hours, I found exactly five of the longed-for red berries. Happily and hastily, I ran the many kilometres I had walked during my search, back to the temple. I was allowed to enter. I thanked the Goddess and gave Priestess Mudima my five berries, with a huge smile.

For three days and three nights I have to remain awake in the anteroom, until the decision is taken whether I am allowed to sleep the sacred sleep on one of the sacred stones during full moon, where I would receive my initiatory dream. On this night it will be decided whether my future profession will be inside the temple or whether I will have to fulfil my task somewhere else.

I have been sitting in the anteroom of waking visions for two days already. Three times a day one of the priestesses looks in through the window and asks for my intuitions and special experiences. This evening I will get to know whether I will be accepted for the night of the round moon.

THE TEACHINGS OF MUDIMA

My dream has come true. I have been accepted for the night of the round moon, and to the school for Mirjas. I will learn the arts of dreaming and oracle. Already in Ggantija, the temple on Gozo, my name had been announced to me: Nudime. It means 'She who studies with Mudima'. How much I had to practice to let this dream go, to stay unattached to it! This is one of the most important exercises which every prospective oracle-priestess has to learn: not to become attached to one's own wishes. Only then is it possible that their universal effectiveness and their sacred law of growth can unfold freely and thereby manifest. I have made this important first learning step successfully. Nammu has heard my dream; I can go to the school of Malta. It takes seven years. Afterwards it will be decided whether I will be sent on pilgrimage for some time or whether I will learn the higher levels of the sacred oracle. This would then lead me to the centre, to the Hypogeum of Hal Saflieni. Our three ancestors, Tamara, Newar and Vatsala, hold their sacred sleep of death there, under the earth. I hope that one day I will be called by one of them for further education. Three women have been chosen for the school of the Mirjas. Two for the sacred dances of the snake, and I for the art of dreaming. For one revolution of the moon we will not leave the temple, and will be prepared for the important initial stages of knowledge.

Today is the day on which Mudima wants to gather us all to tell us in more detail about the school on Malta and the development of our peoples. We are to be introduced more deeply into the secrets of the guardians of peace and our tasks as prospective Mirjas. We have all gathered in the big anteroom of the southern temple of Mnajdra, to listen to the words of Mudima. Mudima arrives, sits down on one of the flat altar stones which are dedicated to the sleeping Nammu, and starts to talk.

"Some thousands of years ago the first people came to this island on ships from nearby Sicily. They were a peaceful people who had learned the art of dreaming and were therefore in direct contact with mother Nammu. The spirit of the fish had appeared to them as a sign of peace. It told them that some of them were to cross the water to settle on Malta. They were to found a place on the island of Gozo, which was one of the centres of the world according to Nammu. This place was especially suitable for the arts of dreaming and reception. They would come into contact from here with guardians of peace all over the Earth and be able to communicate with them in dreams.

They built the first stone circle on Gozo. Over time, caves and a labyrinth developed underneath it, in which they buried their dead with presents for Nammu and their ancestors. Their small clay godesses which were to serve the fertility of following generations still rest there. Mudima, who then had the name I am allowed to carry today, was the custodian of the lying stone. She had telepathic contact from here with a tribe in the south of Portugal. It was the tribe of the dream-guardians who lived in Portugal close to a powerful stone circle which had been there for several centuries already and had collected peace knowledge in condensed form. She also had contact with Eritrea, Asia, Tibet and India, and also with the tribes who were on the way to strengthen the sacred streams of Mother Earth, to nourish them and receive important information from them. Together with related tribes they started geistig preparation for the coming culture and oracle school of Malta which was intended to make it possible to maintain the coming peace culture for as long as possible despite the rise of the first opposing powers.

It was a thousand years ago that Tamara, Newar and Vatsala arrived here from Portugal. More boats arrived shortly after them, from Eritrea and the country of the fertile crescent, later called Egypt, from Anatolya, Nubia, India and other places of the Earth. Later generations built the temples in Zebbiegh and Buggiba to honour the Fish-Goddess Nun, the guardian of

114

peace. And over the course of the next centuries the school of Malta arose.

The first signs of violence had appeared on Earth two thousand years ago. They spread like wildfire, but at the same time our arising peace-culture was being further developed and refined. Conscious contact to mother Nammu became ever more important. In many parts of Europe the Earth was quaking, and natural catastrophes occurred as mother Nammu was gravely injured. Intense outbreaks of violence started throughout Europe 1300 years ago, and many guardians of peace left their original homes and set off to protect Nammu and guard Her dream. They could not allow themselves to become infected with the concepts of violence and fear.

Then, about four hundred years ago there was another peak of violence, not only in Europe, but also in India and Asia. Our guardians of peace on Malta had expanded the sacred temples and partly surrounded the places where there were originally only domes with huge protection walls. These stones have been carrying our memories since ancient times. We had to guard and protect them. The influx of people to Malta has increased since the armies have been marching through the land again and have killed many tribes. Students who want to connect to the knowledge of the guardians of peace have been coming and are chosen by Nammu to enter this school. More and more temples are being built so that we are prepared for all the coming tasks. Meanwhile, powerful priest-castes have developed at various places on the mainland. They all worship mainly male gods; gods of war. This arose from a concept which long ago became independent and which is not compatible with the dreams of Nammu: the concept of power. Men wanted to gain power and domination over others. At first, they wanted to gain power over the woman. Then this concept of power expanded and transformed into the concept of domination of whole countries and peoples. This self-created dream grew in men, and took on its own momentum.

Even in the old cultures, women are starting to neglect their original dreams. A certain amnesia is slipping in. They like it when their men become ever stronger and take over more of the women's tasks. They also like it when the men approach them in a new, more masculine way, as it is their desire in love that men transform from the son archetype towards a more masculine archetype who can be partner and lover for the women in all areas, particularly the sensual. As this longing is so huge in the women, they do not notice that the men are only feigning potency, following a false concept of power. It does not correspond to the actual archetypical true nature of the men.

The women do not pay attention to the coming danger which lies in the new development. They thereby allow invasive powers to creep into their dreams. When the nomads with the new powerful priests visit them and tell them of the new belief systems, some of the women are willing to ally with them against Nammu. This is what led the Arya in India, the Mitanni in Egypt, the Luwians in Anatolia, the Kurgans in the north and east of Europe, and the Acheans and later also the Dorians of Greece, to wage war. They have even forged powerful weapons from the sacred treasures of Nammu: the metals of this Earth. This is a great offence against the sacred laws of Nammu. These metals, in which important knowledge is stored, are not created for killing, but serve organic flows within the Earth. It is only permitted to take from them when Nammu commands it in dreams, for example to create jewellery for the sacred dances of the fertility and love celebrations. The theft of these treasures of the Earth is increasingly causing catastrophes which take away the conditions necessary for life from people in some parts of the world.

You will ask yourselves why Nammu allows humans to destroy the conditions necessary for life for so many beings. But Nammu has Her authority only in cooperation with the human being. The human being is an important part of Her. If humans step out of this context, they have a huge destructive power, as the whole is disturbed by this action.

116

You can imagine how important it is becoming to guard our knowledge and to lay out the sacred corridors for the protection of the Earth and Nammu. Humans have created a power which is starting to spread and which continues to take effect even after death. It even makes it possible that the dead spread disinformation from Sirius or the Pleiades on Earth, which serves the unfolding of new gods of war. The new conquerors have to somehow manage to dethrone the ancient female goddesses.

Desertification is coming, caused by the disinformation and great destruction, closing like a ring around the Earth and blocking the sacred flow of information. The ritual of circumcision was introduced in Africa as a sin against sensuality, as they have also started to believe in punishing goddesses and gods there. Some tribes even sacrifice humans to influence the punishing goddess or the punishing god. All this is happening because of immense confusion and amnesia. A shift of power is taking place that few people are able to understand. Ever fewer people can avoid its effect. Some tribes are introducing a religion which transforms the religion of the original mother Jehovah as some call her into a religion of a male god which they call Jahwe or also Jehovah. Immense religions of male anger and destruction will thereby spread.

Our task is to protect and further develop our culture despite the increasing spread of these religions.

This male image of god carries an inherent power of destruction which in no way corresponds to the original divine aspect of the male in Creation. Religion is being used as a tool of power. It is a spiritual drug which distracts humans from freedom and presence for the world they are carrying within themselves. People separate from their own knowledge and from themselves to believe the promises of the religions, which postpone paradise to a life in the beyond. But the world itself is sacred and divine. We do not need religions to perceive this. Religions were created to make humans more submissive, dependent and controllable than ever before. And they have *an unimaginable effect. The whole world has become infected with the concept of power and submission. They will even try to destroy our stonework so that no memory of us and our culture will remain. Hatred of women and their knowledge has increased in these warlike peoples. Their only wish is to dominate Nammu and all women, and all knowledge which is guarded by women.*

All this has happened as a process of field-building. It was triggered by the premature birth of the dream of Manu and Meret. It is as if this dream has cosmically miscarried. The lover, born too early, is now enraged over his lost connection to the mother Goddess. Men will use all means possible to drive the human being away from the paradise which is germinating. They will do anything to condemn the female and will murder millions of women. They will particularly condemn sexual knowledge as the original female power lies there.

We have to take care that the messages of peace can develop further despite this. We must not allow the poison of anger and revenge to enter our hearts, as this is what causes the great amnesia and allows the anger which destroys life to extend over everything.

Those who follow anger too early cloud the purity of elementary and connected thought within themselves. We too have to get to know and carefully unfold the powers of rage within us. We need power to concentrate the anger within us into sacred rage. This gives us the ability to remain connected with Nammu, the powers of encompassing love and Creation even in the most difficult situations. In connection with sacred rage we will be able to develop the higher power which will eventually be able to save this planet Earth.

But first we have to guard and further manifest the germinating dream of Mother Earth. It is still young in the historical context of the universe. The war-cultures will reach this island in some centuries. Our task is to postpone this moment for as long as possible. By then we will have found other islands where we can manifest this knowledge further. As long as the dark gnawing thoughts do not reach our hearts, we can maintain this island. On your pilgrimages, be careful and discrete. It is not good to tell everyone of our knowledge as it could be misused. None of these peoples will know about the existence of Malta for a long time. We still have some centuries ahead of us to bring our culture to its full bloom and voice.

Tomorrow I will tell you about the guardians of knowledge on the mainland. We here on the island have the task of accompanying their actions with protective thoughts and dreams. To do this, we have to know their ways and methods. You have now learned many new things. We will protect you from too much knowledge of war and violence until you reach maturity, as you are not yet safe from the powers of anger and revenge. Destructive thoughts could reach your hearts. In the first years of your life it is important to get to know the cycle of life in its unclouded form. Your chakras and energetic centres of the body had to train themselves in knowing about your organism so that you are spiritually prepared for the coming tasks. Guard this knowledge. Also do not talk too much about it at your home-fires. Talkativeness attracts disinformation. Be reliable and discrete like the fish.

Your task is now to witness the powers of anger for three days and three nights. These will arise in everyone who hears the story of our ancestors. The anger might be directed against Nammu, against the powers of Creation that allowed human freedom to develop its own momentum. The anger might also be directed against those people who spread war over the Earth. Or it might rage inside you as an undirected power which eventually turns against you by transforming into an immense feeling of powerlessness. These possibilities are dangerous and they do not open the channel to sacred rage. Keep the balance, also in your anger. Be aware of the anger inside yourself and observe what happens because of it. You can witness the birth of violence. Don't fall for it! Pay attention which thoughts are created in you by anger. Then you become a witness of the formation inside you of a new, growing revolutionary creative power. *If you prevail, sacred rage will awaken within you. It carries the answers necessary for further development.*

You have to support the growth of this power in our men, as they have the task of healing the hurt caused by Manu. Take care that the anger connects with the power of the heart and the luminance of the sun in your body. Only then is it an elementary power which is necessary for development, and not a union with the arising thoughts of revenge and violence. Without a connection to the heart, anger is dangerous and destructive. In three days you will tell me what you have experienced, and from that it will be possible to draw conclusions about your further tasks."

Mudima finishes with these words, and we all go silently outside, to look at the sea, listen to the sounds of nature and think about what we have just learned. I feel a powerful grief and huge pain inside me. I would love to just surrender to my tears. But something inside me warns me to pause. I can feel and observe how the grief transforms into a so-far unknown power. My fists clench, and then I know that it is anger which is visiting me for the first time. It is simultaneously a feared and welcome guest, which I will observe during the next days. I will become the witness of the thoughts which arise from anger, and I have the task of transforming it into a sacred peaceful power.

LABYRINTH AND SPIRAL –
IN THE TEMPLE SCHOOL OF KNOWLEDGE

We are gathered together again.

Mudima has listened profoundly and precisely to the dreams and thoughts on the nature of sacred rage which we brought to her. Now we will find out what each of us has to do to get to know the secret of anger and to protect ourselves and Malta from its threat. Today she will tell us about our friends and tribal members who are on the mainland, guarding knowledge of peace through the centuries, and keeping it alive. She will also talk about the secrets of the labyrinth.

"*The germinating power of every new life grows through the labyrinth. All those who die are also led through the labyrinth once they have passed the threshold of death. In our culture it is guarded by Rashnim. It corresponds to the meanderings in our abdomen; it also corresponds to the spirals of our brain. You can also call the labyrinth the location and origin of the Goddess.*

Geographically, Malta and Gozo lie at the centre of our peace-culture. They are the geistig navel, from which new thoughts spread and to which they return. The spiral movement that can be recognised in the Milky Way is mirrored on Earth. Malta lies on such a spiral. From here we can easily reach Africa. From here, geodesic lines of knowledge lead to other countries. All lines of consciousness are connected with each other in some form of spiral. They can be recognised and perceived by a highly educated consciousness. One leads, for example, over Scandinavia, one over Sumer and Babylon, one over France, Spain and Portugal. These lines are connected with the life-creating movements of the double spiral, which is the origin of all beings and the beginning of every process of creation.

121

All spiritual processes can be explained by means of the spiral. This is also true of telepathy. It is spiral movements of light which spiritually lead you to those you want to reach. The more you learn to observe this process, the more consciously you can direct it. It is very important that you know the directions of the compass and their connection with the energetic streams of the Earth. Our ancestors wandered on these energy streams around the whole planet, as the information and healing mana streams of Nammu flow along them. They set stones at the important power places and energy nodes, which are continually recharged with the flowing and breathing vortex movements of the energies of Nammu.

Geomancy, alchemy and astronomy form a trinity. The same laws of life, which we have to protect, work in all three. They follow the creative processes of the spiral; the processes of materialisation and dematerialisation which are encoded in the double spiral. Become researchers, and observe vortices in water! Sit down in front of it for some hours and you can study all laws of mana and life-power. You will find the secret of stability hidden there, as well as the secret of becoming and passing away. True stability is always created by movement. The vortex follows the movements of the double spiral. The finer and quicker the movements become, the more stable the outer form appears.

A stone also follows this basic movement as it forms. But in this case your eyes cannot perceive the movement. It is only possible for us to use stone as an encoded store of human consciousness because we know these movements.

Our opponents think that we consider the stones to be gods and that this is why we worship them. They do not know that the reason a stone speaks a living language is that it is a part of Nammu and the whole of life. Only those who are in connection with Creation are able to understand the language of the stones. Our opponents have no knowledge of the laws of eternal Creation and the power of Nammu from which we all originate. They have forgotten that life itself is permanently talking to us.

We do not need religion to understand its many languages and signs. We are able to understand these elemental processes of Creation because we ourselves originate from them and we are connected in an elementary way with all that lives. Life speaks with us directly, through stones, animals, plants, water and light, and we do not need gods and idols as intermediaries.

There is only one existence. There is only one divine power in the universe, out of which all life comes. It might have a thousand names, but it always remains the same. Here on Earth this power of Creation is first expressed as a female entity, and is represented by Nammu. All material birth processes go through a female cycle in their elementary level before they switch to their special individuation. And this process connects all material existence. Secrets of Creation of the female aspect of the universe are to be manifested and realised ever more profoundly here on Earth. The male power also wants to be born into this. It is Creation's original longing for the male power to unfold in matter on Earth. Here in our bodies lies a secret of Creation, of planet Earth and human beings. Creation as a whole is both female and male. It is polar and it is the eternal source. Life can only form because of the polar tension which is always creating. It connects all thoughts and all dreams. The double spiral is the most elementary form in which these processes can be expressed. It has no beginning and no end. Within the spiral, the energy movement can expand in every direction and cyclically change its direction. Every change of existence happens through the spiral. We all come from it and all return to it. It is an expression of the life-giving power. This is why you find the sign of the spiral at all of our temples, usually as the double spiral.

You can follow the web of sound of the whole world through knowledge of the spiral, which is also guarded by our ancestors in the Milky Way. You will see and understand that the world is made of sound. Our master builders use their knowledge of light and sound to transport huge stones and erect them in new locations. Light and sound frequencies of consciousness inform the stone. A light and sound frequency also materialises memory in the stones, which is able to store human information and activate it whenever needed. The stones erected by humans are a library of human history which our descendants will be able to read to acquire the knowledge they need. This is all activated by certain patterns of sound and light. If you listen finely you can hear the energetic web of sound and perceive the energy movements around the stones. They connect with the energy movements of the stars, the sun and the moon and unite into new forms.

Nammu, Mother Earth, is a living organism. She breathes and pulses as we do. She hosts infinitely many organisms and micro-organisms, which all carry knowledge within them. The microcosmos works like the macrocosmos. We are a doll within a doll within a doll. All life moves towards new levels and forms. The seed of an apple transforms into a tree, the caterpillar into a butterfly, but the being remains the same. It is processes of consciousness which develop ever-new levels of life and bring them to evolutionary birth. The energy flow of love, a wild light, sound and vortex movement, unites everything. All beings and all new thoughts arise out of this.

Become guardians of the metals: of bronze, copper, gold and silver. They ensure that the magnetic streams on Earth take the right paths. A system of immense power regularly contracts and expands on Earth. It is an eternal pulsation, which also permanently creates sound. This is how the song of the Earth comes into being. We assign a certain sound to each metal. It can be heard as far as the Pleiades. You are guardians of sounds and dreams. Conscientiously offer your songs and the images which you have dreamt, to the Earth. She needs your song as we need hers. We keep our knowledge and our telepathic powers alive by singing. The dolphins in the oceans are our special friends. Nobody guards the secret of the sound-world better than they do. They are connected with Nammu's dream of peace. You can call the dolphins with a certain rhythmic tapping; through sound connected with the right thoughts.

Spiralling energy forms a web of sound and light in the universe and thereby moulds the growth of all life. It is responsible for the moments of conception and birth; it is responsible for the moment and the place where our ancestors incarnate. With the help of the spirals you can also learn to travel through time or to visit other planets in your dreams. Moon and Earth are connected with each other through the spiral. These energies are transported further through waters, influence the tides and precisely connect with each other. The umbilical cord through which a mother nourishes her child is created through spiral movement. An umbilical cord comparable to this exists between Sun and Earth, and Moon and Earth.

The law of mutual attraction is the cause of everything. The deepest secret of love lies here, including sensual love between the genders. The guardians of knowledge on the mainland walk along these sacred streams. These are the 'leylines' which encircle the planet in straight lines, transporting certain streams of energy. Other lines of power meander like snakes around the Earth. Yet others form a particular branching system. The stone circles which were built by our ancestors in various countries are oriented according to these sacred streams. Encircling the energy protects life processes. Erecting large stones on the lines of power increases the power. This eases the processes of information flow around the Earth. At such places you almost always find special treasures such as iron ore, copper, gold, silver or uranium. Such places also serve to calculate the positions of the Sun, Moon and stars.

The energy processes which shape all life on Earth are a permanent interplay of change and continuity. All life moves between these two poles as long as it can be kept in balance. The stone circles are all located at special power centres to bring Mother Earth back into balance. At these places you will find sacred water, which is protected and kept pure there. These places are often at fountains which are especially meaningful for the female cycle. This is also why the places where we give birth are located close to sacred waters from such fountains.

You can observe how the animals find these places and return to them. These underground waters have a sacred power at particular times, which we need for healing and purification. They are the amniotic waters of the Earth. Their healing power can be used only in connection with the information they transport, which can be accessed at certain times which depend on the movements of the Moon, the Sun and the stars.

The stone circles often have the form of an ellipse, or an egg, as this is the basic form of all life. It develops from the spiral. The egg is the basic shape for all harmonic laws on this Earth; it is the sound body which stores the perfect bioenergetic knowledge within itself. This is why the form of the egg is the most stable, and gives the greatest staying power for peace knowledge during the millennia of destruction.

All guardians of peace follow the energy paths which connect them with the Earth. These energy paths will also bring together the people who are meant to meet. They transfer harmony and knowledge to all those who walk this path while consciously inviting the messages of Nammu. It is usually easy to find these paths. You will recognise them by certain stone formations, certain plants and certain characteristic ways the plants grow. Animals also usually follow these paths.

When people started to breed animals and keep them on fenced meadows they noticed that domestic animals became ill more often than wild animals. Giving birth is often also more difficult for domestic animals. The reason is that the animals cannot follow their natural paths. They can no longer drink healing water at the right times. Animals would often escape to give birth at the right places, at the fertile fountains.

One way to find the routes of the sacred energy flows in the forest is to follow the paths of the animals. Pay attention which animals appear to you in your dreams and take them as guides. Disturbances of these energy flows can lead to difficulties. In cases where this could make you insecure, you can dowse using willow, yew or rowan, which react particularly sensitively to the vibrations of the Earth, even when they are disturbed by overlaid energy flows.

Now take on your task for the next week. Let your dreams assign your metal and your stone to you. It is possible that you will be sent very abruptly on the path to your first training. Your personal metal and your stone can be a great support in finding this path.

The whole universe opens to those who know the path. Those who have lost it see only chaos. Later religions will express this extensively in detailed pictures of Heaven and Hell."

Mudima said this all laughingly. And this is how her second lesson ended. She did not say a word about anger. She did not give us any further explanations or hints. But we are already used to lessons which are very different than we had expected. What we have learned today is not really new for us. We were already introduced to these issues at a young age. Children of our tribes are able to find power paths in the forest by the age of six, by noticing plants and by observing the birds and other signs. And still, the material reaches us on new levels each time. In earlier years we understood these contexts mainly intuitively. Now we are challenged to understand and use them on a geistig level.

We leave the temple and climb up to Hagar Qim, where we will study dance and the body.

The Fish

Dark clouds were announcing heavy rain. I stood on a hill above a busy street where I had a date with Jo. I looked out over the stony landscape of the island, seeing it as the work of an artist who was exploring a particular style here. What a genius artist! She has managed to keep the colours delicate, but in a way that they still shine as if everything is radiating light from within. This view gave me wings.

I wanted to make a day-trip with Jo, perhaps to Valletta to visit the Hypogeum where the famous terracotta figure of the sleeping priestess had been found. It was one of the main reasons I had come to Malta. At the very beginning of the trip I had learned that the Hypogeum was closed, but I was still determined to do anything to get inside.

At exactly two o'clock, Jo arrived around the corner in his old rattling rusty white car. It was hard to believe that this car could still run. It was starting to rain, and the windscreen wiper barely managed to clear a small patch of the screen so that we could see the street. The great artwork of this island became colourless. The weather became so much worse that a day trip was impossible, and after we had made a creative break down a side road, Jo drove me back to my hotel. We set a date for next Tuesday and casually said good-bye. We did not know then that this would be our last meeting. Some days later when I visited Mnajdra I learned that Jo had not returned there.

"Probably he suddenly had to visit his family. His mother is very ill," said one of the guards who worked with him. I wasn't sad about the situation. Jo had given me a huge present, for which I had opened sexually to him and enjoyed it a lot myself. This situation did not require more at the moment. I thanked the Goddess for this wonderful and wilful guidance, and left it up to her whether Jo and I would meet again.

Some fairly uneventful days passed. I worked in concentration in my apartment, enjoying the big and beautiful space. One interruption in these work days was a phone call from a friend named Marisi. Surprisingly, she had just arrived on Malta and heard that I was here. I invited her to stay at my apartment with me for a while as I had enough space.

As soon as she arrived, we took a day-trip together. We sat in a café, reading an exhibition catalogue which showed many finds from the labyrinth below the stone circle of Gozo. I was astonished by the richness of the finds. One of the finds caught my attention because of its individual style. It was a large stone on which a few lines depicted a friendly face. I knew similar pieces from Portugal and Southern France. It made me think of the tribe in Portugal who had had to leave their country. I had received the information that a small nomadic group had travelled from Portugal to Malta carrying a stone figure as a gift.

In the exhibition catalogue I was also astonished by a small figure which had been found in the Hypogeum. It was a small stone figure similar to the famous sleeping priestess, but in place of the woman lying on the stone, there was a fish. Of course, I immediately remembered the message with which I had been sent on this journey.

You must write a book. You must travel to Malta this winter. Follow the track of the fish from here, via Malta to Crete and to Egypt, until you reach early Christianity.

I had now found the symbol of the fish on Malta for the second time. And I would also find it a third time. What was this all about? Had it already been used then as a symbol of power for peace? Does this symbol of the early Christians, who used it as a secret sign, refer to their connection to ancient peace cultures? I knew that the letters of the Greek word for fish were the initial letters of the Greek for 'Jesus Christ, son of God, the saviour', but maybe there had been a much older meaning of the fish symbol before then. Did it perhaps represent an ancient source, a peaceful past epoch? Was it perhaps a reference that Jesus can also be understood as a recurring son-archetype of the ancient mother? Was Jesus's protection the fact that he could unite the male and the female aspects of the divine world? Maybe he was one of the first who were preparing a deep reconnection to the female culture, by loving and admiring the feminine. Many of his exceptional acts could be signs of this. Didn't he respect women in a way that was unusual for his times? There are also Gnostic traditions which say that Jesus did not only pray to Abba, his 'Dear Father' but also to Sophia, the mother. I am aware that I am in the realm of speculation, but it is striking that the fish had been a special symbol of this early culture and that without knowing that, I had been guided in the stone circle onto this track.

At the start of my journey I had already noticed a relief of a snake with the tail of a fish in the Temple of Ggantija. The snake is known as an ancient symbol of female culture. But why did it have the tail of a fish there? And I would find a third fish in Buggiba, where we would go this very afternoon.

But for now we were enjoying the sun in the café in the centre of Valetta, allowing the sound of the church bells to move us and eating the spicy vegetarian quiche which was offered in many delicious varieties. We decided to visit a temple whose picture had attracted my attention.

I had seen its photograph in a book, but I could find no more information about it, even in the detailed book I had received from the married couple. I had asked several people, but nobody seemed to know this temple. The young man at the reception of my hotel had already wanted to give my book back to me when he suddenly laughed, "Ah, that's in the New Dolmen Hotel, very close to here." I wanted to see this temple, without knowing exactly why it attracted me so much. So we took a bus and searched for the small relatively unknown site. In the middle of a tourist city, we found the New Dolmen Hotel, a huge square modern building beside the sea. At first there was no sign of a dolmen. Instead we entered the elegantly furnished reception hall. We found signposts leading to rooms named after oracle sites: Dodona, Delphi, Delos... Someone had found a clever idea to make a stylish business with old oracle schools. The receptionist showed us the way into the inner courtyard, where we found the old temple ruins surrounded by the balconies of the sun-hungry visitors. Probably these ruins had been found while building the hotel, otherwise it would be difficult to imagine how they would have been given permission to build such a monstrous hotel here. I immediately got a headache, even though the place was beautiful, and one could get an impression of how strong a source of power it must have once been for the inhabitants of the island. The temple was located directly by the sea, where it might also have served a navigational purpose. Here we found the symbol of the fish again. A large stone tablet with three engraved fish had been found here. I immediately received an image of people arriving from different countries landing here and erecting a stone tablet to honour the fish and thank for its company and protection on the sea voyage.

I perceived the way the stones stood here, and memorised it deeply; I would have to leave the place soon as my headache was becoming too strong. This is one disadvantage of mediumistic work. Those who start to open for different spaces of perception often become as sensitive as a mimosa. Disturbance fields, like the field which seemed to be present here, take immediate effect on the whole body. I felt nauseous, as if I would vomit, but this quickly passed once we left the hotel. It was already late in the evening when we finally returned from our day-trip.

A Spiritual Experiment

Marisi was as disappointed as I was that the Hypogeum and the archaeological museum were closed. One of the main reasons for her journey to Malta had also been to see the Hypogeum and the sleeping priestess. Marisi is an artist and she carves small figures of women out of stone. To inspire herself she often visits historical sites where figurines from ancient matriarchal cultures have been found.

I suggested that we dare to make a spiritual experiment together: to go to Valetta and find a key there that would open the gates of the Hypogeum to us.

We quickly agreed to do it. In an ancient rattling bus decorated with pictures of Mother Mary and other saints, we drove to Valetta. I was not very interested in the city and its various historical monuments. I wanted to stay on the track of the early history of Malta and not be distracted by church history, or Roman or Phoenician history, or any kind of history. That could come later. So I just passed by the hustle and bustle of the friendly Maltese as we walked directly to the archaeological museum.

A guard stood in front of the door, "It is closed, Madam. I am very sorry."

"Is there no possibility at all?" I asked.

"No possibility. There is nothing to be done about it."

I did not want to give up so quickly. We went into an information office, from where we were sent on in a friendly but firm way. At the next office, they wanted to send us back to the information office again. We continually received the same negative answer. I was prepared to forego the archaeological museum. But the visit to the Hypogeum was important, and I did not want to give up on it.

I gave Marisi a silent signal, and we just remained standing there. I had a feeling that we would soon receive important information. First we received a brochure with beautiful pictures of the previous exhibition. Then the woman in charge looked thoughtful and gave us an address where we could make another attempt. Down a tiny street we found the administration office of the archaeological museum.

"We were told that it is possible to get the key for the Hypogeum here," Marisi said confidently. An old rotund man looked up a little surprised and indicated a neighbouring desk where a similarly rotund man was reading a newspaper. We repeated our statement. He laughed and told us that we had been misinformed. I told him that we were working on a book. I had made an inner rule for myself to always remain as close as possible to the truth whenever I wanted to reach some goal. Anything else does not serve spiritual life praxis. He looked interested but again gave a negative answer. The renovation of the Hypogeum had taken several years, and might be completed later this year. We would have to come back then.

"This is unfortunately not possible," I answered. Marisi also tried her luck again with different words. We remained standing there silently for a while even though it seemed clear that we would not get through. Time seemed to stretch. I connected with my supporting powers, as I knew that it was a cosmic wish that I would find a way into the Hypogeum. Silence filled the whole room with a huge tension. We held out, as we both felt that something was now possible.

"The only thing I can suggest is that you try to contact the curator of the museum, Mr Melvier," he said finally, breaking the spellbound silence. At my request he wrote the name of the curator on a small piece of paper.

"The museum is officially closed," he said, "but you can go in anyway and ask for Mr Melvier. His office is there. The door is probably open." We returned determinedly to the huge building in front of whose closed door we had already been standing today. Marisi's breasts were bouncing with anticipation and certainty of success. This time there was nobody standing in front of the door to turn us away. We opened the enormous gate and we were inside the building. We saw huge tablets of stone. The rooms were almost empty. A few reliefs stood around, covered with cloths. Our footsteps died away in the emptiness of the huge halls. There was nobody to be seen. I heard a sound from a small back-room, and we went straight there, where we found two construction workers painting the ceiling. We asked for Mr Melvier and they sent us up to the next floor. There, in the only room which seemed to be used in this building, we saw a desk with a telephone. But still there was nobody to be seen.

"Hello!" I called into the empty halls.

From somewhere a woman's voice answered, "Yes, please?" A young woman came towards us and we told her our request. She was very helpful and said regretfully that Mr Melvier was unfortunately not available, but that she could give us his business card. She also asked me to send her my texts as she was in the process of building an archive of all the written material about the temples of Malta. Immediately the question arose in me what she would think about my sexual research. How absurd it is that these beautiful aspects of life have a slightly distasteful character and fit so little into science and research, as if Eros was not a real part of human history.

The woman disappeared to get the card. She had a beautiful figure. I thought to myself that she would also love an erotic adventure. At this moment, a friendly young man entered the room.

"Can I help you?" he asked.

"We are looking for Mr Melvier," I answered, feeling already that it was him. I was right. I told him about the book I was working on, and how important it was for me to visit the Hypogeum. He listened to me with interest and seemed thoughtful. After some hesitation he finally started to speak. He said that he was very sorry but that it was really impossible to visit the exhibition now. But I felt that he was forthcoming. I liked him immediately. One could feel that he was a man who loved his work and took it seriously, filling his position conscientiously. I repeated that it was more important for me to visit the Hypogeum.

"The Hypogeum," he murmured. "I will see what is possible. Wait a moment." Then he went to the telephone and talked to several people.

"I am sure that we will soon be in the Hypogeum," said Marisi joyfully. My feeling was that there would still be some difficulty, but I also felt clearly now that there would be a way. He returned and turned specifically toward Marisi. He seemed to like her. We awaited his words with excitement.

"I am very sorry," he said. "I tried, but at the moment there is really no possibility. The workers would have to stop what they are doing. And at the moment I would not be able guide you."

"That doesn't matter. We will certainly not disturb the workers," I said. We were simply determined to get into the Hypogeum.

He laughed. "How long will you stay here on Malta?"

"Until two weeks on Wednesday," I replied.

"Ah, I did not know that you would be here so long. Call me next Wednesday and I will see what I can make possible."

He gave us his card with his telephone number, and we left. Do not become attached. *Let things take effect.* Let your wish go into the cosmos. A well-tested rule from the spiritual world, which we could now practise.

Dream of the Apostle Paul
and His Fight against the Woman

Before I come to the results of our experiment, I want to follow a line of information I received about the Apostle Paul in a dream.

It was full moon. I had arranged my bed on the couch in the living room so that I could see the moon clearly and enter a more conscious and aware dream-state. And many dreams did indeed come.

I saw myself standing on Gozo, at Ggantija Temple, with a compass in my hand to check the connection to Sirius. A man I did not know was part of this test. He said to me, "Yes. Based on the Jefferson Method, it all seems right."

I awoke abruptly. The term 'Jefferson Method' seemed to me to be very important, but no matter how much I thought about it, it meant nothing to me. Surely it couldn't have anything to do with the famous American president.

I fell asleep again, and dreamt of the Apostle Paul. Scientists are still arguing today whether it is even possible, considering the currents and winds of the Mediterranean Sea, that Paul actually landed on Malta. Whether he was here or not, legend says that he landed on this island, and this took effect on my dreams. A huge anger against Paul and his actions had gathered in me during my theological studies. It was Paul who ensured that women were not allowed to speak in church. He also ensured that the bible prevailed as the only recognised source of revelation in Christianity. So far I had considered Paul to be a power-hungry misogynist who contributed to the development of early Christianity into a dogmatic church.

In my dream, I was surprisingly forgiving towards Paul. I saw him preaching and awoke with the sentence, "Forgive those who are pure in heart."

I told my dreams to Marisi, and she looked through her guidebook. The legend says that Paul was bitten by a snake after becoming stranded on Malta. As he had survived both the shipwreck and the snakebite, he was considered to be a saint. This enabled him to preach Christianity wherever he went. The symbol of the fish, which had originally been a symbol of the Goddess, now found its way back to Malta through a strange detour, as a symbol of early Christianity. Paul was probably not aware that he was bringing an ancient symbol of the Goddess back to the island.

I was not surprised that Paul had been bitten by a snake. This event is a simple expression of how the ancient female culture, symbolised by the snake, defended itself against male dogma. Many legends tell of monks who came to convert people in foreign countries being bitten or attacked by snakes. For example, the abbot Pirmin, when he had the task of building a monastery on Reichenau Island in Lake Constance, to convert the region to Christianity, had to fight against a whole army of snakes.

Paul fought like no other against sexual and therefore female mystery knowledge.

"And those who belong to Christ Jesus have crucified the flesh with its passions and desires." (Galations 5:24)

He implies that he is one of the godly eunuchs and therefore thought that it was "good for a man not to touch a woman" (1 Corinthians 7:1). Paul wrote to the Galatians, "I wish those who unsettle you would emasculate themselves" (Galations 5:12).

He made it clear in his preaching that those who bite and intertwine with each other, terms which are often used for sexual union, thereby destroy each other. The fact that Paul concerned himself so much with sexuality and women was a sign that women had regained the courage to speak about their issues again in early Christian times as many had seen Jesus as a messenger of the Goddess.

Paul's victory over the snake which bit him on Malta is a symbolic representation of his fight against a culture which positively affirmed sexual union.

It is interesting that despite the fights and attempts to defeat the snake, it still prevailed as a positive symbol in Christianity. Many Gnostic traditions equated the snake with Jesus. In the Pistis Sophia, Jesus was the snake who talked about the tree of knowledge and the tree of life. Traces of the Goddess are visible in simple mythological images even where She was fought. Lilith found her anarchistic ways to plant signs of the Goddess. Sometimes it was the bite of a snake. Or the fig tree or the symbol of the fish at the threshold. And Nammu is waiting patiently until the first people decipher the traces of the Goddess scattered throughout the history of humankind. It is possible that this knowledge has developed further despite the many perversions and false representations made by the Church, religious books and the state. Despite Paul's many efforts to eliminate the woman from cultural history, Mary continues to be worshipped in the Catholic Church. And although Paul wanted revelation to be carried only by the written word, it was impossible to prevent others experiencing even greater revelation through the appearance of a snake or the sound of a toad. How could he hope to extinguish the living impulses that he himself could not understand any longer?

According to Paul's attitude of opposition to lust, which is very different from that of Jesus, woman should be worshipped only as an asexual being. The peak of this attitude is the Church's concept of the virgin birth.

When one thinks of the *Virgin Mary* one thinks of chastity and asceticism. When Paul turned towards Mary as the *sacred virgin,* he certainly did not know that the holy whores in the service of the temples had been called sacred virgins in former cultures. Despite all efforts to promote chastity, sexuality always found its way back into the Christian tradition and terminology. According to Paul, women were no longer part of the sacred mysteries, and had to be silent in church. This is where God and the world separate and become strangers and contradictory to each other. This is one core aspect of the fight between the genders which has lasted until today.

But despite the most brutal attempts at eradication, the female voice could not be silenced. Later traces in church history show that even the most extreme persecution could not eliminate the voice of the Goddess and the sensual and sacred concept of life.

It is enough to elevate the spirit to God. And then no action is sinful – whatever it might be... Loving God and loving your neighbour are the most important commandments. A man who unites with God with the help of a woman follows both of these commandments. And it is the same for one who elevates his spirit to God in this way together with a person of his own gender, or alone. In doing so, that which is wrongly called impure is the true purity wished for by God, without which no human can gain any knowledge of Him.

This was written by a nun at the beginning of the 19th century. The quote expresses how matriarchal knowledge prevailed throughout the centuries despite all persecution and alienation from the Church and the inquisition.

I wrote down my dream and my thoughts. The moonlight was falling on my bed, just as it had fallen two thousand years ago on Apostle Paul, to whom I had found a more forgiving attitude through this dream.

Looking at the moon thoughtfully, I fell asleep again into iridescent dreams. I dreamt of the Hypogeum. I had never seen it so clearly. I followed the steps down into the innermost labyrinth, to the shrine of the sleeping priestesses. It was a relatively abstract dream which followed its own very individual logic. It was as if I could follow the lines of energy and information deep into the Earth. I perceived how the energy of this place itself greatly increased my power of concentration and vision. I awoke again after about two hours. I took this dream as a good sign that we would actually find a way into the Hypogeum.

During the day, the sacred world was invisible. The visible world was surrounded by the invisible world, just as millions of stars exist that are invisible during the day, and not only one sun. Non-human beings appeared not only in myths, but also in dreams. The dream was the intermediary between the profane world of everyday life and the sacred world, as only a dream was able to create an intimate contact between each individual and the sacred world.
Elisabeth Lenk[18]

JOURNEY INTO THE EARTH

I had clearly seen the cave-like space of the Hypogeum in my dream. It is amazing how clearly our subconscious can produce images, impressions, smells and sounds in dreams. It can be so clear that we succumb to the illusion that we are actually directly experiencing them. And sometimes it is more than an illusion. I have often received evidence that our subconscious is indeed able to reach places and study the surroundings there in detail. The oracle priestesses of ancient times were probably educated and trained in this art. They were able to really see with the help of the art of dreaming, and to travel with their spirit to specific places. I awoke with the clear wish to get into the Hypogeum.

It was Wednesday morning, the day we were to call the director of the archaeological museum, Mr Melvier. Today it would be decided whether or not it would be possible for us to get into this millennia-old labyrinth.

In a profound meditation, I managed to see a clear picture. I saw us in the corridors of the Hypogeum. The conscious *geistig* work now was to remain unattached to my own images and wishes. In the meditation I was told to let go of the picture, not to react with disappointment and not to make my happiness dependent on its manifestation. When one works on a *geistig* level with situations in advance, it is easier when one actually encounters them. I clearly felt that I managed to do this. I felt free and light.

It is a decision to stay with the divine power of life. You notice that the Goddess is with you when joy enters your cells.

This was my power-sentence for today. Now I was able to send my clear wish into the ether. The rest I put into the hands of the Goddess. I had detached from my goal sufficiently that I was able to be flexible and open to the situations that life would bring. Now I needed to remain aware of my inner voice and take care that my contact with Marisi functioned well. Her intuition told her to call Mr Melvier, but she did not reach him. While she followed up various leads on the telephone, I stayed with my inner voice and continued working on the book as if I had no other special intentions. The outer signs were not encouraging. Marisi could not reach him in the archaeological museum, the Hypogeum or the temple of Tarxien. But I did not react in myself. I was ready to accept anything, and at the same time I was oriented towards success.

A master does not wait for his or her destiny. He places the figures on his chessboard in a way that they can reach their highest possible effectiveness. A true will attracts the conditions needed for its fulfilment.

Connected with these thoughts, I felt free and confident about whatever the day would bring. I was accompanied by the thought of being in a cosmic lesson which required me to be as unattached and precise as possible.

We agreed very quickly to choose different paths, each going our own way that connected us to our source of inspiration and joy. I had the clear intuition to stay in the hotel and just continue working.

In order to achieve a result, it is sometimes wiser to stay in one's own room and think the right thoughts than to take hectic action too early, my inner voice had clearly told me, with Lilith smiling mischievously in the background. In her meditation, Marisi saw herself going to Tarxien and to the Hypogeum. We both had the feeling that she would meet Mr Melvier at one of these places, and we talked everything over in detail so that we could stay in touch during the day. I would try to reach him once more in about two hours. So we each followed our plans. I was just summarising my experiences on Gozo when the telephone rang. One of the attendants from the Hypogeum told me that a visit there was unfortunately – my breath stopped but I continued listening – only possible at a particular time. My heart raced with joy but I remained very focused. We agreed it would be on Thursday morning at ten o'clock. That was tomorrow, Marisi's birthday.

She came home happily in the late afternoon. She already knew everything as she had met Mr Melvier in Tarxien as we had foreseen that morning.

Next morning we left the house early and took the bus to Valetta. The driver's cabin looked like a living room, with a lively chirping canary in a cage. Like most drivers, he took the curves as if we were in a rally. One needs a strong stomach for these rides.

We received a warm welcome from an attendant at the Hypogeum. At exactly ten o'clock we entered the atrium, which was being renovated. After a short introduction, the attendant, a friendly man of about fifty, led us to a steep stairway. We climbed down into the depths of a past which for a while came so close to us that it was as if we could still hear the soft breath of the sleeping priestess.

It was as if the walls of the cave were alive and pulsing. I felt like a cosmic embryo in the body of the original mother who is guarding knowledge of a peace-culture here and preparing a new birth. How short one's own life appears in the face of the ages and cultures that this Earth has experienced and will still experience. The five thousand years of patriarchy and the misery of the present culture which

142

now need correcting also seem to be tiny compared to the span of life on Earth.

What a huge change of outlook it must have been when life diversified in the Cambrian explosion! What an immense new beginning! What a huge *geistig* and historical leap took place at this time!

A close look at history shows that historical change almost always occurs through field-building, initiated by an important *geistig* step which takes hold of the whole of evolution and causes a change in every cell. The next field-building change might set in just as suddenly as the *geistig* confusion of patriarchy did. It has long been in preparation here inside the Earth.

The Earth needs the revolutionary and perceptive *geist* of humans. We are simultaneously an active part and a witness of this process. We are the seeing eye of Creation and organs of its manifestation. The Earth is in pain because the human being, an important part of Creation, has separated from her.

I felt a deep shiver and immense gratitude for the processes of life on this planet. How often I have walked this Earth, time and again confronted with the riddles of existence! Will we one day succeed in reversing the great amnesia so that full memory can return?

Why have humans neglected the secrets of the Earth for so long? Why do they search for God in the life beyond, ignoring the divine miracles in front of them every day?

Imagine that you are dying. You pass through a gate, beyond which paradise opens to you. This paradise is the Earth. What would you do?

I heard this question as if it came to me from the walls of the cave. Was it Nammu? Was it Lilith? It was the aspect of the feminine in Creation asking through me, wanting to be perceived. Connected to this aspect, I was not searching for a life beyond. The life beyond will shine through everything as soon as the full step into the present is made. The Goddess demands affirmation of this life wherever we are.

The divine power lies in presence.

It was as if every cell of the cave walls breathed this state of presence towards me as a healing source and at the same time as an appeal. I had a deep feeling of home in these caves of Nammu, the mother of all existence.

For about two hours, the attendant told us everything he knew about the history of this place. Time raced by. We could feel his happiness at having two such deeply interested listeners. He was intimately connected with every rock, every nook and cranny, and showed us the tiniest hidden corners. He often showed us traces of red ochre. It had been the sacred colour of the early ancient cultures. He talked of the beliefs of the ancient cultures, connected to the Great Mother, from which everything came and everything would return. He did not seem to be in any way worried about this form of belief. It did not hurt his male pride. He did not follow the male vanity of having to repeatedly emphasise our present superiority over such a 'primitive' early culture.

Only female figurines had been found in the Hypogeum. He showed us the so-called tree of life, which was ornamentally depicted on a wall. I remembered my introductory dream of Lilith, in which she had told me about the tree of life of the ancient mother. He told us enthusiastically how he had often sat in front of it, and he was convinced that it was a pictorial script similar to Chinese or Egyptian scripts. It was possible that content was transmitted by means of images in these times.

After our tour he left us alone. Now I could go into my meditation. What a stroke of luck that the Hypogeum was closed! We had it all to ourselves. At the very beginning of my meditation, my whole body was seized by an energy movement which I can hardly put into words. It was as if my whole body was a prayer, as if time ceased to exist. I was filled with a deep silence, undisturbed by any thought or feeling: a purely energetic space. I had lost all perception of time. I felt as if I was directly connected to the heartbeat of the Earth, as if I could feel into every animal, every rock, plant and human being carried by this Earth. Everything was connected with her heartbeat, her breath, her rhythm and her sound. This perception was beyond time: tautness and presence together, beyond words or thoughts, and yet a space of dense information.

Only later would this process be translated into pictures and words.

I came into direct contact with experienced oracle priestesses of the early ancient culture who guarded peace knowledge here when it had already long been threatened.

Whole historical contexts seemed to open up to me in a very new way in these few moments. I had no voice recorder nor any other way to record this flood of information.

In ancient times, they had neither writing nor recording apparatus. They had to be able to come into contact with their memory, to the source of information to which you are now connected, at any time. Treasure the memory of this moment. Treasure its quality and special character. Then you will also be able to access it later.

I gratefully received this information and spoke a prayer of gratitude and power. I could have stayed down here for hours. I knew that experienced priestesses had stayed here for weeks, fasting, praying and dreaming to receive messages from all over the world and if necessary to transform them and pass them on.

We climbed the stairs again, opened the door and stepped into the bright daylight of modern city life as if awakening from a dream. We walked silently through the city, which seemed unreal to us. What we had experienced down there seemed more real in this moment than the noise of the car horns, the many shops and the people dressed up like puppets, rushing through the streets, distracted and busy. We caught the next bus, speaking hardly a word on the journey, and gave space for what we had just experienced.

In the Temple of Love

The sun was shining in its full beauty. I had decided to visit Hagar Qim once more as there were still some pieces of information missing. Marisi and I took the bus to Qrendi, a nearby village, from which we walked about three kilometres to the temples. On the walk we saw Maltese women sitting in the sun in front of their houses, letting the day pass by. An old man on the way to his garden accompanied us for part of our walk. He proudly said some German sentences, which he could indeed pronounce astonishingly well.

I knew that this would be my last visit to this area and I wanted to receive the messages which were still missing. Mnajdra had revealed itself fully to me; in Hagar Qim some questions were still unanswered.

At the slope close to the two temples we took a rest, looking over the sea and the nearby rocky island of Filfla. Lizards ran over the rocks, and a small gecko was sitting in a crevice. I closed my eyes for a moment and turned my face towards the sun. Then I went once more to Mnajdra, to say goodbye. The rooms welcomed me as if I had stayed there for weeks. Every corner breathed its story for me. One last time I walked up the hill on a little path to see the temple as a whole. On the path I discovered a spiral engraved simply into a rock. This picture reminded me of my own dream, in which I had drawn a spiral to practice concentration and conscious thought. The spiral served concentration and the power of thoughts to create reality.

I sat down on the slope above the temple and my eyes rested once more on the whole building. Then I tried to do the exercise with the spiral. I could observe the chaos created by a thought which is not thought through to its end. If it is left to the unconsciousness only half-thought, it creates confusion. It is often our thoughts which separate us from reality. Like a movie, they separate us from the

146

world. Failure is often a consequence of ideas which have not been thought through to their end. Different thoughts and wishes which have been started fight each other in our unconscious, becoming entangled and cancelling each other out. It is not a coincidence that success and succession are linguistically connected. Failure is often a result of an inner chain of thoughts and processes which we have not consciously finished. They often lead to physical symptoms, fears and disturbances. They can be the cause of all kinds of disturbances in life. It can be quite a revelation to witness one's own thinking processes for some time. The pace at which I was thinking my thoughts while I concentrated on the spiral was very important. I had to take care that no side-thoughts got lost. I also had to take care that my thinking did not gallop away and pull me out of the present. My task was to go into stillness, open my senses of perception, concentrate on the spiral and from there consciously follow all the thoughts which came up. I witnessed the birth of ideas, could see which thoughts immediately gave power and which created fear. I saw the high responsibility that one has to be aware of one's thinking processes.

After I managed to let go of the everyday thoughts, the following sentences came to me from deep inside.

Those who are able to reach the origin of their thoughts can look into the mirror of their own soul. New decisions can be taken here. In the mirror of your soul you will also find the mirror of the world. Once you have found peace within yourself, you will also be able to bring peace into the world. It is decided here whether war or peace guides your actions. Those who fully understand this secret are able to move the whole world as if it were turning on the palm of their hand.

The last sentence reminded me of a similar statement in the *I Ching*. But who actually consciously accepts their abundance of ideas as a power that creates reality – knowing that every conscious thought creates reality? These connections are innumerable and highly complex. They are not linear. There is a trend today to try to react to these connections too early with recipes and advice such as "You just have to think positively!"

These attempts to make a recipe book from the secrets of life are like a small wave in the immensity of the ocean in the face of the composition of the whole. They come and go; they fade just like a small ripple. They remain attached to the arbitrary play of the surface and do not have the power to reach the depths where true revelation and the *geistig* shifts of life itself occur, where reality-creating revolutions take place.

A new school for a peace movement would include a school of thinking. Today people are against all intellectual thought, against "being too much in your head". This is because we long ago lost contact with the simple elementary thinking which comes from conscious perception. Thinking, in its original power, is as elementary as breathing, eating, drinking and loving. It belongs absolutely to a healthily functioning human organism. I assume that there is a connection between the verbs 'to think' and 'to thank'. Thoughts which are connected with Creation and universal perception always have an intimate connection to gratitude.

"With the conscious decision to live in a sacred way we attract the teaching, information and understanding that we need to unfold our talents for the benefit of all."[23]

This is a sentence from Dhyani Ywahoo, a Cherokee Indian. I could directly observe the reality-creating mantric power of this sentence. I spoke it aloud and remembered how often it had served me in a healing and helping way when I had suddenly got lost in the thicket of my own thoughts.

The attendant waved to me from a distance, giving me a sign that it was time to leave, as he wanted to close. I took a small stone and put it into my pocket as a thank-you and reminder of my experiences in Mnajdra. We went towards

Hagar Qim, which would stay open two hours longer. On the way to the exit, we spoke a few words with the attendant. Although he was responsible for the temples every day, they did not have much meaning for him. He yearned rather for the forests and mountains of distant lands. With a laugh I suggested to him that we swap places for a while. He was an attractive young Maltese man, whose heart beat fully for the present, and who had not yet questioned the Western world and its culture.

Hagar Qim drew my attention again. I said goodbye to the attendant and went to the inner area of the temple. I walked between the tall stones which shone in the sunlight of the late afternoon. They shone as if they had their own inner light. As I was standing there in front of the supposedly biggest temple building on this island, I was suddenly grasped by a wave of energy. It was as if my heart became one with the heart of the Earth: exactly the same feeling as I had just experienced in the Hypogeum. With this energy wave, a rich world of images opened naturally. The temple seemed to want to open its whole history to me. It was the first time that Hagar Qim had opened for this kind of contact. It was as if I was seeing with my heart. I no longer had to meditate or make great efforts. I now saw the living history of the temple in front of me as if it had just happened yesterday. The temple shone in sublime radiance as if it was still ready for living celebration. I recognised Hagar Qim as the temple which had served as a school of love and temple of love. Men had also been educated here. I could see that the whole temple had been created especially for the male *geist*. I saw the stones in the outer area of the temple where the men had slept, saw the love-places where they had been received by the Mirjas, the representatives of the Goddess of Love. I saw the places for dance and celebration which had been used particularly at the times of the fertile moon, solstices and equinoxes. I had a strong feeling that this place was particularly dedicated to the sun. Some stones loomed like symbolic phalluses into the sky, as a sign of fertility and arising male potency. One stood as if accompanied by three goddesses.

At one place I suddenly had to laugh. An inner, but clear and vivid picture suddenly leapt at me. I saw a power-centre in front of me where the young men could test their physical potency. Here they could energetically test if they felt ready for an encounter with a female Mirja for sensual love service with her, and for initiation into contact with the Goddess. I had to laugh because the picture was so natural and at the same time so strange and unknown to today's culture. Religion and Eros were directly connected with each other here in these temples. This picture of Hagar Qim opened up to me in such a simple naturalistic, almost normal way, that it touched me deeply.

Walking on, I discovered a place which seemed to be directly connected with the power of the sun. A stone, also shining particularly beautifully in the late afternoon sun, had a huge round hole in the middle which gave the me impression of a special gate. I instinctively named it the Gate of the Sun.

"Where could one get to know more about these connections, about the relationship of this temple to the moon, sun and stars? There must be research on this." Suddenly the attendant was standing next to me. I noticed that he was talking to me. He talked about Jo, and how he had suddenly needed to travel to Germany. But if I still had questions, the attendant would love to help me. He had worked here for 27 years, and knew every stone on the island.

At first I wanted to get rid of him, and then I remembered my question. Maybe I would receive the answer right here and now! I asked him, and indeed received interesting news. He pointed to the stone that I had called the Gate of the Sun and told me that someone had discovered that the first rays of sunrise at solstice fall into the interior of the temple through this hole. Then he showed me a similarly prominent stone at which the same happened at sunset on the solstice. So the temple had indeed been designed and built according to the sun. I asked whether he knew similar things about certain star formations. He mentioned a book about Malta which had been written by a specialist on stone circles. He could show me a copy. We went into his room, where he dug out a book. Fascinated, I took it into my hands and saw immediately that it contained a lot of information that I was looking for. I asked whether it was possible to obtain it somewhere. He said no, and then paused thoughtfully for a moment as if he had just received information from the cosmos.

"Okay, I made a copy," he said. "Take it. If I have died by the time you come back, take it as a present from Franz."

I looked at him, hardly able to believe it. I almost had the feeling that I could not simply accept it. How could this man, who I did not know at all, give me such a present! *Of course you have to take it. It is a present from the cosmos*, said my inner voice. I took the book and thanked him.

Together with Marisi I drove home on our beloved Malta Express bus. It had become dark by now. As we sat next to each other in silence, the day passed once again in front of my eyes. I felt intimately connected with the divine source of love and I wished that it would stay with me in this simple way for ever. It was almost a mystical state of love. I loved everything around me. I loved the people sitting in the bus, and the driver. I loved the slightly disabled simple Maltese man who had sat down in front of me and kept glancing at me. It was a simple, unostentatious and uplifting love that had taken hold of me. Everything around me gave me the feeling that I was a servant of life, and I was filled with a profound feeling of being fully at home on this planet.

Not only the past, but also present life unfolded in front of me with its many idyllic possibilities, giving me the courage to open my heart fully for the pictures of a growing longing for a future worth living. From this perspective I could only be amazed by the banality and meaninglessness in which many, including myself, often spend our days. How could one pass by the sacredness of life and the original power of love! I invited Marisi for dinner, and we talked all evening about our many impressions of the day.

REDISCOVERY OF THE STONE CIRCLE

I had become curious whether it would be possible to find the stone circle on Gozo of which I had dreamt in Portugal. So I went there once more by ferry, planning to stay there for a night if necessary. Early in the morning, after tea with Marisi, I took the bus to the ferry. I wanted to arrive at Ggantija temple as it opened, so that there would be a chance I could be there alone for a while.

It had rained during the night, and the island shone at me as if it had been freshly polished. The weather was wonderful. I found the right bus surprisingly quickly and easily, and arrived in front of the still-closed gates of the temple a few minutes before 9 am. I was lucky. The attendant was just arriving on a rickety old moped, with his lunch bag in his hand. When he saw me waiting he opened the gates, even though the official opening time was still some way off. For almost two hours I would have the temple all to myself. By now it had become very easy to find mediumistic access to the historical information. It did not take long until many intuitions and images unfolded in front of my eyes.

I had the impression that the stones here were scanning me energetically. Some of them had a very personal radiance, in a similar way to the stones from the stone circle. On the left of the entrance I saw a stone which immediately gave me the image of female students learning to speak their soul free here. Directly in front of it was a 'talking stone', which seemed to be a symbol for the voice from the depths of Mother Earth. Here they practised making themselves completely empty to be able to listen to the universal voice. It was astonishing how clearly I was now able to see the complete history of this temple in front of me, in complete contrast to my first visit to Gozo. I felt connected with the interior of the Earth, from which answers rose up to me. I perceive this building as the former temple of women and of birth. The stories opened up to me as intimately as they would if I had lived here in those times. I saw the women in front of me, gathering here some days before giving birth. I saw how young women were prepared for sexual life, and how women were here when they cleansed their bodies, souls and *geist* at the times of their menstruation. This is why the temple has the form of a womb. By opening mediumistically, Í felt as if I was in the womb of the ancient mother who now wanted to bring forth new births. The time passed astonishingly fast. After almost two hours the first visitors arrived.

Go, and come back later. Take a room in the village. Buy a new film. You need it for documentation. Take care that you are always well-equipped. Ask more only then. There are many important things to be discovered here! My guidance gave me this information quite strictly. Slightly angry with myself, I noticed that my film was indeed finished and that I had forgotten to bring a new one with me. As I left the temple, I asked the attendant about the nearby stone circle, and asked where to find a camera shop. He shrugged and said that this temple was the only historical site in the area, and could not suggest a shop which would be open, as the Maltese respect the holy nature of Sunday. I had to walk for over an hour to find a shop which luckily sold films. On this odyssey, I also found a hotel, unexpected in such a small village. Even though it gave a quite elegant impression, it was astonishingly cheap, and I took a room immediately. It was now noon, and as I had become hungry, I ate a little before letting myself be guided onwards. I thought about how strongly an existence in connection with the universe requires high awareness and the right pace. A small mistake, such as forgetting the film in my case, can throw you out of connection with cosmic perception. As soon as you are identified with the feeling of having done something wrong, the spirit is no longer free to perceive direct presence. You are immediately entangled in inner dialogues which very soon lead to an unconscious expectation of misery and overshadow all other perceptions. As I had accompanied my inner processes with high awareness this time, I was able to move out of this state relatively quickly. I have repeatedly noticed that one's own mistakes are most easily overcome by first accepting them as mistakes. Only after I have noticed my mistake can I leave it fully behind. If I am conscious of this process, I can use my mistakes to raise my actions onto a higher level of energy. I invest the anger in my own development instead of throwing it blindly at others.

An intuition interrupted my chain of thoughts:

Find the place of vision and the stone circle before you go back to the temple. The place of vision is the place where the young women were sent before they were introduced to their next level of development in the temple. The place of vision is one of the few remaining ancient megaliths. It still has high energy.

Now I was challenged once more to listen clearly to my inner guidance without following the inner dialogues or doubts. I knew from experience that this is a high exercise, and that it would be necessary to stay fully centred to be able to hear the detailed information. The first hint came right away.

Look at the book you received from the married couple whom you met here on your first visit. In the appendix is a map indicating the locations of the stone circle and the vision place.

I indeed found a map which I had not previously noticed. The drawing was not precise, but I could get an idea of the location. As I left the hotel, I asked the concierge, but he knew nothing of either a stone circle or a megalith. He said that a new excavation site had recently been opened, but that it was covered with boards and sandbags, and completely inaccessible. During the last years I had learned a lot about the hints of my inner guidance, and by now I often trusted it more than information from the locals. Confidently, I walked through the village in the direction where I expected to find the stone. As I arrived at the edge of the village, I received astonishingly clear directions from my inner voice. It led me along small roads to a field about three hundred metres from the village, where I found a lying megalith without any difficulty. A gorgeous place, with a wonderful view over the sea! I knew right away that this was the place. This is where the future priestesses were sent in former times when they were to receive new visions. I could easily imagine it. I sat down on the stone and sank into my thoughts. After I had been sitting there for a while, I looked up, surprised by an inner message I had received. In the middle of my dreams about prehistory, I suddenly received the sentences, *"Stand up and look around! You will find something here!"*

I walked around the stone. What should I find here, except for the many dreams and hints coming from within? Then I discovered a little bunch of reeds which had been bound together with a string, as if to make a broom, and placed very deliberately at the stone. I took it as an indication that this stone was still being visited today by women, who speak their prayers for weather or a good harvest while in intimate connection to nature. Maybe they bring Mother Earth presents like these to support their prayers. I took a photograph of this relic and returned it to its place. Surprised, I noticed that I had been sitting here for more than two hours. By now I filled a whole tape on my voice recorder. I could easily imagine how they spent several days here in former times, fasting, sometimes sleeping, sometimes waking, before returning to the temples with new visions. I knew that I had to move on now if I wanted to find the stone circle before dark and visit the temples at sunrise.

I went in the direction where I expected to find the temple. On the way there I would certainly also find the stone circle, as the book indicated that it was only a few metres away from the temples. I followed my intuition confidently. Within the village once more, I discovered a small trampled track leading into the thickets. I received a clear intuition to take it. I followed the track excitedly for about three hundred metres through the bushes and came to a high wooden fence and a big gate. This was either a construction site or the goal I was searching for. I saw joyfully that the gate was open.

Yes. Go in. This is the right place, I was encouraged. I passed carefully through the narrow opening at the entrance. I saw two men in a makeshift hut. They looked a little rough and stared at me as if I came from a different planet. I forgot to breathe for a moment. Then I asked if I could enter, but they seemed not to understand me. They also did nothing to send me away; they only stared at me. So I gathered all my courage and went in. I knew that this was the place where a complete stone circle had once stood. I had it clearly in front of my inner eye from my dreams. From here the priestesses had communicated with people from Almendres in Portugal, even before the construction of the temples had been started and before people from the mainland had arrived here. The picture in the book I had received from the married couple had confirmed that the stone circle I knew only from my dreams had existed in reality. Now I was at exactly this spot, which had only recently been rediscovered. It was also the place where the fish on the altar had been found – the small clay figure. I knew that I was at one of the oldest sacred places on the archipelago, where the vision of the peace school had started. I closed my eyes in admiration for a moment and went into silence. This place had been built a long time before the Hypogeum, and before the school on Malta had existed, it had had a similar function. I was sure that in the excavation they would now find important items which would give further information about the early culture on Malta.

I also saw that destructive forces had raged here. This was where the stone half-buried in the earth and the two pillars that I had seen in my dream had once stood. One could still sense it. Unfortunately there was not much left of the stone circle. The farmers, who did not want their fields to be taken away from them, had succeeded in removing almost all of the stones. Later I came to know that some of the menhirs had been erected at other places.

This is also the site of the subterranean passageways where they had discovered the stone which I think was brought as a present from the mainland. This was probably also the location of the subterranean labyrinth about which I had received information during my first visit. There is something moving about finding places from your own dreamworld in reality. I was completely sure I was at the right place. I felt as if I could hear the silence, as if it were a very personal entity which welcomed me. I knew that this was a very central historical focal point. This was probably the starting point of the original visions of all further temples on Malta. For a while I examined the area, taking in information as well as I could despite the presence of the two rough characters. But I was also relieved when I soon received the clear intuition to move on now. Right now there was nothing left for me to do. Inner guidance had worked. This was my lesson for today.

I perceived the original strong healing power of this place, while at the same time feeling a field of disturbance which clouded my soul. It felt as if dark and destructive forces were clinging to this place and sucking out its energy.

I left the place on a narrow path in the direction of the temple. I felt driven, as if I had to get away quickly. A slight undefined fear had slipped in. After I had walked some hundreds of metres, I noticed that one of the two men was hiding behind the bushes observing me, thinking that I would not see him. I walked faster and was happy to finally arrive again on the street, where I felt protected by the presence of other people.

I spent the evening hours in powerful and inspiring calmness in the temple, connected to my impressions and images of the day, and collected the last pieces of information which were important to me for the developing book.

The next morning, after a generous breakfast of fruit, I was sent to the temple once more, to take photographs in the early morning. I found a beautiful postcard showing a megalith. I felt called again to walk across the island to visit individual stones. Such stones. *On this island you will find megaliths and power lines which are still fully intact. Take a walk. This is a good method to access further information.*

I took the bus through the capital Rabat, to a bus station which I assumed was close to the megaliths I was looking for. Then I once again surrendered to the adventure of fully following the guidance of my inner voice. Walking through the narrow streets, I saw beautiful signs with the names of saints at the entrance of almost every house.

I knew that the last bus to the ferry would leave at 2 pm, but I was not disturbed by this. I knew that I would somehow return to the harbour. After walking for only about twenty minutes, I was already in open land. The bright sunlight and the gorgeous view over the rocks and the sea quickly brought me into a mediumistic state, and with a light step I joyfully followed the trail which was shown to me by my intuition. It did not take long before I had the impression that I was walking along one of the lines of power. Every hundred metres or so there were large stones placed in such a way that they were noticeable, and I had the clear impression that they had been placed there by humans. I continued, jumping from stone to stone, feeling astonishingly secure. After about an hour I arrived at the stone I had seen on the postcard. It was smaller than it had seemed in the photo, but it was clearly an erected megalith. I also recognised it because of the huge church in the background, which I had also seen on the postcard. I sat down for a while and started to listen to the inner stories, which I could see like a movie before my inner eye. Then I walked on, to the coast. Once I even thought that I could discern a footprint in the stone. Also clearly visible were the so-called 'cart ruts', tracks gouged into the rock, whose origin nobody can explain. I did not receive any information about them. Probably they developed later, perhaps at the time of the Phoenicians.

I sat at the coast for about an hour, deeply immersed in past cultures. Then I felt that it was time to leave. The walk back seemed to be endless. In the villages, I could not find a bus which would take me to the harbour. Then about five kilometres before the harbour, a car stopped and a young man offered to take me there. His name was Jo, like my first companion, a name which seemed to be common on Malta. He offered to drive me across the whole island, but I did not feel like further adventures, and accepted his offer only as far as the harbour, thanked him and took the ferry back to Malta. Late in the evening, I arrived tired but richly blessed at my apartment, where Marisi was waiting for me.

EDUCATION IN THE WOMEN'S TEMPLE

After I had seen the story of Nudime in Mnajdra, I wanted to know more. Before she had started her education as a Mirja, she had spent one month on Gozo. I wanted to know how she had received her new name at that time, and how she had found her way to the temples in Mnajdra. These questions led me directly to Ggantija on Gozo. Through my mediumistic intuition, the following story unfolded in front of my eyes:

I am walking with a group of other young women up the hill to the heights of the temple. At this time my name is still Surinja. This name comes from Surnja, the name of my grandmother.

We young women have been sent here to the island of Gozo for one month. We are on the threshold between childhood and womanhood. I am expecting my first period, the sign of fertility.

Gozo is the island of women. I feel especially connected with the star of the women, Sirius, which will later be dedicated to the Egyptian goddess Isis. I am in the temple of Ggantija. This temple is older than Mnajdra and Hagar Qim. Only the temple of Zebbieh and the temple of Mgarr on Malta are older. Immigration to our island has been increasing for over three generations, so our school has been greatly enlarged. Even before grandmother's generation this big temple on Gozo was built close to the older stone circle. The labyrinth is also here, the ancient sacred site which is both the place of sleeping and the resting place of the dead.

The temple occupies the lofty heights of the island, with a wide view over the land. Like most of the temples of the island, its entrance is also facing very slightly south of east. When the first rays of the morning sun meet the bright stones, you can see the first lizards moving their curious heads towards the light. Sometimes I even see the dance of a snake in the morning light. They move from the slowness of the cool night to the dance of the day. Although the basic form of the temple is very similar to the temple in Mnajdra, there is one striking difference. The temples in Mnajdra both have two rooms in the shape of a kidney connected to each other. The first, the entrance room, is bigger than the altar room behind. Here it is the other way around. The first room, through which you enter, is smaller, and behind it opens a huge inviting form which gives the impression of a three-leafed clover. One could also say that this temple has a head, while the others represent only the form of the body. This is no coincidence. This temple is built for the education and cleansing of the head centre. The form of the temple is appropriate for this function.

There are certain positions of the sun, and times in spring when the temple is only open for those women who stand under the aspect of the coming new moon shortly before maturity and the arrival of their period. This blood of the women is sacred to us, as it is the life-giving force which makes it possible for new life to develop in us. We also know that this blood cleanses our spirit and our body every month anew. At these times we always withdraw to special places dedicated to this. The blood has healing power for humans and the Earth. We know that and we act accordingly.

The young women who arrive are received by the guardians of this place. They receive an introduction to their tasks and are then sent away once more. There are times for each one to enter the temple alone or in smaller groups.

Now it is later in the morning. After two future-priestesses have been called, and the shadows are already shorter, a woman's voice calls my name. I am received by a Mirja who is not much older than me, and given my first instructions. I am first allowed to enter the smaller temple in the north. Right at the entrance stand two large guardian stones where every future-priestess must stand still and concentrate to check her bodily energy. Certain openings in the stones help us to find our centre in the corresponding areas of the body and to feel them. Before I enter the temple itself, I have been told that it is

162

my task to visualise a spiral of light in front of my eyes. Spiral symbols are engraved here at the entrance.

The stone on the left has a large opening at about head height. I stand still here. It represents the power of listening of the great ancient goddess Nammu. I can tell her my whole story, all my wishes and the hopes with which I enter this temple. I tell her of my greatest wish: to become Mudima's student. I also tell her of my hopes in love. I reveal my wishes, which men I would love to meet first when I soon become a Mirja in the Temple of Love. I talk about the dream which already told me that I will receive a child in two years. I tell my recent dreams of plants and animals. And much more. We are told to talk until our head and our heart feel cleansed. The listening stone provides the power of calm and emptiness, and takes in everything which is given to it.

After we have told everything, a state of emptiness arises. For me this happened after about an hour. Light floods through my heart chakra and my mind. This shows that we are allowed to enter. Now I can ask the questions that I have brought with me. Some young women do not immediately receive the sign to enter. Then they leave once more to find the things they still have to tell. When we have received the sign and have put our questions, our bodily energy spiral is cleansed and ready for the inner experiences in the temple. I have received that light. The joyful state of emptiness has reached me and the warm light floods my heart chakra. My voice is excited when I bring my wishes and questions to the oracle. Now I am asked to go to the other side of the temple entrance. There is also a hole at about head height here on the other entrance stone, and behind it stands a stone with two small openings. It represents the speaking aspect of Nammu. Here we are to learn to focus ourselves on listening and to hear all the messages that Nammu provides for us. My task is now to stay connected with the inner emptiness and light which I received on the other side. In this opened state, I can now listen to the voice which arises inside me when I concentrate on the two openings in the stone in front *of me. Now the first information comes, as I gratefully receive the answers which unfold from my light-flooded heart chakra.*

"Two different ways still live as wishes in your heart. Your wish to become Mudima's student is not compatible with your dream of receiving a child in two years. A child needs your full awareness and presence. This does not fit together with the way of an oracle priestess, who gives her full awareness to the messages of Nammu. Many oracle priestesses do not receive children at all. For at least four years, the way of an oracle priestess cannot be brought together with becoming a mother. Some only enter the way of a Mirja or priestess when they have already given birth to a child and the child has found its home fully in the community. Listen to the voice of your own soul and to your dreams. They will know which path is right for you. An oracle priestess must not be driven by other wishes. That would cloud her service and damage her soul."

These words came clearly to me. It is my task not to give any inner comments but to gratefully accept everything that I receive as an answer. These answers are the material for my further work.

Now I am allowed to step over the next threshold into the inner area of the temple. I enter the empty apsides and purify my body and soul once again. Then I sit down for a moment and wait until I have the feeling that everything that I have just learned has arrived in my cells. I am allowed to sit down and rest here, depending on how I feel and on the messages I have received. Sometimes students are also sent away from here again to clarify open questions.

Sometimes whole groups of women of the same age are brought here together. When they are here they tell each other what has happened to them. On the left side sit those who listen, and on the right sit those who speak. They are told to tell everything that they have just experienced, in their own words, as clearly and precisely as possible. Then they swap sides. Those who listened before, now have the task of telling what they have *just experienced. And those who spoke before now listen. In this exercise they learn to deal precisely with language and memory.*

In front of the next entrance are two more stones, each of which looks like a throne before a sacred altar. We sit down here when we are ready for the next step. The right side is where we practise sending, and the left is where we practise receiving. It is a similar game to the one before, but without words. On the right side is a deep opening in the earth, Nammu's speaking oracle which gives us information. The aspect of sending, which we now have to practise, is embodied here. On the other side it is about practising the art of listening, the art of receiving. We train our telepathic abilities here. Sometimes we do it in pairs. One woman sits on the stone on the right side and has the task of sending a message to the one sitting on the stone on the left side, while remaining in concentration until the message is received.

I am alone and I practise reaching Mudima with my message and my wish to become her student. For me this wish is higher than the wish for a child, and I hope that the Goddess has the same opinion as I do. I sit on this stone for a long time. First I concentrate on the spiral. This is the start of every new geistig action. Then I imagine the image of the double spiral in front of my inner eye, and finally I start to search for Mudima with my power of imagination. It takes about twenty minutes, then I feel flooded by a soft warm wave of light. I take it as a sign that Mudima has heard me. I see her eyes in front of me and concentrate on them. I reveal my wish. Then I move to the stone of receiving and listen for any sign from her. Again it is a wave of energy that gives me the certainty that I am now connected with Mudima, the Temple Priestess of Mnajdra. I clearly receive the messages that she sends to me.

After I have finished my cycle in the temple, she says, I should go for one day and one night to Santa Verna, the place of vision. "There you will receive a new name. This name will show you your next tasks." Soon I would also receive the message of when I would be received in Mnajdra.

Now I enter the two sleeping chambers where every student here has time for further training in the art of dreaming inside the temple. We are all trained in this, whether or not we will later become oracle priestesses. We are also all trained in taking the directions of the compass as an orientation. A further exercise is to attain geistig clarity in what we send or receive. It is not about practising deep sleep here, but about practising concentrated and aware dreaming, connected with certain topics and questions. It is about training and cleansing the right and left halves of the brain. Even though this is a women's temple, men are also taken into this area at special times to consciously practise the female aspect of bodily cleansing of the head chakra.

"All misfortune starts when wrong thoughts which are not connected with the energy of Nammu slip into the head centre. One aspect of the Creation of Nammu thereby falls back into chaos."

We have been told this from an early age. The centre of the temple, which represents the head chakra, is the place of the women who are the caretakers of the temple. The altar on which we put the offerings which we have brought as a sign of respect and gratitude to Nammu stands here. Most of the time these offerings are certain dried herbs. The priestesses light them and send their cleansing smoke in all directions to give power and blessing to the wishes. I bring rosemary and lavender as offerings. They are two plants which have accompanied me on my way of inner cleansing.

Now I am led to the neighbouring temple. It is bigger and rounder than the first. It expresses the inside of the body, and especially the heart chakra as an organ of recognition. The head and the body have to be cleansed so that the heart chakra can fully open. There is always a fire burning here inside the temple. This is the place where the physical chakras are cleansed and strengthened. This is the place for dancing and dreaming in all directions of the compass. The women get to know the inner functions of their organs. They know that every organ is connected to a corresponding geistig power of insight. As all matter is organised in the sense of the connection of microcosmos and macrocosmos, there is an equivalent on a different level for everything that exists. If someone from the tribe has an injury to a certain organ, one question that is always asked is where something is not right in the community and where the injury has taken place on this level. An injury in the organism of the individual always has an equivalent in the whole organism. When healing the individual, we also always ask what needs to be healed in the whole.

Certain persons are caretakers of certain organs. I, for example, know from my dreams that I have a special relationship to the kidneys, and on the level of the bones, to the knees. So I am a caretaker for these areas of the human organism and have already been called by the tribe as a young girl when healing or special attention was required in these areas. Every organ also has an equivalent in the plant world.

Ggantija temple is not only for initiation rituals. At other times it is a meeting point for women. They come here shortly before giving birth, as there is a fertile well nearby which makes giving birth easy. This place is accessible to all women. Female knowledge is nurtured and passed on here. Before a woman steps into the cycle of adulthood, before she is allowed to receive men and deliver children, she visits this place for one month to be introduced more deeply into the secret of the feminine. Only later does she come into Mnajdra temple, or Hagar Qim, the temple of the Mirjas, love celebrations and fertility.

Now I am in the temple which symbolises the abdomen and the heart chakra of women. Last night while I was half asleep, a curled up snake appeared to me in my abdomen. I saw how she slowly danced upwards to my heart chakra. This is the sign that my body wants to open for sensual love. I also know now that I will be invited to Mnajdra and Hagar Qim on the other side of the water within the next six moons.

At Santa Verna, as it will later be called, the place of visions, I am to receive the next signs. On the next morning I set off to spend 24 hours there practising remaining unattached to the wish to become Mudima's student. Despite this strong longing, I have to be ready for anything that comes to me, as Nammu knows best what corresponds to our true gestalt. Once a state of deep inner emptiness and calm takes hold of me and I do not feel any wish inside me any longer, but only a firm and clear connection with my goal and becoming – once every longing in my body calms down, I fall into a light sleep. I am awoken with the word Nudime, to which I dream a very clear melody. I know that this is my sign. Mudima has answered my wish. I have passed the test. I am accepted to start studying in Mnajdra temple on Malta. Nudime is my new name. It means, "She who will be Mudima's student."

I walk blissfully back to the women's temple and spend the next days in the women's community. We talk about everything that moves our hearts. The cleansing, life-giving blood has visited me for the first time. At the same time, the same is happening to other young women. We often sit around the fire until late at night. The younger women ask all their questions to the more knowing women. We want to know more about how it will be in Hagar Qim, the temple of love. Every young woman who has not visited it is joyfully and excitedly looking forward to her first visit. Some women tell of their first sensual encounter with a man. One tells how she felt when she fell out of her balance because she wanted the same man as another woman. The love-priestesses helped her to rediscover her inner shining ball and to strengthen it. Others tell of their dreams. For example how they were told of ancestors who want to come to them and incarnate as their children. Now they have come to the temple to find out from the Goddess when this time will come. Of course, they also ask who is meant to be the father, if they do not already know.

We are never bored. The four weeks on the women's island are a great present for all of us. Women also visit this island after their education, usually at the time of new moon, always *joyfully looking forward to the wisdom they will share with the other women.*

ABOUT THE SACRIFICE OF ANIMALS

I repeatedly had the question during my many temple visits whether animals had been sacrificed on Malta. If so, what did this mean? Did the people eat meat? I had found pictures of animals on many stone tablets. This was definitely an indication that there had been domesticated animals at these times. But were they also killed and eaten? Or were they kept because they were worshipped, as is still the case today in some areas of India?

In the stone circle in Portugal, a tribal life had revealed itself to me in which the people had lived as vegetarians. They neither kept animals, nor killed any other living beings. I wanted to know more about this. When I saw the everyday life of the people in front of me during a meditation, I also asked questions about this topic. I again saw the world of Malta through Nudime's eyes, and learned the following through her:

When our ancestors settled on this island, they met a tribe who took care of animals. It was mainly the task of the men to travel across the island with them, following the sacred tracks which the animals had chosen naturally. It was mainly goats and pigs, but they were much wilder and much more vital than the domesticated animals of later times, as they still lived in direct connection with the elements and with nature.

It is not the custom of our tribe to keep herds of animals, but we have contact to the elephants, the bison and the wild buffalo. Sometimes we get milk from the wild buffalo, which we give mainly to the pregnant women. The wild buffalo is especially sacred to us. The female buffalo is a representative of the Goddess who takes care of the spirit of this epoch. The buffalo trust us and come when we call them. Each one has a sacred name. Nobody on this island follows the later habit of many peoples of killing the superfluous young male animals of a herd. As animals are respected everywhere on the island, they can move to another herd whenever they want, for example if there are too many animals of one gender in a particular herd. The native inhabitants of the island also watch over this.

Animals are our friends and are respected as such. But one event on the island changed this situation. It was two generations ago. A foreign man landed his boat on Malta, accompanied by some women and children. He had been sent to Malta in a dream, to use this place as a sanctuary for his healing. He prayed to a different goddess: the goddess of protection of animals and of the hunt. Immediately after his arrival, he told the priestesses about his difficult situation. He himself was being pursued and sought protection on the island. A fish had appeared to him, giving him the task of finding his way to Malta to take care of animals there, and also to hunt them when the goddess told him to do so. He asked for permission to sacrifice an animal in the temple once a year to worship his goddess. He loved animals and took attentive care of them. But he believed in other gods, and his religion required him to sacrifice an animal once a year. He told this story to the priestesses. They accepted him on the island and made it possible for him to take care of animals. But they did not allow him to hunt them. One year later he came to them with the request to sacrifice one of the animals of his herd who wanted to die, to worship his goddess. The priestesses considered his request for a long time. They did not love the concept of sacrifice, and they knew about its shadow side.

The dangerous point where Manu had taken a wrong turning many centuries ago was very close now. Manu had discovered that humans themselves had the power to decide about life and death, and that they can use this power. With that he had discovered and entered a path which made it possible to disconnect from Creation and to live in opposition to the laws of life of Nammu. Disconnected destructive dreams which were directed against life and against love had developed, and everywhere on Earth a similar process had occurred as a field arose, finally leading to war, abuse of power and violence. But we are caretakers of life, and therefore the priestesses refused his request at first. But by now more people of his religion had arrived on Malta looking for protection.

The priestesses knew that this man was not lying. He was a true servant of life, and took good care of the women, children and animals of his clan. The other members of his clan had also become friends of the inhabitants of our island.

When the man came a third time to the temple and asked once again for his way of service to the goddess to be acknowledged, the priestesses considered it for a whole night. If they again forbade the clan to follow its customs, they would perhaps create a situation where the clan would do so secretly, conducting their own hidden rituals, and a new movement would develop on the island. This was certainly not Nammu's wish. A priestess asked for a dream that would give an answer to this difficult situation.

In her dream she saw the animal that was meant to be sacrificed. She went into contact with it, and saw that it was actually willing to die. From this moment on, the priestesses allowed animal sacrifice.

At the time that this decision was taken, it was becoming more usual to eat meat on our island. This custom had already existed amongst the original inhabitants of the island when our ancestors arrived on Malta. I find it repulsive. Most of the members of our tribe do not eat meat. Originally none of us considered it natural to kill animals before the moment that Nammu had decided that they would die. Why interfere with the natural cycle of life if there is no obvious reason to do so?

But the new clan on the island often invites members of our tribe to eat with them. And more and more people, particularly men, start to also eat meat on these occasions. Our priestesses do not like it. But Nammu has told us to respect people of other beliefs, as Creation is infinitely varied. Nammu alone knows in which way she wants to reveal her love for other people.

Our priestesses and the Mirjas do not eat the meat of animals. They do not want to cloud the original dream of Nammu in which there is no violence at all. They consider it to be one of their greatest tasks to keep the right balance in our tribe. The priestesses deal very profoundly with this question. They know that prohibition alone will not bring about the wished-for transformation. And they take care that animals are only killed in coherence with dreams. Nobody is allowed to just kill and eat animals. As this process takes place only in contact with the temples, it becomes sacred and is kept in balance.

When we celebrate the day of fertility once a year in the temple and now also sacrifice an animal, our tribe connects in a particular way with the violence on Earth. We ask for the power to stay connected with awareness to understand the drive to kill, and to be able to heal it. We ask for the power which keeps us in balance so we stay connected with the dreams of Creation of Nammu. We ask for the power to heal the dreams of love and life with Her help. Never again should people of our tribe follow the seduction of using their own power of domination over the rules of life and death.

We sadly accept that some of our men have connected to the customs of the other clan and take part in the ritual of killing. We know that behind this process of killing animals there is also a sexual impulse. It is the still unfulfilled sexual contact between men and women that creates the impulse in men to kill an animal. The wish of the men to become able to fully sexually match our original female power, our motherly power and our female grace, is the deeper reason for this process. The wish to touch outer beauty from the inside lies hidden in sexuality. The sexual impulse to create life also lies very close in its nature to the process of death. The wish to kill and eat animals is connected to the wish for transformation and deep embodiment of outer powers. If the wish for union and full realisation of the male and female cannot be fully achieved on a higher level, it seeks its expression on a lower level. An unfulfilled impulse towards sexual love leads to killing. The wish of the men to sexually match the women and to be able to lastingly touch her inner shining ball of sexual fire leads on another level to killing and eating animals. Men hope, consciously or unconsciously, to gain more sexual power of insight by this, as they want to be able to fully understand our inner secret. We are the world for them. And as women long so much for sexual fulfilment, they let all this happen. They allow processes which they would actually love to stop.

I am still young and cannot understand these connections in their full dimension. But when I listen to the voice of my heart I wish that the priestesses would forbid this process. They should connect to the tradition of our ancestors, who did not allow humans to cause suffering to any living being. It is possible that our priestesses act wisely. It is possible that a prohibition on killing animals would only lead to unnecessary conflict on the island. I have never had a dream in which an animal who would volunteer to be killed by humans appeared to me. I perceive it to be natural to leave the process of birth and death to divine guidance. My young female heart, which is not yet ready to think in terms of compromises, perceives the decision of the priestesses as a step of powerlessness.

I often speak with Nammu about these issues. If my professional path leads me to being a priestess, then together with Nammu I will find other solutions which are closer to the original powers of life. I will never be able to trust a goddess who demands that I kill other living beings. The pain which we inflict on the world is a pain that we always also inflict on ourselves in the end.

THE CYCLE OF LIFE, THE CLAN, AND EVERYDAY LIFE IN THE TEMPLE CULTURE

The Day of Fertility is coming closer. One more cycle of the moon, and then the great celebration will start. We are all preparing already. It will take place in Hagar Qim. The hill of Hagar Qim is a good meeting place for the different clans when we have special questions. It is also the place where all our thanksgiving festivals are celebrated. The Celebration of Fertility is one of the most important days of the year, and there is still much to be prepared.

Hagar Qim is a temple that opens to all directions of the compass. It is not dedicated to the birth and nurture of new insights like other temples. The intention is to pass on our insights here. It is about opening to the world and making our knowledge accessible to all the inhabitants of the island. Hagar Qim is the temple of fertility, harvest and love. It is also the temple of studies. It is where we learn astronomy, knowledge about the sun, and geomancy. It is where we learn about the sacred flows of the Earth. The positions of the sun and moon are measured here. Young women and men practise the art of perception and observation of the stars. This is where the art of physical power is studied, the art of stalking, the art of levitation – the ability to move stones more easily through geistig powers and musical sounds, and much more. Hagar Qim is also a place for healing. Gatherings are held several times a year when healing questions for a clan or the whole tribe are to be solved. Disease is always a sign to us that Nammu is asking us to give attention to a particular aspect of Creation which we have so far overlooked. Disease is never a private concern of an individual but is always interpreted and healed from the perspective of the whole.

In the temple area of Hagar Qim, a little aside from the main building, there is the place of the men, where they meet regularly at certain times. They also have their sleeping stones here, on which they practise the art of dreaming. They do not sleep inside the temple, but outside. It is not so much their task to connect to the depths of Nammu, but rather to train in the powers of observation, perception, the art of stalking, smelling, hearing and seeing. It is a miracle how many different frequencies a human being is able to see and hear. It is especially the men who practise these ways of seeing and hearing. They know the art of estimating distances. By precisely observing the stars they are able to calculate the rising and setting of the sun and the moon. Sounds also make it possible for them to estimate distances quite precisely. The whistle of a bird in the distance is enough for them to know its exact location. By clearly concentrating on items with their eyes, and by fully concentrating on sounds with their ears, they know the distance and location of items precisely over many kilometres.

Another way of seeing requires exactly the opposite from them: they learn to look past things and to perceive what is behind them. In this way they come into contact with the soul of all existence. This perspective, which gives the impression that one is looking through things as if one were absent, enables the young men to recognise the energy processes of the whole.

So we learn to perceive the auras of plants and animals in various ways. We perceive flows of communication, foresee changes in the weather, and much more. We also learn to see and recognise the higher self of all beings using this method. Hearing, on various levels, is trained in a similar way. On a high energy level, this ability makes it possible for us to initiate processes of levitation. These only succeed when they are in harmony with the will of the whole. It is a high art that one studies in later work. The master builders of our temples learn to transport heavy stones to the places where they are to be erected using research in sound. In later times, legends will arise that our men erected the temples using only their power of concentration. This is a one-sided description. It is the combination of many elements which enables the construction of our temples. Of course, physical power is also part of it, and also ingenuity in creating technical tools. It requires cosmic interplay with Nammu's wisdom on many levels. Part of it is the art of mobilising powers of levitation through sound-spaces. In the end, it is full connection with Nammu on all levels of consciousness which reveals Her variety daily in new discoveries.

At the place of dreams in Hagar Qim the men practise their orientation to the directions of the compass during their sleep. It is important for everyone to know the directions of the compass also in their sleep. The men have the task of always falling asleep with the picture of the huge ball of the Earth in front of their eyes. They also practise the art of telepathic communication in this way, with other beings on Earth, from the stars, or ancestors. In the state of light sleep it is particularly easy to find the connection with all of existence. In this state we receive most of our messages and intuitions. Hagar Qim is especially connected with Sirius and the Pleiades. It is like a messenger between these two worlds.

The men often meet here at their favourite place in the temple complex. The older ones introduce the younger ones into the various arts and fields of knowledge. Men often travel over the island but they also love to be close to us women. They recharge their powers with our beauty, our laughter, our dances and our stories, and this is right. Men and women are educated in different ways and processes of insight. While men are rather led towards inner insights through outer perception, for women it is the other way around.

In the course of the last two centuries it has happened that most of us women have stable living places in the caves. This is where we carve our figurines, prepare our vessels and take care of our arts. Men often live with their relatives. They visit us for love. The men usually do not want stable living places. As they are loved by their mothers, their sisters and their clan, they always find a place to stay. Our main living place, where we can all rest our heads, is Nammu, where we are all securely at home.

In everyday life, it has come about that most of the women have up to three stable lovers. These men also accompany them in educating their children if the women want them to. But it is mainly the brothers and the clans of the women who support them in this.

It rarely happens that only one woman in a clan becomes pregnant. Almost always several children are born at the same time. The women who give birth are usually still very young, and still have a big part of their development and growth ahead of them. Therefore the whole tribe takes on responsibility for the children. They grow up together and are often taken care of by our grandmothers.

The children are not our personal children. They are children of the universe. On a different level, they are at least as experienced and wise as we are. They bring new knowledge from the kingdom of death with them, messages from our ancestors. They have returned to support us in accomplishing our tasks. The children are under the protection of the whole tribe. Especially in their first years, the children are taken care of by our elders. They take care that the young beings spend a lot of time on their own, with Nammu and nature, to carefully find their transition into this world. We all want them to remain open for the messages from the world beyond, and that they remember everything that they have brought from that world. If they are too much in contact with this world too early, the risk of forgetting increases.

Women who have reached their fiftieth year are usually sufficiently developed in their lives that they take care of the contact to the universe and our ancestors. They are therefore, together with the mothers, those who accompany the children during their early years.

We all have our firm and reliable web of relationships and friendships which gives us protection and security. Of course, we can always follow erotic adventures if we want to. This does not bring any confusion into our love life. Sexual encounters in the presence of the clan are nothing unusual or even objectionable.

We love variety and the play of Eros. In connection with our dreams of love, it also happens more and more often that couples withdraw a little from communal life for a while. For some time they want to be with only this one partner. This is joyfully accepted if it does not become too much. We have built places for love in the forest. Under the leaves of the palm trees are places for love-couples, where we can all intimately surrender, undisturbed, to the sweet play of love.

It is the clan which gives us calm and security and from which we can discover the adventures of life. When a deep friendship develops to certain lovers, they come to live with us. If one day we no longer want to be with each other, we separate again. Simple signs and dreams support us in this. They indicate that the purpose of our encounter is now fulfilled and that what we wanted to achieve together is accomplished. Only rarely do conflicts develop over this as each person has their security and clan to which they can always return.

Only since the dream of personal love has been coming more strongly into our lives has this started to become more difficult sometimes. There starts to be confusions. If a couple has had a particularly beautiful intimate time for some weeks, one of them suddenly considers the other to be a life-partner. One becomes bound to personal wishes and longings and no longer listens to the voice of Nammu. This happens when someone is in danger of losing their inner shining ball. Sometimes resentments come up in the tribe when a couple withdraws for too long. If a woman, for example, turns more and more to a new lover, going very often to the intimate love places, not taking care of her firm love networks in the clan, this can lead to jealousy. Feelings like envy and resentment can develop. The elders and priestesses pay a lot of attention to this.

If this leads to a seriously difficult situation, one is sent to the temple to ask for support. The priestesses often bring people back together who have separated too early, before their common life-task has been fulfilled. Sometimes it also happens that the inner sexual energy ball of a woman burns too strongly with desire for one man. A woman who experiences this is in a state of severe unrest. It can even lead to physical diseases. She is then obsessed by the sexual fire and confuses this with love to one man.

Men usually become scared of the intensity of this desire and therefore cannot meet such longing. In such difficult situations, the priestesses arrange a healing encounter. Often they bring the woman together with a Shamanu so that the fire burning too strongly inside can be stilled and the woman can find her way back to herself and her calm.

Sometimes these women are only occupied by such a longing because something inside has fallen out of balance. A small shamanistic act on the outside can bring things back into balance on the inside. The priestesses, the Mirjas and the elders provide support in such cases.

We know that Nammu has an answer to all questions of life. Nobody in the tribe has any doubt about this. The experienced women in particular are a great support for us in these personal questions of life. From the age of fifty onwards, women find their deeper fulfilment in preparing the younger women for maturity. They themselves only give their love services in the temple when their age or special knowledge is required. They continue to dance the snake-dances, and they love the play of Eros ever more at their age. It is not at all the case that they renounce this joy of life. The younger inexperienced men still love to visit them, as well as the older ones. These women have realised the aspect of the mature Goddess of Love and Her dream in their lives. They have found their partners, friends and lovers. Together with them, they usually live a full and satisfied life. Now they have the task of supporting younger people through their advice and actions. In their cosmic search they turn towards the aspect of age and wisdom. Gaining deeper knowledge in all areas has become their main interest in life.

Now they also want to get to know more about the other spaces of existence towards which they are turning in the second half *of their lives. They take care of the newborns and accompany the old ones into death. And they learn from their dreams. They are connected in many ways with our ancestors who live over the threshold of death. Together with them, they take care of the love-life of the youth and support them in finding their path.*

The Cosmic Guardians – An Encounter in the Oldest Temples of Malta

My departure was coming closer and every minute was becoming valuable. I often spent almost the whole night writing. The feeling of having to write down the most important experiences, at least in keywords, before leaving the island became more and more urgent. Even though I worked a lot, on the day before I left I had the strange feeling of not having done my homework. While I was sitting restlessly at my desk early in the morning, a clear inner voice told me to pause.

This is your last day on Malta. Stop working! Strengthen your memory and your newly gained inner power. Nothing will get lost. Taking the right action is now decisive for success. Listen to your inner voice to find which tasks you still have to fulfil before you leave the island!

I stopped, filled a bath and went into meditation. In the very moment that I became calmer, I immediately received the first instructions.

Take a walk today, and take in the energies of the island once more. Be awake and follow your intuitions, as there is still something you have to do today. You can start walking directly from the hotel. Visit the oldest temples of the island. There is information waiting for you there.

"Does it mean I should walk to these temples? How will I find the way there? Anyway, they are closed and I will not be able to enter!" I asked in reply, surprised.

Just make a start. You will receive many presents today. Start, and keep yourself open!

So I left the bath and dressed appropriately for a walk. I only had a road map of Malta, which I took with me so that I would have at least a rough orientation. I also took my camera and a little money, and started. As soon as I stepped out of the entrance, I was told to follow a path behind our hotel which led into the wilderness of the island.

After only a few hundred metres, my burdens fell away from me. The landscape was beautiful, with old pine trees and Southern Mediterranean plants which I did not always recognise. The air was filled with spice. In the distance were villages the colour of natural stone, and behind them the blue sea. I followed the path securely and without hesitation, led by my inner intuition. After I had walked for about two hours I reached a small unfrequented road which wound its way over a hill. I followed it for a while and found a cave located directly at the side of the road. The entrance was decorated with flowers. I decided to rest for a while and go into the cave. Amazed, I realised that I was in a church. Behind a wrought iron gate stood a Madonna figurine with old jars and vessels arranged around her. On a small sign I read that this place was a place of pilgrimage and healing for believers of the island, and had an intimate connection with Lourdes.

"This is how some sanctuaries of the feminine have prevailed over the millennia and still fulfil their original function," I thought, and sat down on one of the wooden benches. A silent, almost childlike religious feeling filled me.

Be aware. You will soon find something close-by, I heard from the silence of my childlike prayer. *It is a gift for you from the island.*

I had the feeling that for the first time I could pray to the Mother of God, without any difficulties, without having to think of an arrogant, prudish, anti-sexual saint who still dominates so many families with false morals. The Mother of God to whom I now spoke has remained constant in Her nature. In ancient times She was loved and worshipped as Nammu. She was sensual, vital, elementary, wild and graceful at the same time, joyful and grieving, wise and playful. I remember that I knew this kind of connection in my childhood before I went through the detours and errors of religion and patriarchal education. Later I found it absolutely childish to pray to a Mother of God, and was at most moved by the naivety of believers who could just do it. This childlike religious feeling for the female divinity as I experienced it now had been lost for a long time. I remained in it for quite a while, as it was valuable.

After I while I moved on with a feeling of gratitude, looking around attentively and asking myself what kind of gift might have been meant. After thirty metres I had the clear impulse:

Turn right here!

I had the clear feeling of being at an ancient sacred site. I sat on my haunches and opened all my senses.

Look around you!

I did so, but saw nothing but stones. *Look more precisely!* I discovered that one of the stones, a little bigger than the palm of my hand, had a very clear pattern of a leaf. It was covered with a thin layer of colour reminiscent of the ochre which we had seen in the Hypogeum. All the other stones lying around were normal pieces of rock. I took this one stone, which could have come from a very large jar or pillar and was quite heavy. I had no idea whether I was holding a prehistoric artefact in my hands, or whether it was a relic from Phoenician times. I only knew that this was the gift that the voice in my prayer had meant. I was as happy as a child with this treasure.

After walking on for another thirty minutes I reached the village of Mgarr. Close-by was one of the temples that I should visit. But surprisingly, I was told to walk on to the next village to buy a roll of film.

You will still need it today to document important events.

This time I had taken a roll of film so that I would not repeat the mistake that I had made on Gozo, but this did not seem to be enough for my inner guidance. I had to walk quite fast as it was about twenty minutes to one.

"How can I make it to the next village before one o'clock when the shops close?"

Don't ask. Walk! came the answer.

Sometimes I have to give quite some trust in advance to my inner guidance not to get entangled in unnecessary resistance. At about ten past one I arrived in the next village and found a little shop whose owner was about to close. In a dusty corner she found her last roll of film.

I was quite exhausted and very happy to find a small restaurant. I decided to take a break, ordered a glass of wine, sparkling water and a salad, and enjoyed the siesta. I noticed that I was no longer used to walking long distances. While enjoying my white wine I made some notes in my diary and thought about how to continue from here. There was also an ancient temple here in Zebbieh which I wanted to visit today. I had a full programme ahead of me and by the evening I wanted to be back in the hotel. While I was deep in my thoughts, I suddenly perceived a clear inner message.

You have to be at the temple of Zebbieh at exactly 2:30!

This order came so clearly that I looked up amazed. What did this message mean?

I did not have an appointment nor anything like it. Were these now the first signs of insanity of a spiritual researcher who has lived for too long alone with her inner voice?

No discussions. There is no time to lose! came the firm reply. When I looked at my watch I was surprised to notice that it was already twenty past two. I hesitated for a moment as I was actually still tired, and lazy. Was this really my inner guidance? Or did someone want to make a fool out of me? Was I not at least a free being? But I could clearly see that these thoughts were only an attempt to justify my laziness. I ordered the bill. The waitress was not at all in a hurry and talked with guests at the neighbouring table. "Surely I have a little time," I thought to myself. But my inner mistress was not so easily bribed.

Give her a sign that you are in a hurry.

A bit embarrassed, I looked around as if somebody in the room would notice my inner dialogue. I went directly to the waitress, pointed at my watch to make it clear that I was in a

185

hurry, and paid, giving a generous tip. Then I started running. I had exactly five minutes left.

And I indeed arrived at the temple at exactly 2:30. From a distance I had already seen that a gate was open and that a white car was standing in front of it. Was this the deeper meaning of all this? Would I now maybe have the opportunity to get to know this temple thanks to my inner guidance? Everyone had told me that it is not possible to visit it.

I arrived at the entrance gate out of breath. Two young round Maltese men were standing in front of it.

"Oh! It's open! Is it possible to come in?" I asked in English.

"Yes. Come in. We were already waiting," was the surprising answer. I reacted quickly inside myself. I knew that I had to take this opportunity immediately. I walked erect, with a racing heart, through the gate, feeling like the Queen of Sheba.

"Probably they are waiting for someone else. There must have been some confusion. But a great opportunity to get into the temple," I thought delightedly. I would certainly not rush to clarify things. Then I stood still inside the walls. The place was surprisingly well cared for. This temple was completely familiar to me. It was enchantingly peaceful. I immediately perceived that it was dedicated to the three aspects of the Goddess: the aspect of birth and youth, the aspect of maturity and fertility, and the aspect of old age, death and rebirth. The entire temple culture of Malta had started with the construction of this temple. The first people who had arrived here from the mainland had built their temple of power and gratitude here together with the inhabitants of the island. Here, and soon afterwards in Mgarr, they had started to give education in sacred dreaming and they started to build the school of Malta which then guarded a culture of peace for millennia.

For about twenty minutes I investigated every stone, without being distracted by the knowledge that people were watching me, as I had a task here. The two attendants observed me.

One of them was as round as the ancient mother goddesses. It was as if he was one of these ancient female figures in male form. Eventually he approached and started talking to me. He seemed to be untroubled by any kind of confusion. On the contrary, they both seemed to be sure that I was the person they had been expecting. I started to become insecure that nobody else had come. Were these two maybe in contact with my cosmic guidance? My careful question why they had been waiting was answered only with a friendly smile. Was that because of their bad English, or did they want me to remain uncertain?

They did not seem to be in any hurry, and patiently waited until I had investigated every corner of the temple, which took about an hour. The rounder one offered to take a photo of me at the entrance.

Eventually I had the idea of asking them about the other temple, close to Mgarr, which was also closed. Maybe they could help me to get in there too. The younger one, about thirty years old, immediately offered to drive me there. Surprised, I accepted, and we drove to the neighbouring village in a rattling white jeep. Conversation was difficult as he indeed spoke hardly any English. At the temple of Mgarr, he opened a section of fence, obviously knowing the place well, and we climbed together into the temple grounds.

I was once again surrounded by the same grand silence. Nammu herself seemed to rest here, and to receive me gracefully. I did not receive any special messages. It was simply silent peace, full of light. I went into prayer and formulated my gratitude and my plan to write a book about everything I had experienced and seen. While I was sitting there for some time in silence, a film from prehistoric times ran in front of my inner eye. I felt as if I was standing in front of a priestess of these ancient times to present my intentions. I felt a warm soft positive acceptance of my plan. It was as if I was arriving back at the original source of my power and love after a long time, and was now being accepted as a messenger of the Goddess. My service was being blessed by Her. It was like a silent initiation ritual.

Always return to the origin before you begin something new, came into my mind. This rule of the ancient times had already been presented to me in the stone circle in Portugal as an essential ritual of the ancient humans. Now I had the impression that I had been guided here to follow this rule. This was what I had still had to do before I could start my journey home. With this visit I had fulfilled my tasks on Malta. This contact with the oldest temples on Malta had still been missing from my temple visits. Now the circle was complete and my inner calm returned to me.

The air was perfumed with earth and spice, and I was filled with an inner certainty. I felt initiated into the secrets of the Earth and their healing power, returned to the service of a message of peace which has always existed. The longing of the Earth, her pulse, her knowledge and her power have struggled to survive for millennia, waiting for those who will recognise her knowledge again and seek to manifest it in a form which corresponds to the present time. In the context of the historical background, this planet is young, a love affair of Creation and Her dream of paradise which is waiting for fulfilment.

My companion – I also perceived him as a messenger of the Goddess, although he perhaps did not even know that he was acting in Her service – waited patiently. Then he showed me a place that is commonly called the tombs of Zebugg. As he was standing in front of me showing me the ditches, over which the light played particularly softly, the erotic tension suddenly rose very high, although I had not even thought of it before.

He asked whether he could kiss me. But my inner guidance clearly advised me against it. I had the clear feeling that I would bring turbulence into his life if I did so now. He offered to drive me home, and I accepted gratefully as it was already late afternoon. On the way I got to know that he was newly but not very happily married. I spoke with him about love, faithfulness and sexuality. He was only 28 years old. I felt like a love-priestess of the twentieth century. This time, however, the messages were a little more difficult. His wife did not like sex as she was strictly Catholic. He also could not look for sex outside his marriage because that would be betrayal. Unfortunately there was no social vessel into which the messages of true love and a possible solution could flow. If this had existed I would have happily welcomed him sensually, and he would have returned delightedly and gratefully to his wife to pass on something of his new experience.

I understood the warning from inside. If I had allowed full sexual contact with him, a young marriage would probably have been destroyed. Long and comprehensive work lies ahead of us to develop social vessels so that the widespread misery in love need continue no longer.

After about ten minutes he stopped his car directly in front of our elegant hotel. I said good-bye. This last day on Malta had been another lesson in inner guidance. Sometimes it is about absolute precision. The interplay of guidance and obedience which had occurred today is only possible based on a high degree of trust. I saw this experience as a greeting from the Goddess, showing me clearly that cooperation with Her powers is still possible today.

EDUCATION OF THE MEN

At the gates of Hagar Qim I could observe a strange energy movement. An ocean of dancing dots was carved in a very simple way into a stone. The dots seemed to dissolve into nothingness. The light of the sun started to shimmer upon them, and after observing it for a while my eyes became more sensitive to optical phenomena. I have never seen anything comparable to it anywhere else. It was like a picture of an energy of Creation, which reminded me of the energy which would be called orgone by Wilhelm Reich some millennia later. Other peoples have called it mana, prana or chi.

Maybe it is no coincidence that this strangely abstract picture is carved at the gates of the temple of love. I will now tell the story of Hagar Qim as it revealed itself to me in its flourishing beauty and sensual fullness when I asked about its deeper purpose and meaning. A life of love, free of fear, condemnation or accusation unfolded in front of my eyes, free of everything which would burden it nowadays.

Some may be astonished that so much attention was given to the topic of love and sexuality. Imagine how it would be if questions of love and sexuality were dealt with in our parliaments, instead of questions of tank deliveries or weapons systems. Incredible attention was given to love-life in the temple cultures, as if the life of the whole tribe depended on the question whether the love between two or more people would succeed or not. No experience in love, no matter how banal it seemed, was a private matter. Love always happened in the presence of the Goddess.

It was considered significant for global peace whether or not harmony between the genders could be accomplished and whether or not the longings in love between men and women could find fulfilment. These questions determined whether Nammu's dream of paradise could be fulfilled or not. It was about much more than a personal love experience of two people.

It was about the cosmic balance of polar powers of Creation, and about the fruitful arrangement of the powers of life on planet Earth. A human being whose heart chakra was fully awakened and opened in connection with the sexual chakra looked into the world with different eyes. He or she naturally took on responsibility for plants, animals and humans, naturally becoming a guardian of peace on this planet. Therefore men and women profoundly studied the cosmic laws of love from an early age. These studies were the basis of their whole understanding of the world and for the profession that they would choose later. My inner world of pictures led me into the love school that the men passed through.

At the place where the men sleep when they come to study the stars or when they want to visit the love service at the altar of the Mirjas, stands a huge stone. It is a phallic symbol, supporter of fertility and growth. It is a supporter of their male beauty, integrity and litheness. The young men are sent here to receive dreams. This is their starting point from which they enter the paradise of sensual love. Every man has the possibility of receiving education from the Mirjas before he is sent into the wild world of love adventures. In addition to education and development of personal abilities in love, the sexual act is practised as a service to the world, Nammu and thereby the female aspect of Creation. In the temple of Hagar Qim they learn and experience that something universal and divine reaches into every love relationship and every contact with the woman. Only in connection with the universal aspect can a personal relationship find its fulfilment. In Hagar Qim the men learn to let the world and the Goddess shine into everything they do.

"He who is blind in love and sees only the woman in his desire destroys divine life; but he who recognises the Goddess in every woman and serves Her unfolding lives in the sunrise of eternity."

This is a sentence from the love priestesses which every man receives along his way. Men learn that they can only understand the nature of a woman when they rediscover the Goddess in her.

"*You can discover and take care of the Goddess in every woman. A man who knows this art serves the world and will receive many gifts,*" *is another teaching on that path. The men get to know about the sensual nature of women from the love priestesses. They learn from them what women love and what they do not love. A man who has learned to use his phallus in the service of the Goddess has also learned to properly respect the female gender.*

All men receive a clear sign when it is the time to visit a woman sensually for the first time. Usually the sign comes to them in a dream. From that dream, reality is born. The dream is the guardian of the coming reality of every human being. When a man dreams of a woman sexually, and when he also encounters a snake, it is usually clear that it is time to go to the love school. Nammu has called.

Men practise the art of approaching correctly, the art of sensual language. They learn to strengthen and open their physical chakras. They get to know the core of their sexual chakra which connects them to Nammu like an umbilical cord. They learn to keep this core centred and let themselves be guided by it.

Special attention is given to the opening of the heart chakra. An important shift for the men takes place in the heart chakra. This is not only a personal event. It is connected with the preparation for a new step in the evolution of love. This fruit was injured before it could truly ripen. A closed heart chakra is the place where violence is created. The image of the Goddess of Love should open in the heart chakra of the men. An open heart chakra can immediately change the whole thinking of a human being. Once men are connected with the image of the Goddess of Love it is possible for them to understand love and support women.

The beauty, bodily fullness and grace, the very personal smile of the full and soft lips of the Goddess of Love, Her perfectly shaped breasts and hips can trigger intense desire in a man. It is easy to push a man from his centre through a visionary or real image of the Goddess in Her full beauty.

The men themselves are again and again surprised how easily they become restless when an unknown woman appears. We talk a lot about the deeper meaning of this allure.

"The longing for loving union with the Goddess touches you in every woman. If you do not forget this, and if you trust in the guidance of the Goddess, you can remain connected to your calm. The Goddess will lead you securely to your goal. If you forget the deeper divine aspect because of the beauty of a woman, only the burning desire remains," are the enlightening words of the Mirjas, who themselves usually stand in full beauty before the men. It is the task of the men to follow the longing without getting lost in it.

"Rediscover what you are looking for within yourself first. It lives within you as an image of the Goddess. This protects you, because you know it. Act only after you have found it," is one of the guidelines that provides orientation for the men. It is the task of women to guide and direct the men in this. The scent and radiance of the Goddess can have such an enchanting effect that men forget their own centre. Their senses become foggy and they no longer feel when the right moment to act has come.

The same is true for beautiful young women who come into close contact with the image of the Goddess of Love. They also easily miss the right moment for action, as we already know from the story of Meret.

It is often confusing because the Goddess of Love has a very seductive and personal attraction. Many people continue to try to fulfil the personal longing which the Goddess has triggered, in the contact with a partner. They too quickly throw their whole longing, which originally was for the Goddess, onto one person. This person is of course never able to fulfil this longing. This is how the misery in love unavoidably develops.

This is why the aspect of personal love is given special care on Malta. Men are connected with Nammu and the Goddess *of Love as if through a cosmic umbilical cord. Through this energetic process they also receive the signs for when it is the time for them to directly connect with the sexual aspect of Creation.*

Young men who have never experienced the cosmic energy of the body with a woman, but already went through the school of the first encounter with adolescent girls, and those who have encountered sensual happiness in their dreams and have received the sign of the Goddess, go up to Hagar Qim to tell the priestess of their dream. They know that the temple servants of love will now arrange an encounter for them. Usually they then spend some days at the temple to become familiar with certain tasks. They should strengthen and cleanse their chakras. They are led to a priestess and tell her in detail what is on their hearts. The priestesses listen very precisely to recognise the deeper tracks of the seeking and loving soul, in order to be able to guide them in the right way. Particularly in the times of arising potency, there are often confusing dreams and experiences that the young men are not yet able to interpret for themselves. They are guided by their male companions, the Shamanu, through the temple, and can deepen their knowledge in geomancy and astronomy. The Mirjas ask them how far they already know their personal connection to the stars. One's personal connection to the stars is significant for the path in love, as one can see from this connection which contact to a woman is now the most urgently needed.

A man who is connected with the ancestors from Sirius needs a rather grounded and earthy woman for his first contact. She must know how to securely and firmly guide him.

A man who is connected with Venus is grounded and earthy himself already and needs rather the light and playful element of a woman who expresses dance and movement and who is connected with the airy elements.

After the temple priestesses have listened to the words of the love-student, they decide how to introduce this man to love. Sometimes it is the dream of a man to meet sexually with a particular woman from the tribe. Usually a contact is then created between him and this woman. Probably there is something significant about an encounter between these two. This is checked and the woman is also asked about her dreams. Usually that shows that dreams have brought these two together. If it fits, and if the time has come, they may try their first act of love in a special place which is dedicated to this.

Often it is the wish of the man to first be introduced to love by the temple servants. To find which of them is the right first step for the man, the priestesses often spend several days at the temples, accompanied by the Mirjas and often also by oracle priestesses. The young men are sent away several times to become aware of their own intuition.

There is a certain place overlooking the southern coast where a bench has been carved into the stone. This is one of the men's favourite places to contemplate their questions. It is a place where thousands of men have sat before them. They think about their wishes and hopes here, and wait for further intuition. In addition to the geistig challenges there are also exercises for physical flexibility and control over their physical reactions.

Every man has the task of practising the sexual walk, and being fully aware of the impulses in his sexual chakra. The criteria for this walk are not external; the most important thing is to be aware of the inner snake-power. Whether one is able to hold the power of the snake determines whether one is able to use Eros as a cosmic source of power and let oneself be guided or whether one loses it and slides into restlessness, neediness and agitation.

"Those who know the power of the snake and care for it, enter the path of guardian of peace. They are led along the ways of insight and to the source of all who love, wherever they walk. It is also the snake who teaches us the path of healing," the priestesses tell the men.

There is a small triangular corridor which symbolises the vagina of a woman. They enter it many times to practise awareness of their sexual chakras. While doing so, they connect with the

195

image of going to a Mirja and performing the service to the Goddess of Love for the first time. They are allowed to imagine in detail how it will be when they stand in front of a woman with an erect phallus for the first time to perform the act of love. If their phallus then stands firm and erect, and this despite the excitement is connected with inner centring and calm; if their phallus does not then fall at the thought of their first performance, then they know that Nammu has called them and the time has come for their first sensual contact with a woman. They then go to the priestess who is the keeper of the threshold, to tell her.

The priestesses take special care that the Mirjas give their service in a way that does not lead to any wrong attachment. It is not their task to create a personal relationship to the men, but rather to teach them sensual trust and to show them a path which is connected to the Goddess. It might happen that a man first personally falls in love with a Mirja. But she must take care that this does not lead to any wrong attachment. It is her task to introduce a young man to the art of love and to help him find his way to other women and to those who will become the companions of his heart. These women already live in his heart and only want to be recognised. Insight in love will take place if the sexual aspect of the heart chakra is opened fully, and thereby reveals its still-hidden pictures from the inside. It is sexual energy which makes this happen. The Mirjas represent a certain aspect of Nammu which can contribute to this opening and this insight. A Mirja works as a representative of the whole within which a man can rediscover the universal aspect of the feminine. A man learns from the Mirjas what it means to love and embrace the universal aspect in the woman. He learns to hold a woman in a way that she feels secure in his arms, without wanting to own her. The concept of wanting to own a woman would suffocate the seed of universal love immediately. In this case the Goddess withdraws, and with Her the source of universal love also disappears. The beauty of the lustful embrace then fades and it becomes empty of content.

Our men are of course told early on about such and similar false orientations. Every man in the tribe knows the story of our early ancestors. Everyone knows about the incident of Manu, who fell for the wish to own a woman. And everyone knows about Meret, who gave the apple of love too early to Manu. Manu and Meret acted against the laws of Nammu and all the warnings of the priestesses. The deeper sexual longing of the men is not about owning a woman. The deeper wish is to fully interfuse with her, to embrace her with his male arms so that for a short moment nothing is hidden from him any more. This is connected with complete revelation under the protection of the Goddess. Nothing female will then be unknown to him any longer; he has fully dived into the depths of the female being. No part of her soul will withdraw from him any more, and for one eternal moment he will be suffused with universal love together with her, and reach the deepest ground of existence. He wants to add his powerful male energy to her soft female giving aspect, to then be able to dissolve for some moments in it.

The evolutionary birth of partnership takes place in the longing of every man. The woman wants to be liberated from being perceived only as a mother. The woman does love to be a mother for the son-archetype, but a very different longing also burns in her. The aspect of her full sensuality demands liberation and seeks sensual recognition by the fully awakened man and partner. Nothing less than the birth of a new archetype in Creation takes place through this process. It is the birth of the new archetype of the lover and his beloved. Every man in whom this longing is burning wants to reach the inner core of the woman in a soft and agile way, wants to touch her in her inner nature, wants to recognise and experience her. He is midwife for the aspect of the growing erotic love of the Goddess of Love. He wants to nourish the shining fire inside the female soul with his phallus. If he is connected by the cosmic umbilical cord with Nammu, he need do nothing else to find fulfilment. He only has to strengthen his trust in the Goddess. Once he *has learned to surrender to the play of love, his body knows when his phallus is to erect or fall, when it should become soft or strong, depending on the wishes of the Goddess of Love. The Goddess knows precisely what serves insight and fulfilment. According to that, power, insight and love flow to him from the female body. The art is to activate the knowledge of the snake in such a way that he is able to hear the voice of the Goddess at any time and therefore no longer needs to leave his inner centre.*

Fully touching the universal point of love of the woman is like drinking from the well of eternal love. The Goddess alone decides when we experience this bliss. It is independent of age, profession, or outer beauty. It is not the size of the phallus which is the measure for the art of love, but the inner connection with the Goddess and the agility that arises from this, the suppleness, awareness, sensitivity and flexibility.

I see Tamara in front of me, giving her service of love. She has called a student of love into the love room. In the way he is moving she can see clearly that he is not visiting a Mirja for the first time. They surrender to the play of love in a meditative and calm way. Only when there is no rush, restlessness or impatience do they get in touch with Nammu's inner radiance and only then are the two lovers led together through the bodily centres and gates of sexual insight by the sexual energy. They feel how life energy spreads in their bodies, how they are flooded by it. It starts in their abdomens but then this power increases, filling all of their chakras and centres. The fire of love moves in spirals through them, and they follow the power of transformation of the snake energy in their bodies. This power dances through their entire bodies, filling their cells with the most healthy and most creative power of life they know. Sometimes the sexual power concentrates in one centre and in certain areas of the body, curling up like a snake, then burns again throughout the whole body. When this power takes hold of them, the sexual power is suddenly also directed through their gaze. For some

198

seconds it is possible to look into each others' eyes with the gaze of sexual recognition. They recognise the divine origin in the other, look into the deepest ground of polar Creation, and they recognise each other, a man and a woman in their elementary and true nakedness, wildness and beauty. They recognise that they are one; two complementary poles of a vast play of Creation.

Entwined in varying positions, their only task is to surrender and to follow the pictures of their soul which come to them during the encounter. The Mirja, the more experienced of the two, guides the process smoothly, letting herself be guided by her inner sensual knowledge. She senses precisely where the sexual energy of the student of love is in every moment. Sometimes she tells him to remain still and not to move, to pause in calm concentration until a new soul picture takes hold of their bodies and they follow its dance. Time stretches to eternity. They go on until he feels that he can no longer hold the power of his seed, and ejaculates in her. Like two resting animals, they lie still together for a while, looking at the pictures of the inner world of the soul and listening to the voice of Nammu. Then the Mirja gets up, wraps herself in her cloak, and leads the young man to a bowl of sacred water, where he can wash and refresh himself. He gives her a present to thank her for this experience of love. She also thanks him for his act of love which she has received as a representative of Nammu. She tells him to go to the cliffs to contemplate on what has happened, and to return after one hour to tell her what he experienced.

While a Mirja is giving this service in love, she usually sees the whole nature of the young man who is together with her. She now knows more about what he must take care of on his path in love; with which women he can continue learning, and to which women he can go if his desire needs a knowing woman. She also knows more about the deeper wish of his soul for a personal companion of the heart and beloved at his side. She will give him hints for his further path. Usually great happiness shines from the eyes of a man when he returns from

199

the temple service of the Mirjas. Actually it is always a great experience. Sometimes a man is not yet able to hold the tension long enough and ejaculates at the beginning into the lap of the Goddess. Nobody judges him for that. He will come back often to learn and experience more. After a love lesson with the Mirjas he feels born as a man. Now he has reached the nature of sexual love. Now he is ready for the young women who are joyfully awaiting his growing power of love. Over years, the men are repeatedly invited into the temple of love, and the more often they are initiated, the deeper they can reach the inner seeing and recognition of female nature. They become ever more knowing, and can put their maturity and insight into the service of the women of their tribe.

Sometimes a man has a repeating sexual dream of a snake. For the Mirjas this is a sign that Nammu has special plans for this man. He is to be educated in the service of sexuality and healing. He will support the initiation of the birth of the new lover. Such men are called into the service of the temple. They are educated as Shamanu to give the sexual healing service for women whose inner fire has for some reason been injured. This education takes several years. They become guardians of the temple until their advancing age calls them to other forms of service.

THE FESTIVAL OF FERTILITY

It is the night before the big summer solstice celebration. From tomorrow onward, the days will become shorter again. The day of fertility is the day when the sun spreads her radiance longest over our island. Every inhabitant of the island has come to the temple. All of the tribes and their clans meet on this holiday to honour Nammu as the Goddess of fullness, fruits and the harvest.

The men have prepared their fertility costumes. They have carved various symbolic phalluses which they will wear when they dance in honour of Nammu. The women have prepared beautiful clothes. They will be adorned with jewellery and body paint. New goddess figures have been shaped from stone. Large jars stand ready. The passing of days from one fertility celebration to the next is marked on them each day. Tomorrow at sunrise the final mark will be celebrated. The jars are filled with the drink of fermented fruits. Everybody has been preparing this festival for weeks. The summer and winter solstices are our biggest holidays of the year. The transitions from spring to summer and autumn to winter are also celebrated, but in a calmer way. These days are rather about certain geistig insights which we are to receive in order to bring them to maturity.

Today is the holiday on which we give thanks, honour our ancestors, and celebrate the whole of Nammu's creation and its peaceful continuation. The festival starts with the first rays of light in the morning. Most people spend the night close to Hagar Qim, by the huge water storage basins above the temple, or in the numerous caves close-by. Some spend the night awake at the sacred temple itself. Some have asked for dreams of fertility and spend the night on one of the sleeping stones.

By sunrise the area is filled with movement. At dawn one can already see men and women climbing the hill from all directions. They gather at the east side of the temple. Quietly, modestly, and in awe, they are anticipating the great event of the first rays of light. Inside the temple are the oracle priestesses, some of the Mirjas and snake dancers, and some of the male snake dancers and Shamanu.

South of the temple stand three particularly large stones. They represent the three aspects of the Goddess: birth and youthful power, maturity of sexual femininity, and the wisdom of old age and dying. Between them rises a single big stone. It is a phallic symbol, the sign of great fertility. Another phallic symbol, the biggest of our megaliths, stands in the north. This is the power-symbol for the men. The temple represents the cycle of the becoming-man. Male power is less connected with matter, and incarnates more slowly than female power. It is called to incarnate by us. We use our intelligence and beauty to seduce this male power to incarnate more fully in material form and to make this space of existence its home and to manifest here. The coming birth of the male god, who wants to incarnate and be carried to birth by Nammu, announces itself each year anew with the first rays of sun on this special day. When this birth will, after centuries, take place, the dream of Creation of Nammu will be complete. The male power is created by the rays of the sun, and is meant to be carried and brought into reality here in Nammu. The male and the female aspect are in every human being; the female is greater in us women, and the male in the men.

Our temple is also dedicated to the creation of male power and fertility in the way it is constructed. The big phallic symbol in the south represents youthful male power. Young men become students of the Goddess to become able to unfold the gift of male power and fertility with Her help. In the east lies the biggest block of stone we have ever used to build our temples: more than three metres high and about seven metres long. It was brought here accompanied by music and dance, hundreds of years ago. The Goddess stones in the south and the big phallus megalith in the north were already standing at this time as guardians to protect the development of the temple. The rising sun should show its first signs of new creation on the big stone in the east. This stone will energetically help to store the memory and manifest Nammu's dream. Behind this stone is a depression in the ground with a smaller triangular stone. It symbolises the fertility of Nammu, Her sacred gate leading into the centre of Her body, and Her life-giving fullness. Directly beside it is an opening, an oval hole through which one can look into the interior of the sanctuary. One's view falls into a circular room. It symbolises the womb of the Goddess, protected in the body of the temple. This temple represents the union of the male and female powers, the most exciting experiment of our evolutionary intention.

We all stand in front of this opening at exactly this moment every year, waiting for the coming events to unfold. The opening symbolises the vagina of Nammu, but also Her geistig birth channel, Her geistig umbilical cord from which everything comes and to which every new creation goes. The light of the sun is to unite with the inner sun and radiance of the Earth here. This is why this place lies embedded within the protection of the temple walls. It is the conception of new ideas of Creation which is celebrated here every year.

Now we hear soft drumming from inside the temple. It symbolises the heartbeat of Nammu awakening. The people start to stamp their feet quietly and rhythmically on the earth. Then it really starts. The first rays of sun from the east fall directly into the opening to the sacred centre of the temple. Those who built the temple planned it so that the sunlight meets the right point. Long calculations and precise observations were necessary. Every year we are amazed anew by this great event. We take it as a good sign for the coming year that there are no clouds and the first light of this day is received directly by Nammu. It is as a good omen for the celebration of the male and female powers of love, and for the harvest and growth of plants, animals and humans.

After a first ripple of amazement, it becomes completely quiet again. Through the hole we see an oracle priestess step into the room. We hear the soft stamping of her feet and we can imagine *how her hips move rhythmically in circles; every now and then we see her shadow falling on the sunlit earth. Then we hear her song. She sings the song of gratitude to Nammu and to the first rays of the sun which have brought the powers of masculinity into Nammu's womb where they can further mature. The priestesses work all year on this song, which is sung, in a new way each time, at every fertility festival. The priestess is singing of love and longing, birth, Eros and death. She sings the prayer for Manu and Meret and their healing. Then it becomes quiet once more.*

Now we ask for a rich harvest and fertility, for the Earth and for our women who will become mothers this year. Today is the day of fertility and of sanctification of our sexual powers, through which Nammu wants to further manifest, in the human being and in the whole of Creation.

Manava, Manu, Tewlett and other snake priests have carved their new flutes. They now come out of the temple and start to softly whistle their snake-songs. They are accompanied by the rhythmic drumming from the heart of the temple.

"Nammu, from whom all life comes. Nammu, into whom all life returns, we dance for You. Together with You we weave our dream of love. We call the male powers of Creation to make us their home, to anchor inside us through Nammu, to become and grow in Her so that their light can care for, love and honour Nammu. This will bring Her body to fulfilment, Her light to eternal radiance. It shall make the song of the Earth sound until it is heard by the most distant stars. With Her light, and at Her body, he shall nourish himself and for that give Her his fertile seed. In Her, Nammu, male power and female grace shall unite to one whole with the power of eternal Creation, the Great Mother from whom all life comes and to whom all life returns. The eternal act of creation and conception shall take its ever-new beginning in sensual love, into which the seed of new creation shall be put, into a new order of universal power of love. He shall become Her lover and care for Her, he who will be at Her side in eternity, who fills Her fertile body, who

makes Her grace shine even more beautifully and keeps Her body forever youthful. He is to be the keeper of light so that even in the state of chaos he will not fall from the higher order and security. May chaos be the beginning of every new order. Chaos is the gateway of the Goddess which wants to be guarded carefully. All becoming came from chaos. May it forever develop anew. Manu, Manu, give your radiance, give your beauty, give your growth and power back to the Goddess. Become healthy at Her body, growing and becoming with Her."

This is how the men sang. And they danced with it. They were wearing their carved phallic symbols, the sign of potency and arising masculinity. The women joined the choir, "Nammu, Nammu, give Your beauty, give Your body, give Your kindness, give Your eternal fullness, give Your calmness, give Your dance and arising life, give Your protection and Your patience. Give all this to the arising Manu. Give Yourself to him fully. Give him back Your dream of Creation and let him grow in You so that the new lover shall be born and can give us all his protecting loving, caring and potent power. Give birth to us together with the lover who stands at our side and who makes Creation more beautiful, finer and sweeter for us. Let his phallus grow with us and in us, so that he nourishes and cares for the shining fire in our bodies for ever and ever. We wash our body in beauty and happiness by enjoying Your joy. Thank you, Fullness. Thank you Nammu. Let us together celebrate the sacred marriage." The temple priestesses and Mirjas step out of the temple. The youngest amongst them are still students, not older than seventeen. The more experienced ones dance first. They dance with such grace and beauty that no phallus present remains unmoved. The men accompany them with their flutes. Snakes they have brought in big stone vessels come out of the pots, rising with their small heads, hissing and tasting the air, and move gracefully to the music. Some of them are more than two metres long. They come further and further out of their pots. The women dance with them and let them encircle their bodies as if they and the snakes were one. The dance takes almost an hour. Everyone has brought rattles, drums or other instruments. After some time it feels as if the earth is shaking under us, moving with us in our rhythm. Some dancers are visited by Nammu herself during the dance. They are moved and they stand in the light of enlightenment. In their dance they receive a dream of Creation which they want to bring to reality. When this happens, the other dancers notice immediately. They turn their dancing power and attention fully to the one who is being visited by Nammu, circling around her and supporting her with their movements and insights.

The men also start to dance now. They dance around the women, courting them. It is playful. It becomes visible which women and men are attracted to each other and meant for each other in this dance. Sometimes one can clearly see how the shining fire of Eros enters their bodies. After they have danced for another hour, courting each other, it is time for the first ones to leave the line of dancers and go into the temple. They are received by one of the elders, who has once given the service of the Mirjas herself, and led to one of the love-rooms.

Usually the Mirjas and love priestesses give their service of love in the love temple until the age of fifty. Many of the older women show their knowledge of love today in the dance. Often this is filled with serene joy, but also with a deep and colourful abundance which comes from their experience of life. They observe us with laughter, giving advice and hints, often stepping into the middle of our group. They radiate the joy of life and the serenity of their age. They usually sit a little aside so that we can always go to them with our questions. We love and honour our elders. They are the guardians of our maturing knowledge, and of our past, for which we have great respect.

The first hours of the morning have passed. The most important part of our ritual has been performed. Now the festivities can start. So that everything runs smoothly, we now give our attention to those clans who did not originally belong to our tribe, and who pray to a different goddess.

In front of the temple a Mirja opens a prayer for the clan which wants to bring a sacrifice to the goddess of the hunt. A priestess steps to her side.

When the people eat the meat of the sacrificed animals today, they shall do so in the name of healing and sanctification. In this context, the priestesses speak the prayer as representatives of us all. They thank the souls of the animals, wish them a good journey and invite them to come back in their next lives. Many of us believe that the animals' souls leave voluntarily because they want to incarnate next time as human beings, and wish for geistig accompaniment from us for this transition. Their soul wishes for a change of bodies. The animal keepers then start the preparation for the coming banquet.

Every part of the animals is used. There is nothing that is not honoured. Respect is shown to the animals by using them for the fertile life of the humans. At noon, when the sun reaches its zenith, the banquet has been prepared, and further prayers are spoken.

NUDIME AND HER LOVE CELEBRATION

I am in the second group of student Mirjas to dance, and I watch the first dance of the rising sun with amazement. It is the first time I have been allowed to take part in this snake-dance. My whole body is quivering with anticipation. Then it happens. Mudima calls my name. Now it is my turn to perform the sun-dance which I have been practising in the temple for weeks. My hands are resting on my heart chakra and I feel my heart racing. Slowly my arms are led upwards towards the sun. My whole body draws the rays of shining light into me. A dance of the soul starts, fully led by my intuition. My dance is prayer. My prayer is dance. Nammu has come into me from the very beginning and is guiding all of my movements. I follow them as if in a trance. After I have danced for about twenty minutes I clearly hear her voice inside me.

"Circle around the Shamanu. Circle around those who are dedicated to the Goddess. Approach Manava, Manu and Tewlett. Surrender to the movements of your inner snake and let yourself be guided by her. Today you will come in touch with the aspect of the sexual heart for the first time. This is the area of life which needs special attention, healing and care."

I follow my inner voice. Shy and yet decisive, I approach the three snake priests in my dance. My body is still young and inexperienced in love. It is only half a year since I was first introduced to love, when for the first time I surrendered sensually to more experienced men and was initiated into the happiness of sexual life. For some time now a new feeling has been taking hold of me. It is the personal aspect of the Goddess of Love. For weeks I have been constantly thinking of Kareen. He is the slim, dark skinned man from the neighbouring clan, who I find particularly beautiful and intelligent, different from most of the men, and to whose sensual voice I love to listen. Some days ago he appeared to me in a sexual dream. My heart was touched by love, and I know that I now have to bring this aspect of love to Nammu and that I have to learn from her. Two nights ago I asked for permission to meet Kareen in the temple today for the first time, on the festival of fertility. Like me, Kareen has been accepted into the service of the temple of Hagar Qim. We see each other every morning when we are at school, and walk together to the studies of the stars.

But now I am led to the Shamanu. This is a change I had not expected. But I know that Nammu often takes over guidance in mysterious ways to reveal Her teachings of Creation to us. I dance for Her and give my whole concentration into my body. I feel the snake in my body moving up and down like a spiral. The fire of sensuality has never before filled my body as it does in this moment. I feel that the magic lies in my inner shining sexual sun in the centre of my womb, and takes control from there over all of my movements. I enchant the men with my dance.

It is Manava who most strongly attracts me. He dances powerfully around me, and when another man wants to approach me he playfully defends his territory. He charmingly woos me in this way. Flirtation and other playful elements are part of Nammu's beauty and we love to live and celebrate them. After some time Manava asks me to go into the temple with him. I follow him, shy and excited. I know that he will ask me to dance the sacred dance of fertility with him, and I know that his body longs for mine.

"Follow him!" is Nammu's clear instruction. I follow him happily, as his beautiful body and his radiance have enchanted me.

"Are you ready to serve the Goddess with me on this day of fertility?" he asks me. "Nammu told me to introduce you into the sexual aspect of the heart chakra."

I am so excited that I can hardly speak. I show him with a nod that I am ready. We are in the part of the temple that is dedicated to love, which is now brightly illuminated by the sun. Through an opening we can look over the hills of the island out to the sea. Manava embraces me firmly from behind with both *his arms, and calls Nammu to us. It does not take long until we sink to the ground. I am on my knees, leaning on a stone of the temple, directly facing the sun. Manava is behind me. This is a position that all of us on the island particularly love when the contact is particularly dedicated to connection with Nammu. I open myself for him to enter me. Manava holds my waist from behind with his strong hands. Our sexual act is a single prayer. It is the most abundant, richest and fullest prayer that we are able to pray. An essential aspect of Nammu's creation fulfils itself through our bodies. I feel how his phallus, which is firm while still soft and sensitive, touches my inner shining ball more deeply than it has ever been touched before. It feels as if my sexual snake moves in a spiral up to my heart chakra and opens it in a completely new way. After this first powerful greeting, we interrupt the sexual act and I turn towards him. I kneel in front of him and am fascinated by what I see. I see his erect penis, and look at it more attentively than I have ever looked before. He nods towards me and encourages me, "Yes. Take your time to follow whatever you long for. The Goddess wishes from you that you now get to know and experience the deeper aspects of Eros."*

I bend down and take his erect penis between my soft breasts. I can see how it moves and pulses. My long hair covers my face. I breathe his scent. Carefully I surround his phallus with my lips. He strokes my hair, and after a while he softly withdraws. "Take care of its arising power in the centre of your heart," he whispers to me. "Guide it to where it can always be protected in service to the woman and the Goddess. Follow the fire of your love fully. Do not do anything you do not love, and never do something before your inner voice tells you to do so. Your heart beats for Kareen, and probably you will go to him today. Longing for you burns in his heart. Still it as soon as you feel that the time has come, and offer him your open heart chakra so that his phallus erects with you and finds protection in your heart. It is your protection that keeps him from falling into the trap of power and vanity."

Then he takes me once more from behind, this time fully. He fills my body with powerful thrusts. I feel how the shining sun-power of sexuality which falls on my face from the outside anchors itself inside my heart. The sexual power of my heart is fully awakened in this moment. Never before has my body been in such jubilation. Manava keeps his seed; he wants to be ready for many other women today. He withdraws his still erect penis, slaps me lightly on my well-formed ass and says laughingly, "Now you have become more knowledgeable. Your sexual fire is burning strongly. That can make a man's loins explode. Take care that men are not burned by it. Let them move on when you feel that it has been enough for them. I have to keep my power now for others who are becoming Mirjas who will still come to me."

I blush, and my eyes shine. As I stand up, my long hair falls over my breasts, covering my womanly body. I thank Manava from the fullness of my heart. He is indeed a servant of the Goddess. He embodies much of what I have always imagined a lover would be.

I now know what I can give to Kareen. My open sensual loving heart is my gift to him. I know now how I can lead him there without being driven by impatience. I go to the basin of water, and then return to the others. They are still drumming outside. The fire for the meat has been lit. A huge crowd of people is sitting in front of the open gates of the temple. I see bright shining faces everywhere. I observe how the men cut the meat and give it to those who are hungry. With it they drink the fermented juice. I do not join this meal. Most of the women do not. I know the smell of roasted meat mixed with herbs. When I smelled it consciously for the first time I was surprised that it smelled good. Only the awareness of where the smell came from created a deep inner "No!". I still do not like this custom. Too often I have observed how a certain greed becomes visible in the faces of the men when it comes to killing the animals. I do not want to be part of that, as I cannot understand this kind of death. I identify with the animal. Why should it, unlike

211

us, die an unnatural death, even if it is said that is does so voluntarily? The men should rather give themselves into education in love and keep their power for that, instead of the substitute of lustfully dismembering flesh. There is another way to experience the inner nature of a living being. I put my arms around the neck of a living buffalo which is consecrated to the temple and is sacred to us. I whisper loving words to the soul of the animal. I do this for all the animals who have been sacrificed. How long will it take until the priestesses go back to forbidding this custom of sacrificing animals?

I see Manava coming out of the temple, beautiful and fulfilled. I walk to him and thank him once more. He also does not eat the meat of the animals, which increases my love and respect for him.

Then I walk away, sit down at the cliffs and reflect on what I have just experienced. Soon I will go to Kareen and bring him my new gift. I will show him my newly gained knowledge of sensual love. I know that he lives in my heart. It is the wish of the Goddess that he will be my friend for many years. I will accompany him on his path of becoming a lover and Shamanu, as this is what his beauty is meant for. This I also know deep in my heart. All this revealed itself to me fully when Manava's sexual power fully touched me in my heart centre. Through the guidance of other Mirjas, but particularly through my guidance and my sensual company in partnership, Kareen will learn to give his sexual healing power to the women. He will thank me with a huge power of love. My beauty and bodily abundance is here so that he can often re-energise with me, and make new discoveries. These will grow in the intimate space of trust and he will then also pass them on as gifts to others. A vast happiness of growing love lives within me. I am not in a hurry any more, and this is right. Kareen and I will meet in the right moment. I know that now. I thank Nammu for the great gift She has already revealed to me today while the day is still so young.

THE END OF THE ANCIENT CULTURE ON MALTA

Centuries passed while we lived this peaceful and sensual existence. Our arts and abilities became deeper and more refined. Our men became more mature and more powerful. Ever increasing numbers of travellers arrived from the mainland and attended our peace school. We knew that the wars and conquests on the mainland continued to increase. Ever more messages of destruction and violence reached us. People told us of the inversion of all values and about the religions of other peoples, in which the Goddess was no longer the mother of all life. Woman had become the personification of evil. The snake, which for us was a symbol of the Goddess, had been condemned together with her. It was said that the woman had allied with the snake to seduce the man into sensuality, and that this had led to his ruin. Sexuality, the original source of all earthly life, was made evil. Many women – saints and priestesses – were persecuted and killed. We knew that some of our sacred places on the mainland had already been discovered and destroyed. The first priests of foreign religions had found their way to us. We tolerated them, but we knew that they brought great danger.

One night, the priestess Raschnin had a dream in the Hypogeum in Hal Saflieni temple. She awoke with a new message and gathered all the people to tell them. Foreign priests of revenge and anger had appeared to her in her dream. They planned to attack the island. They wanted to destroy the culture which we had built and guarded for millennia. Our dream was not yet mature enough to manifest. It had not yet reached the peak of its glory. We could not allow our temples to be destroyed, as this would mean the downfall and destruction of the dream of our culture. The dream had to be preserved for the coming centuries.

The priests in Raschnin's dream had weapons made of metal. They would take all women who had not yet been with a man and force them to have sex with them. Our Mirjas, temple servants, oracle priestesses and all other women who had been touched by a man already would have to die a violent death. All men would be first circumcised and their foreskins would be brought to the vengeful perverted temple priests, as proof that their power had really been taken away. Then they would be killed. Not a single man of the soft power, who believed in the Goddess, would be allowed to remain alive. The priests were driven by the god of war, the god of power and domination. Never before had Raschnin experienced a dream so directly and physically. She knew that something must be taking place inside our tribe to make such danger possible. Probably the priests who had already visited us had been successful with their spiritual poison and had already touched some of our souls with the idea of wealth, power and cultural convenience. Now something special had to happen for the continued protection of our cosmic dream of life. That this dream could have reached inside the earth to Hal Saflieni, was a sign of huge vulnerability. The Hypogeum rested inside the earth and had the form of a cosmic egg, a form which had so far given the dreams a particularly high power of protection.

Raschnin knew that our people were in real danger. All of the oracle priestesses of the island gathered for one whole cycle of the moon. Everyone in the tribe knew that something special would happen. Finally our elders decided that we would all leave the island, just as our ancestors had left the stone circle in Portugal centuries ago. Some of the elders would voluntarily leave this Earth. Those who felt called were allowed to go with them. They had to do this to increase the protection from the cosmic realm. They would leave this planet uninjured, free of fear and untouched by the destructive rage of other people. They would let our cosmic dream mature in space and on the stars until the time would come to manifest it fully here on planet Earth. The others would leave the island on ships. They would be guided to another island where a few peaceful people lived, with whom we were in contact. There we would continue the development of our culture and connect with their culture.

214

Ships were built. Not even a month passed before everything was prepared. Earnest and obedient, we followed the orders. It was a painful step for all of us, but we knew that we had to do it. So we left the island, and not one single soul of our tribe was injured.

When the foreign priests and their weapons reached our island with their ships they did not find a single soul. Our temples were energetically protected so that they did not destroy them. The priests did not see a reason to destroy them as they did not know their healing function.

So our culture could unfold its further blossoms, at first on Crete, and then in early ancient Egypt and also other countries. This is how the ideas of our culture could continue despite all attempts at their destruction. You will still find people today who lead a conscious life which has its roots in our prehistoric culture. Most of them lead a very simple life connected with the spirit of community. They know the art of speaking with stones and live in such a way that they can hear our ancestors and have contact with them. Some still take care of the culture of the temple priestesses who sleep on Nammu's stone. They lead a life based on the culture of the Goddess which sanctifies and honours the sexual love between men and women. As they have been persecuted in all cultures, they live in hidden places, unrecognised somewhere in the mountains or overlooked regions. The regions where they live are threatened. The Earth is so destroyed that their living conditions in connection with nature are increasingly taken away from them. Peace-loving peoples have been persecuted and their culture destroyed by all means possible even to your present times. Some are violently eradicated, others forced by more subtle means to take on another way of life that is not theirs. They are christianised and converted to patriarchy. They are forced to marry and told that their original forms of life are inhumane. Their forests are destroyed and used for the production of meaningless consumer goods. They are forced to live in houses even though their natural living space would be in nature. The arrogance of your western cultures has become limitless. The original peoples of the Earth and the few wise people of the remaining old cultures are not able to save the planet alone.

But guardians of peace can also be found in the western cultures. Often they have forgotten their origin in the peace cultures. They do not have conscious contact to their ancestors and they do not remember the art of talking with plants and animals, and still they are guided by the Goddess. Their hearts have not lost the connection to Her and to truth. They fight with unflinching power for truth and peace on Earth.

The cooperation of all guardians of peace is now urgently needed. It has become essential to make an immense shift in thinking in all cultures to change the field.

The guardians of peace are challenged to develop new forms of living together which make it possible to return freedom to the Earth and enable the Goddess to breathe again. They have to find their way back to a form of culture which understands, honours and respects the zeitgeist of the Goddess, or they will destroy themselves and the Earth.

If many people remember the dream of Nammu at the right time; if many people remember their own original beauty and knowledge and their peaceful and sensual power, then it will be possible for this dream to be dreamt to its end, and the dream of paradise can find fulfilment. For this it is necessary that these people find the courage to raise their voices again. They must no longer allow themselves to be ruled by the power of destruction and bear this in silence. They must form a powerful network of the heart which has the power to make others remember their loving origin. When the heart chakra is touched by the vast power of the Goddess, worlds can change. Now the time has come for this change. When the first people raise their voices so that they can be heard, they will be able to remember their cosmic dream of eternal love in its full extent. They will know once more why they came onto this planet, and they will do everything they can for the healing of this planet. This can only happen when they have left behind vanity, concepts of power

216

and possession, and revenge and hatred, as they are then ready to notice and take on a more comprehensive power within themselves.

But we do not have much time to lose. This is an emergency call of the Earth, coming with thunderstorms and catastrophes, which drives people to madness and species to extinction. Those who now as dictators lead whole nations into war, are also tortured and separated parts of lost souls who have lost their source and their connection to the Goddess. It is the cry of those who are drowning who now rear up in a last struggle and once more use all means at their disposal for attack. They do not know what they are doing. It is the desperate cry of all beings, the call of the Goddess: Remember a power which is greater than all violence. Remember a way of life which comes from abundance and love. Start perceiving this planet Earth. Take on responsibility for this Earth and your co-creatures by learning again to lead a fulfilled life. Make your life a prayer. Be midwives in the development of a new cultural idea which is now germinating deep inside the Earth and in you. Understand yourself as a source and power of a new culture. All the power is needed. It is the last possibility for salvation which the Earth can offer you. Awakening or downfall. This is the decision which all life on planet Earth stands in front of today. Humankind, which holds the means of destruction of life in its hands, also holds the means of its healing in its hands.

FAREWELL AND THE JOURNEY HOME

My journey home developed once more into an important lesson in the cosmic classroom, an essential element of my spiritual experience. It showed me again that an end is never only the end, but also always a new beginning. It was as if the Goddess wanted to show Her presence to me once more with all Her means.

A friend had called me and asked me to change my flight back to return via Berlin. There were important issues to discuss. She told me on the telephone that she had already reserved a flight from Berlin to Portugal.

My heart would have preferred to return to Portugal as soon as possible, but I understood that this meeting was necessary. After several unproductive attempts, supported by Marisi who also needed a flight back, I gave up.

I went into prayer and told my cosmic companions how important this detour via Berlin was for me. I had planned to stay there for one night and to continue my journey the next morning.

You need a very precise and aware contact to reality to be able to create a different reality with the power of your universal will. This journey will be a high training for you. Go into it with the power of your trust. You face high tasks in the coming time. Just go to the airport and try there! was the very clear instruction I received. I followed it. The lady at the counter told me once more that it was impossible to change flights. But after I had checked in, she gave me the hint to go to a certain counter to just get a boarding pass for Berlin. The travellers to Berlin and to Cologne would be on the same aircraft until London anyway. So she suggested that I could make an unofficial switch en route. My luggage was already checked in to Cologne. I wanted to give up because of the many different pieces of information. But my cosmic telephone rang.

Go! Hurry up! Right now there is a person at the counter who will make it possible.

So I ran. They really did give me a boarding card to Berlin even though I still had a flight ticket to Cologne. My luggage was still on its way to Cologne, containing important material that I would need for the meeting in Berlin. The following thought came into my mind:

Everything that happens to me on the outside is in resonance with inner processes. These form my destiny. As within, so without.

I telephoned 'upwards': "Could you somehow make it possible that my luggage also goes to Berlin?"

At that very moment a member of the airport staff tapped me on the shoulder. He was a dark skinned young man. "I was watching you. If you want your luggage to go to Berlin too, I can help you."

I was completely stunned. Now my prayers were answered immediately by people I had never met!

"Come quickly," he said as he started to run. I followed him.

Luggage was being distributed by conveyor belt to individual flights. He asked me to show him my suitcase, which was just passing by. The young man lifted the heavy suitcase off the belt and took it to the belt for the flight to Berlin. Then he ran with me to a counter to give me a slip of paper so that I would be able to collect it at the airport.

"Hurry up, you have to board now!" he said. I thanked him and ran to the queue. Most of the people had already boarded. Finally I sank exhausted into my seat.

Marisi, who flew with me to London, said laughingly, "That was cosmic guidance. The spirits are on your side."

We saw the island of Malta one last time from above. I thanked my cosmic companions for the deep insights I had gained on Malta, and greeted the guardians of the temples and the peace culture on Malta one last time.

Berlin was a radical cultural change to city life from my contemplative life. Many people wanted to meet me and hear how my journey had been, and in parallel we had to solve some organisational questions. I tried as well as I could to stay connected. I realised with a shock that my flight to Portugal was not yet confirmed. They had tried to reach me on Malta to tell me, but I had just left the hotel. Despite all our attempts, there did not seem to be any flight to Portugal available at the moment.

I actually did not feel like new adventures. But I definitely wanted to be back quickly. Important tasks were awaiting me in Tamera.

Eventually I found a flight from Munich. I would have to travel there by train overnight, as my flight would leave early next morning.

"I hope that this will work out. Maybe the train is full in the end, and I don't get to Munich!" I thought, a little ironically.

A friend took me to the train station, where I immediately went to the ticket counter. And there what I had meant as a joke, happened. The lady at the counter looked at me and told me that the train was completely full. My world fell apart.

"Maybe someone will cancel, or just not arrive," I tried to convince the woman at the counter. I explained to her that I had to be at the airport at six o'clock the next morning.

But she only repeated that she could not help.

A debilitating anger arose in me. I could not, and did not want to, believe that there was no space for me on this train.

This debilitating anger against others, or resignation, only develops in a situation of inner desperation. You then perceive reality as an outer situation that is separated from yourself and overlook your creative freedom to manifest reality. When you are connected to this freedom, the Goddess acts through you in every moment.

I did not know immediately how to translate this hint into practice. I tried to let go innerly, and to let go of my fixation on absolutely needing to catch this train.

"Is there any other possibility to get to Munich in time?" I asked.

"Yes. Another train comes in one hour. But you would have to make four changes, and you would probably not have enough time in Munich to reach the airport," was the reply.

My world fell apart for a second time. To be with a heavy suitcase and computer, printer, books and heavy stone, in the middle of the night in February, in unknown train stations, freezing cold, and continually worried about missing the flight, was not an inviting picture.

"What is the right thing to do?" I asked upwards desperately.

As long as you think that outer circumstances are the reason for this situation that you are in, you make yourself a victim of the situation and do not go with the frequency in which the freedom to create a new reality lies. First, calm down. Go to that bar over there and drink a beer.

I followed. A little disheartened, we left the counter. In the bar we started to play with possible solutions, until a very strict cosmic voice told me, *You are full of reaction and are not leaving any space for possible solutions. Remember Malta and everything you learned there. First, let go fully. Talk about very different things, but not about the journey.*

Stunned by this strict instruction, I followed it immediately, and my heart became instantly lighter. I remembered that I was under guidance whenever I was in trust. So I changed topic. We talked about trivia. Then our talk gained depth, so that I really forgot my difficulties for some time. For some time I became almost serene, until I was abruptly interrupted again.

Go to the counter right now. Your friend must bring your luggage.

My friend may have been a little surprised when I interrupted our talk and told her the instructions, but she followed them. I paid, and went to the ticket counter while my friend went to collect the luggage. The lady at the counter was transformed. "Great that you came back! I just noticed that someone did not collect their ticket. It's a compartment with two beds. Get your suitcase. You need to be quick and I need to contact the conductor." She started to telephone. I wanted to take money from a cash machine and pay, but she waved that I should go directly to the platform. "Wait there until someone collects you. You can pay on the train. The train is arriving and I can't reach the conductor right now," she said in a way that was both friendly and assertive.

My friend arrived with the luggage and we carried it together to the platform. And there I stood, curious what would happen next.

"Please stand back from the edge of the platform. Please stand away from the closing doors. This train is about to depart," came over the loudspeakers.

"Just get on," said my friend. Was it right to just get onto the train? I listened to my inner voice.

No. Wait. Everything is happening exactly as it should.

I waited. Then I heard another announcement over the loudspeakers. "Will the conductor please contact the ticket counter. Conductor, please contact ticket counter 21." Time passed. It is amazing how much peace enters one's organism when one fully re-enters trust! Meanwhile the train was already twenty minutes late. What a strange feeling that a whole train was stopped because of me. Eventually a man approached me.

"Are you Ms Lichtenfels? Get on board quickly and come with me." I said goodbye to my friend.

"Now I have seen your spiritual approach to travel," she said. Then I walked with my heavy luggage behind the man through the long train. He gave me a ticket. I paid an astonishingly low price for the compartment: a two-bed room with a shower, almost like a hotel room.

I lay awake almost the whole night, but it was deeply restful. The rhythmic clicking of the wheels on the tracks, the announcements at stops and occasional whistles as we passed through tunnels provided the perfect soundscape for me to look back over my experiences on Malta once more. I spent the night in a *geistig* review of all my experiences there and in reflection on the future. Lilith came to me once more.

THE ESSENCE: THE DESTINY OF LOVE

I was asking myself how it is possible that information can flow between past and present. Half asleep, half awake, I saw the face of Lilith, this time as a decisive adult woman. The spiral turned before my eyes. I was almost asleep but my mind remained agile and awake. The following words came to me:

The many spiritual experiences on your journey have only been possible as ultimately, all reality is made of information. The whole biosphere is a system of information and communication. The continuous flow of information is as basic as breathing.

The human being and his forms of society have become sick in the last millennia as the human has catapulted himself out of the universal context of life. Because of the human being, the cosmic powers have become imbalanced. Powers which would otherwise have healing effects can now cause destruction. The human being has followed the information and spiritual law of fear for thousands of years because of a historical accident. The consequences are blocked anger, hatred, jealousy, inability to love, loss of contact, violence, oppression, domination and destruction. Spiritual practice demands a life which is utterly free of lies and contradiction and it demands trust as the basic power.

A system which arises from the basic power of trust must be created. As a result, human qualities will arise such as beauty – for example the movements of a body free of fear; truth; responsibility; contact and communication; participation in the world; nurturing; care and the ability to love freely and universally. Trust is a conscious decision. This is the power with which a grass seedling is able to break through a layer of asphalt. The power which is able to heal fear lies only in the reconnection with a calm certainty of home in the universe and life.

I entered a different reality. I felt as if I was travelling through time. I was on a bridge over time. I now faced the task of transmitting all of my experiences into the present. I would give myself the task of letting the prehistoric utopia and the spirit of the Goddess shine into our everyday life in Tamera.

My decision was made: "I will support the creation of the axioms of a new and non-violent culture. Fear must disappear from the Earth. Whether we were perpetrators or victims in the past: at the core there is always fear which arose from separation. We need the universal information which makes it possible for an organism to develop based on the laws of trust and knowledge."

I faced the challenge of bringing the many new experiences into my present life and of further developing our community with my friends and co-workers in such a way that it would become a contemporary non-violent culture. I have tried for many years to understand and bring into reality the rules of free love and social transparency. But what should I give my readers for their path?

The idea of actually living community is completely foreign to our culture. Although everyone knows that most marriages and relationships fail, we nevertheless keep trying, again and again. If one relationship doesn't work, maybe the next one will. The attempt to live in free sexuality outside community often causes more confusion than healing. It is difficult to live in free sexuality outside of a community and it is also difficult to live in lasting, truthful community without truth in sexuality. A group cannot achieve real transparency if the members have to conceal a large part of their inner processes.

There is a huge longing for the numinous in sexuality and it requires revelation and a fully lived life. The longing for personal love and partnership is still as vast and unsolved today as it was thousands of years ago.

We have repeatedly experienced this in practice in our community. Free love is for many only interesting until they meet their big love. When "the one" arrives, everything is forgotten. It is unbelievable to witness how people throw their already-won knowledge overboard when they meet their big love. When a couple is seized by the high voltage of passion and unfulfilled longing there is no holding back. They resist all reason. It is useless to tell them what misery they are running towards. Community counts for nothing. Transparency in the group is uninteresting. Advice to be patient has less power than the attraction between two lovers. I know from my own experience how feelings of inferiority and fear of loss can then irrationally grip me, cloud my perceptions and overshadow me with feelings of pain and grief. There need not even be any real reason. Once this fear is there it is so strong and powerful that it distorts all other perceptions. I also know how out of this fear one then seizes upon defensive manoeuvres and how malice seems to become the only means of protection.

What power can overcome these distorted mental processes? When will we finally be able to develop forms of living which match our longings? The power of anonymous Eros and the power of personal love are forces which need answers that serve healing. They must no longer threaten and fight each other. Neither moral appeals nor old rituals are enough to solve the issues of the longing for love and the longing for anonymous sexuality in our present culture. How will sexuality once more be acknowledged as the sacred force which it actually is in its being and origin? And how will this book become for its readers more than just a pretty fairytale from the distant past?

I asked for guidance for a contemporary spiritual life practice for myself, our community and the readers of my book.

I called Lilith, who has been a witness of the misery in love for many hundreds of years, who fell into the traps of hatred and revenge herself and who has now returned on a higher level to remind women of their original freedom. I called Nammu, the caretaker of all life. I called the universal powers of love to find words of awakening and healing.

How can we become able to communicate with the Goddess today? How will women regain their freedom without fighting men? And which male divine power will stand at their side today? What lover will be able to give women strength and trust without further damage and destruction? How will men recognise their mistake and find a new spiritual life practice and new trust in their original true masculinity? A masculinity which can be obtained without fraudulent misuse of a wrong power. How will men rediscover and accept the aspect of the Goddess in themselves and in others? How will women break through their own silence? How will they start their true emancipation, no longer submit to the rules of a male culture and no longer copy the man but also no longer fight against him? How will they return to their female power and grace, to their wildness and beauty? But above all, how will women find a new and deeper solidarity that does not break down even when two women love and desire the same man?

A higher power told me to pause my storm of questions and to concentrate. I closed my eyes and saw a woman of about forty, sun-darkened, with wild hair who looked at me with her shining eyes. I recognised her as an aspect of Lilith.

You are asking too much at once, she says. *Please concentrate now on the one question which is most important for you.* I thought for a moment and asked to know more about the law of spiritual attraction in our present time which would help us to find new forms of living together and love.

THE LAW OF ATTRACTION: ABOUT THE CONNECTION BETWEEN ALL THINGS

Together we face the task of connecting to the healing powers regardless of our present point in space and time. Each person can contribute an aspect of the solution. The more we gain an overview of the whole, the more we understand our aspect and our possible contribution to healing. First I want to look at the universal law of spiritual attraction with you.

"With the conscious decision to live in a sacred way we attract the understanding, the teachings and the information we need to unfold our talents for the well-being of all." This simple basic power sentence from the spiritual leader of the Cherokee, Dhyani Ywahoo, can open a new understanding of your reality in every moment. This sentence can help every person in every moment if they have decided to build their life on a new foundation.

There is a connection here between inner attitude and outer events. The law of spiritual attraction must be seen and understood from a universal perspective. It is always the whole which causes effects through each individual and through the realities which gather around him or her. Inner and outer are far less separated than one normally thinks from a conventional point of view. Everything that happens to us on the outside is in resonance with inner processes. These inner processes form our destiny. As within, so without.

You ask how to communicate with the Goddess today. Information flows permanently, as simply as breathing. However the human being has brought the cosmic forces out of balance.

Healing occurs through conscious reintegration into the universal organism. Questions of love and sexuality cannot be solved without this reintegration. No-one is able to solve these personal questions in separation from the universal whole. One does not have to believe in a Goddess to see and understand these connections. One only needs to think things through to completion.

Powers which come from the universe also need to be embedded in the universe. The world can only be understood as a hologram. Part of the healing of the whole is of course the reintegration of community into the universe. The community is also part of a communicating organism, part of the universal source from which it has developed. If community no longer functions or completely disappears, an essential part of the chain of the whole is missing. A functioning community is the equivalent of a bodily organ. Your body also cannot function very well when an organ is missing. The complementary powers of the organs are essential to the functioning of the whole. The whole cannot long remain healthy if its parts do not operate and the parts cannot long remain healthy if the whole is injured. The whole is always working through all of its parts and vice-versa. This is a completely new world-view which leads to a completely different form of political activism.

Hearing these words I remembered a quote I had read in a book about the Maya on the previous evening. It always moves me when I see how some indigenous peoples still try to remember the common origin of all things despite the extreme suffering and oppression that they have experienced.

Even today, some of them who continue the traditions of the old tribes refer to an awakening which must and will spread over the whole globe. Master Cirilo, a Mayan prophet, gathered all tribal representatives together in 1979 and said, "Dear brothers and sisters, the time of awakening is upon us. We have come here together to connect to the Great Divine Spirit and Mother Earth. Let us take on our task together. Let us call out to the world that we are all like fingers on a hand. We have come from the same origin and have taken different paths but we are still led by the same powers. We natives have maintained the knowledge about the sacred traditions. Now is the time to set this common knowledge free for a common better future for the whole of humankind. Let us live together as brothers and sisters on this planet Earth. All must awaken.

No nation, no culture, no group may remain behind as it will be a common awakening which will bring happiness and peace to us all."

Again I heard Lilith's cosmic voice.

This awakening is not only a task of the indigenous tribes. People from western cultures can and must make their contribution to this awakening and healing. You also come from the whole. Due to your long experience of separation you have many important insights to contribute for the healing of the whole. These insights have only become possible because of this long separation.

The will is the decisive factor in the process of change. Study the fate of one human being and place it within the inner context of what they wanted. What information did they give into the world?

It is helpful to imagine that we are in a cosmic classroom and that it is we who create our realities as life-lessons. In difficult situations it is helpful to know that I am here because at least one part of me wanted it to be so. Each event that is happening to me has been created in cooperation with my higher self so that we can learn something together. Every reality serves a higher insight. The more comprehensive my understanding of reality becomes, the more different powers can be unified through my life. The more different powers can be unified within one life system, the more stable it becomes.

THE CONNECTION BETWEEN THE STATES OF VICTIM AND PERPETRATOR

These connections are not new to me. And still, questions repeatedly rear up. What about all the victims? What about the children who died in the cellars of Grozny? What about all the people who die an involuntary death? Did they themselves create this life? And what about the perpetrators?

When I think about the dying children who are tortured and killed and know that it could be my own children, how can I then hold still? I addressed Lilith directly:

"You know it yourself. You know how it feels when your original sources of love and life have been torn away from you. You experienced how revenge is more powerful in such moments than any holding still or forgiving. What has to be done here? Which life-power is actually stronger than any violence and is not just comfort for the weak?" I listened to Lilith's answer.

The drama of victim and perpetrator can only be understood in its historical context. It is only possible because humankind long ago fell out of its healing integration in the whole. You can no longer use the yardstick of guilt or innocence here. In a certain way, of course we have all created our situations ourselves. But most people no longer know that. From where should they know that? We have all been driven into dependency by the cruellest of means and have lost contact with the core of our own beings and our connection to the Goddess. Nobody can escape this drama any longer using only their own power. But each person who takes the path of awakening can really help. As long as help is limited to external actions it will have little effect in the long term. The cycle of victims and perpetrators that has persisted for thousands of years must be broken. The perpetrator is also the victim of a driving structure, although he long ago stopped realising it. Perpetrator and victim alike need help from the outside. They need to awaken and they need reconnection to the whole. Healing can only come about on this level. Neither judgement nor punishment can help here. Only insight helps. A change of culture is needed to create a field which is able to lift the whole of existence to a new level.

Yes, I have experienced how much satisfaction revenge can bring. For some lives the power of revenge can replace the power of life and love for you. This is how those who were victims themselves became perpetrators. At some point this insane cycle began. It was like an obsession of mind and spirit. But at some point even this power ends. Just before that, it gives one final push. People whose heart chakra is already closed keep themselves alive with revenge. Revenge is able to keep the whole organism running for some more time. But then the source dries up. Revenge cannot stand in the face of eternity. It eventually leads to a vast dependency, to a chain of despair and fear, power and powerlessness, satisfaction and depression.

A peaceworker reaches the insight that enmity attracts enmity. If you kill your enemies because they have committed injustices against you, they will usually return and take revenge on you. This way the mechanism of fear and violence will never really stop. At some point, every avenger will stand in front of the gate of insight. By destroying others they have destroyed life and the Goddess within themselves. They suddenly understand that those whom they have hated and killed were originally their friends. They then go once more through the chain of grief, despair and anger, which is even more painful this time as they can no longer direct their anger towards others. They regain a concept of the truth of the whole of creation and ask themselves why the Goddess would let this mistake happen. They do not yet know that the Goddess does not have any power over those who have turned away from Her. They do not know that a diabolical divine force arose from the very idea of turning away. The human being himself has created the divine forces of destruction by separating from the original divine truth. The power of a possible new decision lies inside the human being. Sometime every human being will face a deeper decision. At some point the insight will come that there is a more comprehensive freedom, a force of life which comes out of connection and love. Real freedom only exists in connection with the loving divine powers of the universe.

A spiritual person will do anything to regain this possible freedom. First he will stop murdering and killing. But he will discover that thoughts of hatred and anger still rage inside him. As long as these powers do not find expression, they cause destruction on the inside and will eventually also be directed outside. It is not enough to renounce evil actions. You will discover how many unused powers are raging inside you which are bound up with anger that the world is as it is. You will decisively take back to yourself as a source of power, the power previously bound in the destructive forces you directed towards yourself or others. You will take on responsibility for your thoughts. You will invest in your own development by transforming anger and hatred into sacred rage.

In the end, it is always a question of integrating life-forces. Energy is never lost. Energies which have a destructive effect on a lower frequency-level can be healing factors on other frequency-levels. Always go to the place which has information of the whole. If a thought or a power is destructive then look for the direction in which it can transform. When I have found higher information into which I can send or transform the "negative information" it is more effective and especially more healing. If this process has been done fully, you experience it as a boost of health, power, healing and abundance of life.

Sacred rage is the higher power which is able to transform anger and hatred. It will no longer destroy. It will liberate the powers of healing and truth within you. It has the power to leave fear behind. It will no longer allow life to be destroyed in your surroundings, or allow that which was originally sacred to be destroyed.

IT IS FEAR WHICH PARALYSES

It is fear which paralyses. Fear continually creates dependencies. This is why one basic principle of the Goddess and of Life is: Leave fear and choose trust. You are protected whenever the powers of trust can act freely and consciously within you. It is not about trusting blindly. It is about awareness and a perceptive presence out of which true trust can arise. It is a conscious decision to walk the path of trust.

Most of the time human beings completely unconsciously follow fear. It is lodged within their organism and guides their thoughts and actions. An important healing process is that humans recognise their fear again and become aware of it. Fear creates constriction. Constriction creates violence. Understanding this connection is already the first step towards healing.

As long as humans permanently live in the state of fear, they exclude a large part of themselves. It is fear which makes humans governable. They remain dependent and can be hypnotised. If you follow fear, you do not follow the universal powers of healing. You will understand that the Goddess could be expelled from the societies, communities and cells of each organism because the people were made fearful. Fear is the cellular disease of existing societies and each individual organism. Whoever overcomes fear will also overcome the great amnesia and will find access to the healing information of the universe.

Do not follow fear, but instead call upon your powers of insight to show you what you fear so much. Try carefully to replace fear with trust and you will be led to your path of healing.

Those who consciously walk a new path will especially often experience situations of fear and meet the things of which they are afraid. If they follow old reactions, they will become desperate. If they choose a new direction they will learn to pause. They will see that there is actually a cosmic message encoded in the situations of fear. In these situations there are often cosmic friends talking to the person involved, wanting to point out that it is time for something new, and that the structures the person wants to cling to are old. Where a butterfly has been wanting to unfold inside them, they have been thinking like a caterpillar which has lost its cocoon, instead of developing with the powers of the universe. Sometimes there is also a question from the universe behind your fear: Is this what you are afraid of? Is this the situation which seems so difficult to you? Please, let us see it with your eyes! Stay with us, even in this difficult situation! And tell us precisely what you need and what is a true support for you in this situation! Often the support cannot come as the flow of information is interrupted.

Situations of fear do not always come from powers which support you. A spiritually connected person also attracts negative information. We are not only cosmic beings, but unfortunately also a part of the disease and destruction which is caused by the capitalistic system. It makes no sense to close your eyes in front of this reality. Do not close your eyes to the situation of the world. Take in the information you need but do not identify with it. You have to know the situation of the world in order to be able to heal it. Connect with the protection of a higher power. But also sense where it seems at first to be unpleasant. Sometimes the cosmos wants to warn you. If you get frightened at these points, the information cannot fully reach you. Fear makes it easier for the negative powers to possess you. You give away your power as soon as you follow fear. If you feel clearly disturbed by cosmic energies, then send them away. Even an order can be a prayer. If you do not align with the fear, your prayer is powerful and is able to dispel negative energies.

The situation of fear is never a private matter as you were told to believe. You were made silent particularly in situations of fear, where communication was needed the most.

This is how lies and distrust came into all parts of your life. People were depoliticised in the core of their longings and in the true issues of their lives. Private therapy alone cannot bring healing because even if you have found the cause of the disease within yourself, in the end only different living conditions can bring about the wished-for change and healing. There is no private disease.

The dysfunction of an individual is always also a sign of dysfunction of the whole organism. True healing can only be achieved if the whole is addressed. Children are already made desperate in their early childhood and then silenced with substitute satisfaction. Children are forced in their first years of life to forget their cosmic origin and to make a vow directed

235

against life and universal love. An abscess of fear and violence has been implanted in their innermost soul.

Fear has become a global disease and needs comprehensive healing. Each individual has the potential power to contribute to this healing. Each human now faces the challenge of rediscovering his cosmic will. Those who connect to this will have the whole universe as placenta for their work. The higher and more comprehensive a will is, the more universal powers it can attract.

These words came to me in one flow. I felt so connected that I could barely distinguish whether their origin was me, Lilith, the Goddess or my higher self. But I found this question was no longer so important. What was important was that I perceived these words to be true and that I was ready to make my own life a measure of this truth.

LILITH AND THE CONFUSED SPOUSES: THE UNANSWERED LONGING IN LOVE

I called Lilith one last time. I asked for answers about love and sexuality. What has to be done today so that the power inherent in Eros can be lived? How can the great longing for partnership and personal love be embedded in community? How will women succeed in overcoming their jealousy when they love and desire the same man? And what about the intense longing that is triggered by anonymous Eros? How can the blue ball of intimate female knowledge be kept even under these circumstances? Why is the fear in this area so strong and how can it be overcome?

I went deeply into contemplation and silence. By now it had become early morning, and the shadow of the night still rested over the world. I heard only the sounds of the wheels of the night train. I thought of the legend of Lilith: how she visits men in their dreams at night to celebrate anonymous encounters with them.

How much care jealous wives take that their husbands are not visited by Lilith. They know that she would awaken the longing of the man in a way that would extend his longing to other women. Lilith's coming brings a restless longing to the man, and that longing would make him go to other women.

The wives also know that their own longing cannot be fulfilled now that they live in a golden cage with their longed-for "one-and-only". Even though they have promised eternal love and faithfulness, drunk on the first happiness of love, and even though they believed that they had reached the goal of their greatest wishes and desires, now everything has become very different. The unstilled longing and the worries cause restless nights. Every seductive smile of a beautiful woman, every beautiful buttock or breast becomes a threat. The thorn of envy and resentment suddenly poisons her originally pure and loving heart. This also makes her best friends leave, and she finds herself isolated in loneliness with the formerly so-desired husband who now often seems unknown to her. She feels that her body will remain hungry. The nights of love no longer bring the longed-for fulfilment. The previously ecstatic contacts of deep and sensual encounter become flat and normal. You start to see frustration and disappointment in her face. And so, during the years her original wildness and beauty gradually take on monstrous form, the form of a dragon. And just as she jealously controls her husband, he controls her. He might look for traces of Lilith in the distance, in the bars on business journeys or in dimly-lit brothels, spending a lot of money. But he does it secretly. This hidden life shall not come to light. In his daily life he plays the good husband who protects his woman. She has become his security, the mama he has bought. The adventure he allows himself is certainly not allowed for her. He is happy about her jealousy as it gives him the certainty that he can keep and control her. Every now and then they fulfil their marital duty. And except for this, it is about cars, television, money, travel, children and good food. They pave over their life in order to avoid remembering the pain of their unredeemed love and the great promise they once gave to each other.

And while all this is happening, Lilith continues to visit millions of bedrooms. Millions upon millions of couples experience the same destiny in love. They think that their unhappiness is their personal, private misery and do not even suspect that exactly the same drama is occurring in the neighbouring apartments. Everyone lays a veil of silence over their dark destiny. And while they are sitting in front of the television or managing their daily life, covering their frustration with consumption, they secretly dream of a different, greater and more fulfilling love. They no longer notice that outside, a world is falling apart and that their silence, their numbness and their increasing substitution of consumption and money for love is a significant contribution to the process. They have walled themselves off from the world and its issues. Their marriage has become a miserable attempt to solve problems together that they would never have had if they were alone.

Lilith does not only visit the husbands at night. She also comes to the women. She brings to them the wildest sexual dreams, which usually lie so far beyond what is considered respectable in this society that they hide them from themselves and their friends. Only occasionally is the veil torn apart and one can read in the morning papers: "Jealous wife jumps to her death" or "Husband shoots wife and children. Reason for death: her affair with a young neighbour."

While I had been thinking about this, daylight had come. I concentrated once more. This time not to see the misery of the drama of love, but rather to listen to possible perspectives and answers for our time. I called Lilith, who had already revealed herself to me in her encompassing depths during the first days on Malta. I did not have to wait long for the first sentences to come from inside me:

THE VOICE OF LONGING

During our first encounter on Malta I already gave you many answers to your questions. I want to try again. The longing for the numinous in love, the strong desire which can be triggered by the glance of a stranger or just the form of a body, and the great longing for personal love and partnership are in their core the same. Two beings want to love and recognise each other in their beauty and freedom. They want to give themselves away. They want to reach the deepest ground of communication in elementary bodily presence. It is the essence of the Goddess which hits us in the fleeting glance of an unknown man or woman. And it is the longing for the eternal presence of the Goddess and home in the Goddess which touches us in the longing for lasting intimacy and partnership. It is the memory of the source of creation from which we all originate. It is the recognition that fundamentally we are all connected in one existence. This is what we want to rediscover. Every cell of our body wants to be suffused and illuminated with this realisation. Nothing foreign shall separate us any longer. The light of mutual recognition shall shine into the unknown as strongly as we seek it in the presence and familiarity of everyday life. One cannot be understood and particularly not fulfilled without the other, and neither will find fulfilment or rest without the aspect of the sacred in sexuality.

The longing for transformation and to be lastingly present for the divine seeks fulfilment in the longing of the genders. In both cases it is the Goddess whom the man has briefly seen in the woman and whom he now seeks to meet. The woman seeks in the male lover the manifestation of the male divine power. The sensual Messiah stands behind all great longings of the woman. The longing of creation is reflected in the longings of the human being. Earth and heaven will not rest before this longing has found its true fulfilment. And from each fulfilment, a new longing arises. This is the game of creation which steers all becoming. Your heart still beats today with Manu and Meret. Every new love-couple is carried by the same longing.

And in every promising glance of a woman or man, the same numinous is calling. With all understanding and love for the couple, there is no other area where the historic healing impulse is so urgent. Their actions are the cause of great misery on Earth, even though they seem to be so private.

Nothing demands such balance in one's own centre and nothing demands such security in one's own self, as fulfilment of the longing in love. The rituals and rules of life of our ancestors served to find the balance in one's own centre and served to find the power of calmness and focus in one's own self. Even they could not deal with the issue, otherwise the worldwide misery which is reflected in the story of Manu and Meret would not have occurred. But today, after a long process of experience, the voice of the Goddess is returning to the Earth as the first people start to gain insight.

THE POWER OF CONNECTION

Ultimately, there is only one answer to all of your questions. The issue of love can only be solved in connection with the whole. In this connection lies the healing of jealousy, fear, violence, pain and fear of loss. Practise connection with creation and you will be guided safely to the goal of your longing. Follow the energy, but follow it with an awake and present attitude. The divine voice lives within you. Only those who know that will also be able to meet the Goddess in the outer world. No man and no woman will be able to still your longing unless you have rediscovered this connection inside yourself. Divine action is balanced action which comes from connection and one's own centre. If impatience or fear arises, it is also the voice of the Goddess. It is already a sign of blocked energy. Anger is usually an already disconnected reaction which originally comes from the sacred rage of the Goddess. In its being it is an energy of action which wants to correct wrong circumstances. In connection, anger transforms into sacred rage, which is a great and healing power which is urgently needed. In all cases, it is necessary to listen deeply to yourself. You will find the answer deep within yourself. Find the source of your fears and you will find the answer. Follow your impatience. Try to understand it in your spirit and mind, and you will find a new direction. Find the source of your anger and you will find powerful material for authentic action.

THE TURNING POINT FOR MANU AND MERET

You know and understand Manu and Meret, as many of you would have acted in a similar way. Anyone who has been struck by the power of Eros in his youth knows that this longing is stronger than any community ritual and more important than all the warning words of a priestess. But by now you also know the tragedy of Manu and Meret. They could not find fulfilment. Communities have the task of creating vessels of love and trust in which this power of personal love once more becomes possible, without excluding others. Personal love between two people needs the trustful field of a community.

The thought that you want to conquer, against the will of the whole, that which you love, also leads to the destruction of what you originally loved in your partner. No goddess can ever be conquered and no freedom of love can ever be locked in any cage. Full communion which is in resonance with creation lies very close to the wish to conquer. The wish of a woman to belong fully to a man is a slightly lower and less connected version of the wish to fully love and recognise a person. This wish comes from connection and original freedom. This is also true for same-sex love and all other variations of Eros. As these wishes are very similar in our cells and can be easily confused, the potential for disorientation is especially high when our cells are brought into turmoil by the power of Eros.

The mere thought of not being sufficient for the loved one and the mere thought of still being too weak to reach what you love against all comparison and the looks of the others, originally awoke the wish to completely possess the beloved. A feeling of inadequacy towards someone is always the result of a deep disturbance. It is a thought which immediately separates you and immediately prevents your ability to perceive. When this thought arises in you, it is already a sign that you have fallen out of connection. The comparison and distrust triggered by that thought is poison for every true freedom. Whoever replaces this thought with the clearly formulated wish to become the way he wants to be, immediately gains energy for his development. He will no longer protect himself or separate himself from others or more experienced ones, but he will want to learn from them. Mistrust and envy are replaced by great curiosity. Trust is the precondition for this path. It also provides the courage to stand for what you love and desire.

Only those who truly love will really recognise each other. The healing of the future will arise from the communities of those who truly love. Whatever path an individual might choose, healing will only arise out of connection with the whole.

Whoever reconnects with the certainty of success which comes from full trust and connection with Creation will rediscover the abundance of the world inside themselves and in their surroundings. You will encounter every lover and every unknown man and woman with the necessary awareness. You will allow every encounter enough space and freedom that the nondum of Creation – that which has not yet occurred, which has not been understood – can shine in. It is only fear which makes us build fences around the things we already know. It is also fear of the unknown which prevents two strangers from acting. Two strangers who meet each other and who are struck by the seductive call of Eros are prevented by fear from trustfully following the revelation which the Goddess demands from them in this moment. In both cases we protect the seemingly known part of the world much too quickly and do not give space for the creation and freedom out of which real encounters are born.

Ignorance and Arrogance:
the Cause of Seperation

When you reconnect with the divine source within you, it is quite possible that you will have to occasionally act against the rules and rituals of your community. All habits and rules need the continual creative spirit of renewal. Creation might want you to act for something you love against the spirit of a whole group, even a whole country, as something completely new and so far unseen by the others germinates within you.

Out of trust you will hear and respect the voice of the others. You will not just place yourself above them, but will remain faithful to what you love. Through this, processes of transformation are initiated. Whoever truly loves will take care that others will also see and love what he or she loves. This path always leads into community.

It is even possible that you will rise up against the laws of Creation. When you also remain connected at these points and let the whole of Creation look through your eyes, this can be an essential contribution to the processes of transformation in Creation. You should also not forget here that it is the Goddess herself who wants to transform through you and your insights. The pain of separation is not yet in this process. It only starts when you put yourself above others. Only when you become deaf to the voice of the world and your own heart, only when you become lost in the process of enmity, when you no longer respect the laws of Creation and only when desire can disconnect you from yourself, does the misery of amnesia begin. This is why they say "Love is blind". You look outside for what you have forgotten or betrayed inside yourself. You will encounter an unknown man or a lover in a different way when you trust that an answer from the world and the Goddess comes to you instead of following despair in the belief that your longing cannot be fulfilled. Out of despair you will run after women or men and still be led again and again to the same point of pain in your soul. In trust, you will dare more courageous things. Connected to the Goddess, you act out of certainty of your path, just as if fulfilment is already with you. Even if your body is seized by desire and shivering with arousal, you will not leave your inner centre. You invite the Goddess to see through your eyes and to feel with your heart. Already this decision provides you with the protection you need. You will listen to the voice of your heart and you will know whether you have to act or not.

Do not believe that this is always easy and rosy. Nobody has said that it is always easy to find inner fulfilment. If we do not learn to act from connection even in difficult situations, we will destroy ourselves and the Earth.

Arrogance and ignorance are the elements which separate us from Creation. In connection, we will do everything that we do in front of the eyes of the Goddess. No part of us belongs to us. Everything that you are, no matter how beautiful, intelligent or rich you are, comes from the Goddess and will only experience healing through Her. Unfortunately, those who have received many gifts forget this connection particularly often and run into the trap of self-inflation and egomania. This is how intelligence often creates the pain of loneliness, as you consider yourself superior to others and separate from them. This is how beauty creates the pain of narcissism, as you are no longer able to perceive and love the beauty of others which often resides in the seemingly ugly aspects of life. This is how outer wealth creates sickness in your own soul as you have forgotten to live simply and to listen to the voice of nature. You no longer know the true wealth of life itself.

But too many have fallen into these traps. Now we are facing a time of awakening. Those who gain insight will direct their actions towards service for the world. In this connection they will naturally act out of compassion. This has nothing to do with renunciation. You will also no longer act like this because others have told you to do so, but out of your own insight. Those who gain insights will unfold all of their talents for the well-being of all and from this source comes their true wealth. No moral appeals and no warnings of others will be able to lead you back to this connection. They can trigger your development.

But in the end it is always one's own decision. Many people have to go through a long process of experience before they find this insight. There is no other way to find fulfilment in sexuality and love. Only those who understand that the power which is flowing in connection is more comprehensive, more healing and more powerful, will once again walk this path.

THE THEOLOGY OF DECISION

I myself was often searching and feeling powerless. That is why I know that this helplessness only arises from the thought of separation.

Connected to the Goddess, you will never feel helpless.

The koan here is that you cannot find God or Goddess outside of yourself. You will only find them on the outside after you have made the full inner decision. The divine will only enlighten your outer life when you have also found it on the inside. And you will only find it inside when you have decided for it. This is the great koan for all atheists.

This process needs high awareness. The divine source is always in the present. Fear always extends into our lives from a past which we have not yet mastered and from a projected future. When I am fully in the present I am protected from fear.

This is a big secret, but actually a very obvious secret. You feel the connection to the source by the joy that the messages you receive create in you. Joy, security and awareness. A deep opening is created in your cellular system when the thought arises that you are allowed to feel completely secure in this world. The mere fact that this thought can trigger so much beauty already leads to the inner duty to act accordingly.

This thought will turn you into a revolutionary in love wherever you are. The divine voice lives that deeply within you. This is ever again anew the great revelation, decision and freedom. It is your decision whether you allow it.

Peace-information on this Earth can spread when you follow it fully. It can be downloaded in every moment. It exists in parallel with war, destruction and decline. The more people who understand this connection, the more comprehensively and unerringly this truth can manifest and become effective. When it is fully manifested in a community it will take effect as a field and will attract all further necessary information.

LEAVE FEAR – IT IS A DECISION

You will continually ask: And how do we leave fear? And how do we receive the power which can create peace on Earth?

And you will continually receive the answer. It is a decision to walk the path of trust and through that also enable others to walk this path. Leave fear. Fear has to disappear from the Earth. Stay with fearlessness. Every day. Hour by hour. By studying ever more deeply how this becomes possible, you will ever more deeply understand the laws of the universe. Peace is a question of balancing energies. Rediscover the core of the thoughts which create fear in you and in others and transform them into thoughts which generate trust. This is a historic deed which creates new realities. It leads to a new direction in love. This leads to a new direction in community and, in the end, in religion. This is the task of the culture-creating field building at this time. Through comprehensive and existential studies, the answers will come to you. On this path, fulfilment in partnership, in community and in anonymous encounters can be rediscovered. You will discover that they all belong together and cannot be lived separately from each other. In connection, they all shine in a completely different light. As life is a chain of decisions, it makes sense to take the deepest of all decisions at a certain point. It is a basic decision. Once it is taken, you no longer need so much power for the other decisions, as they are no longer blocked by fear. All this does not happen from one's own power, but is a consequence of the basic decision. The basic decision is trust. Walk the path of trust. Leave fear. It seems to be the deepest, most basic and most urgent decision which is needed.

Decisions are never arbitrary. They always take place in the interaction between the self and the world. Decisions can never be taken alone. They are an interaction between the whole and the individual and gain their healing power through this contact.

When one sometimes does not know how to continue, the only answer from the universe is: Wait until the power has fully formed in you. Stop wasting energy on the gaps. Wait until you know what needs to be done. In the end, everything is a secret of energy. Learn how to deal with energy in the right way. You can listen to every detail of the world. You always find the whole in it and you will always receive an answer. Concentration is an important element here.

One of the first steps of the universal school is to gain the power of calmness now for your long path. A huge healing power comes from calmness. Calmness contains a high power in magic. Learn to see, walk, ask and understand at your own pace. In this process, the universe will give you those encounters which carry the power of insight and healing within them. When you are in this state, everything is very simple and clear. You know that you are walking at the right pace when you are on the path of inner resonance.

These answers were carried by a clear and decisive power. I needed a whole day to digest them. To manifest them, I might need a whole lifetime.

It was at the same time the conclusion of my journey. Equipped with new power and hope, with even deeper decisiveness and newly gained knowledge, I travelled back to Tamera.

WORDS OF THE PRIESTESS OF MALTA TO TODAY'S MAN

I wrote this text some time after my journey to Malta. The pain in love of a man had profoundly touched me. I connected deeply with the school of love on Malta and with its priestess. The answer which came is an answer for all men.

Sleeps a song in things abounding
That keep dreaming to be heard:
Earth's tunes will start resounding
If you find the magic word.
Joseph von Eichendorff

The pain which gathers in your soul is the pain of all men, who lost their mother too soon. All loving sons experienced this pain as all mothers were oppressed into inner slavery. Your soul thirsts with a great longing to be the lover and liberator of the mother. A secret seduction and sweet promise of the un-redeemed mother calls within you. It was her heavenly sweetness which called you to this planet. But when you arrived on Earth the circumstances quickly changed and became confused. You soon felt it: a part of her was absent, wrapped in silent grief. She was always gone. Unreachable, hidden behind a thousand veils, she always evoked in you a memory of an unfulfilled promise calling for fulfilment. Early on, this made your soul delirious with longing and desire. An early pain marked your growth as a man.

You were never able to truly arrive with your mother. You only experienced a mother who was a slave of a husband, who had to hide the loving heart she had for you from the jealous observation of her master. Not only her husband was her master; the whole of society was her master, her tyrant, the yoke on her loving soul. In this way, the sweet and holy sensual fairy you adored transformed over centuries into an overbearing hissing

248

beast-mother who lured and threatened you, who demanded your strength and yet from early on dominated you with her frustration. Here was the woman who sensually enticed you and yet rejected you when you followed her enticement. And here was the beast who punished you when your soul raged with anger and disappointment. Suddenly you met rejection where you had originally wanted to love. You find an enslaved mother although you had originally been called by a free soul.

At the same time you are the secret object of her longing, her craving and her desires. You are her secret lover, her knight, her prince who shall free her from the claws of a boring tyrant and monster: the husband who has not been able to fulfil her longings. In her silent, frustrated arrogance and disrespect towards him you sense the disrespect of the entire female gender towards men. Your young child's soul also senses this: father failed, and with him the entire male gender. Now it is you who she hopes will return to her the sweetness and vitality of life which she had lost for so long. She hopes that you will develop the strength, beauty and fineness to return her to a free land of sensual beauty and love. Sometimes the full joy and hope shine in her gaze for which you would do anything.

You read in her eyes: perhaps you are able to accomplish what the father could not, to lead me back to my true beauty as a loving being, to my wildness and playfulness. Maybe you will be able to reawaken my original female song, make my heart feel again and my body pulse again by liberating in me the lover who I actually am.

It is the secret desperate love between mother and son which lays itself like a ring around your heart and which causes this huge pain and despair in you. This ring lies around the hearts of millions of men and has made them become steely warriors, soldiers and heroes, scientists, salesmen and office workers instead of becoming lovers and caretakers of all creatures.

Know that the whole world is calling for a new step in love at exactly those points where your heart most wants to give up *hope. Your heart will heal when you support the liberation of the lover in every mother. It is still your mother who separates you from your lover today. The core of all your desperation and reactions in love is an underlying thought which you consciously or unconsciously follow: mummy is only there for daddy. When I really need her she has no time. This deep childhood experience of original pain is carried over unconsciously to all your subsequent love relationships and you unconsciously repeat the same cycle again and again. Jealousy sets in as soon as your lover even looks at another. So many of your attempts to love had to fail at the same point. When you were with a lover you were always seeking the lost love of the mother. And while you were seeking this lost love in your lover and wanted to fully arrive, an unredeemed longing heart was burning within her. An unanswered longing was burning in her; a longing for a strong man who does not ask but simply understands how to take her. While you were becoming needy, she yearned for the redeemer who does not waste time with questions but rather acts, who does not demand but rather stills her desires. This drama repeats itself in all your love relationships.*

It is your mother from whom you run away when you run away from your lover. You are crying for the lost mother when you believe that you have lost your lover. When the jealous lover awakens in you, fighting against the overpowering father, it is because you want to hold on to the mother. And when your lover seems to withdraw in the face of your longing and your wish for her protection and the security her power gives you, she is longing for a strong man and redeemer, protector and lover in one.

The pain you feel is a historical pain. Even when it feels to you so personal, so irresolvable, and so individual, the whole world is in pain and calling for a solution. All sons have experienced this pain as the soul of the mother and the loving woman has been driven out of your culture and your inner world. Although

250

the loving heart of the son-man originally wanted to exalt and honour the woman, she has been humiliated and vilified. And though the young son wanted to awaken in the physical contact with her, all sensuality and all sexuality had been banned from her life as dirty and debauched. The beautiful figure of the mother was thereby transformed into something diabolic and demonic. While the son experienced his awakening as a man at her breast, she changed into a threatening, rejecting and devouring monster. Because she herself was damned for her sexual nature she now rejects everything which reminds her of this.

At the same time her desire is infinite and is burning uncontrollably, but she is not allowed to show it to anyone. The young son feels its overwhelming power which he will never be able to satisfy. He feels the silent forbidden pact with the mother which nobody may discover, and he suffers under his burden. An unbreakable chain develops between mother and son. Through her silent suffering and her unfulfilled longing, she binds her son to herself. He remains forever bound to her through an unconscious feeling of guilt, inadequacy and a secret love which has never been fulfilled. He begins to mimic the adult, the lover, the potent man which he is not yet, in order to stand his ground in her eyes.

He originally wanted the father to be his friend and companion on his path of sensual awakening. Yet through the unspoken pact between mother and son, the father long ago became his rival in love, a dominating enemy who threatens the mother and against whom he is no match. The father had all the power, he was the only one to whom the mother willingly submitted; she belonged to him and at the same time suffered because of him. Whoever wanted to win the mother would have to defeat the father. As a young son you just could not know that the father had also originally been an unredeemed son-man who had had to overthrow the mother as he had not been able to cope with her sensual desire. This is how he took on the possessive father archetype.

What decision should a son make in such a situation? It seems hopeless if one remains on the level of the problem. If he identifies with the father, the mother becomes a dangerous dragon who must be defeated. If he identifies with the young mother who wants to be liberated, he must fight against the father.

Within the love-system from which you come there is no other solution. You have to leave the whole system if you want healing. An error in love lies behind all these personal destinies. The soft feminine sexual power was banished from history and is painfully missed by everyone. How many sons have already rebelled against their fathers and yet have finally transformed into them? How many fathers have had to step down from their thrones and finally reveal themselves to be unredeemed sons?

We have come to know the male archetypes of magician, priest, warrior, king, father and teacher. What still remains is the female longing for the man who knows love, who no longer rapes the female sources and the mysteries of sexual love. Every mother is eternally calling for the man who recognises her, including sexually in her female nature, and supports her. The archetype of the sensual lover is still waiting to be born.

Was it necessary for men to conquer the land and take possession of knowledge? Did the priests have to demonise the female source? Did they have to suppress the knowledge of the body and of plants, of birth and death? Was it necessary to destroy the key, held by woman, that man himself needed for life? Did men have to vilify the woman, to torture and persecute her to release his male power? Trapped in the position of son-men, they did all this because they could no longer find the way to the source. In this way they inflicted the pain in love on themselves and the world, and from this you still suffer today. It was the wrong level of liberation.

What is it that remains after you have made this long procession through changing times and different levels of civilisation? With each piece of land the male warrior conquered he killed a part of the Goddess and Her culture. Just as he wanted to possess the woman he wanted to possess and rule over the Goddess; but on this path he lost Her ever more. Your fear of loss reflects the historical fact that the man lost the Goddess. The more you conquer and the more you want to possess, the more you will lose Her. Take care now that a new path will be discovered.

Do not direct your anger against your fathers any longer; nor against all the men who represent the father. And do not direct it against the woman who appears to have left you. Direct it against a whole culture that made it impossible to love women. Apply your warrior-knowledge and your intelligence to this task. Use your anger to find the will towards insight which is able to defeat and transform this dragon of a culture. A whole male culture dies through symbolic patricide, a culture which suppressed women and thereby changed them into the evil, all-consuming monster.

Know that actually it is not your mother but ME the Goddess, the female aspect of the lover, for whom all men are longing.

When you rediscover my radiance, when you bring it back into human culture, you will be liberated. You have lost the Goddess and you must find Her again. She can accompany you on your path in love, to still your great longing. She knows what is good for you, and at which time, and She will guide you. To do this, She needs your full trust. When you have rediscovered your home in Her, you will be able to rediscover it in all women. She is able to still your longing, deepen your calmness and to give you the knowledge you need as a lover. She cannot be repressed and She will be liberated by each loving surrender. Find your original human trust through your love of nature, the world and its sensual beauty, and you are part of the historic birth of the new man.

You will say: Why should I look for comfort in religion when I haven't found what I was looking for in any woman? Why should I believe in a Goddess? Isn't this a new philosophy of comfort? Religions have always pushed the fulfilment of our longings into life after death, as we could not fulfil them here. Here you are confusing the patriarchal religions with the sacred source of life.

The Goddess is elementary, utterly worldly. She is not religion. She is life itself. You will find Her in every woman when you look for Her. But through your trust in Her, your contact to all women changes. She gives you home and security and with that, self-acceptance wherever you are. You start to give where previously you demanded. The sting of jealousy can heal when you take responsibility for your spiritual longing, when you no longer banish the sacred from your lives, and when you go to the universal source, which provides power and healing. Only in this state of connection will you experience the truly loving state that you lost. It was not until the mothers in their infinite helplessness bound you to them that you lost this source. Every child knows original trust. It is not connected to any other person.

Healing starts with insight. When you learn to see and accept the personal and historical backgrounds, you have made the first step towards healing. When you reconnect with the Goddess you come into contact with your "Higher Self" which despite all traumas, fears and hardships, is still with you, and which has to slowly become visible again. You can also call it the inner base of God and Creation inside us. There is a universal centre of consciousness in each human being, which carries tremendous accessible knowledge. You need no religion and no specific world-view to believe this.

You ask how this works, how you create contact with the Goddess. Use your power to reconquer those areas of your perception where all judgement becomes silent. Use your will to know. The first step is to want to learn. Learn to be so present and aware that you can be a witness for everything that happens in you and around you. If you want to understand the world you first have to become a witness of your impact. Give up your secret male arrogance, which was meant to protect you from love, and learn that all life has a soul and therefore a meaning. Whoever can reconquer this space enters a spiritual school of life where there are hardly any teachers or therapists. Creation itself will become your teacher. It is highly personal, gracious, physical, elementary and eternal. This school leads to astounding consequences. It forces you to choose the higher frequency and to transform your needy longing into the power of the new warrior and lover who actively discovers the new continent in love.

The new men are able to love women. The new lover is deeply sensual and consciously sensitive of the world in all its radiance. The new lover knows that there is a connected sacred life. He can feel how it is to be a bee, rat, toad, spider or a lichen on a tree. He knows that we do live in a holographic universe. Reflection no longer happens out of separation and division but out of compassion. Manliness no longer means toughness but decisive participation in the whole. With this a new level of insight and perception is reached. Whoever has found the way to the power of the lover instinctively perceives in harmony with the world and the things around him, instead of strengthening his power against them. He senses the hunger and the joy, the sorrow and the happiness of the world of plants, the world of animals and the human world. He takes on the responsibility of the gentle lover and supporter of the birth process of all that is awakening. A new level of insight unfolds as the birth of the new lover is rooted in compassion.

And now a last resistance will rear up in you. You will angrily ask: And the women? Do they know that it is up to them whether or not a new power struggle will arise? As long as fulfilment in love to women is not found, all brotherhoods, all orders and all philosophical schools will continue to spread a comforting theory rather than a new loving everyday reality. As long as women are as they are in love, men are my natural rivals. Why have women put themselves under the sword of male domination for so long? I can see in women that they want to be slaves, that they seek and desire the strong conqueror. Weren't women the mothers of the men that later dominated women? Aren't they therefore also responsible that a new type of man and a new picture of male life will arise? Didn't they try to fight against male domination using the same domination? Didn't they try to destroy our power by luring us into their impenetrable web? They blame us men for being men and for wanting them sexually. They no longer know the spectrum of their own female nature and they refuse to take on responsibility for their beauty, their erotic seductiveness and their natural female power. How can I ever find the trust in women that is necessary to understand their being? An infinite rage separates me from every woman.

Stop directing your anger towards individual women. Women submitted willingly because they no longer wanted to wait for the lover to awaken in the man. Gather your courage to connect to your highest source of insight. Wait no longer for the woman, but give your support to those women who struggle for new love and a new solidarity with men. Know that resistance comes up before each new step of development. It is an education for your willpower. Use this resistance decisively in a new way. Eventually you will learn to use your anger to change the world.

When women and men see through their power struggles, when they no longer wait for each other but see that they are part of one whole, when they recognise that they find their self-confidence within themselves and not within the other, then maybe the birth of insight can start: they recognise each other, a man and a woman, and a wonderful path of sensual love can begin, a path of love which is no longer bound to conditions. Love without jealousy, sexuality without fear, anticipation without secret fears of impotence, a faithfulness which does not break down at the first affair, enduring love and a new path towards partnership. These are roughly the issues you will solve together with others as a representative of all.

Through the Goddess you will connect with the solution and not with the problem. You know that the ring around your heart can only open when you are seen and recognised as you are. You will fight everything which holds you back from love. You will tackle your own inner dragon, even when it seems to be insurmountable, like a too-small penis, a skinny physique, or whatever it is. You know that in the state of connectedness there is a solution to everything and that the first step towards the solution is to decisively step out of despair and out of secrecy.

Stop breaking-up and falling in love again and again, and continually repeating the whole drama with the next one. You fall back into marriage-like roles. Whether you are married or not, as soon as the theme of love in a couple arises, the struggle with roles starts. You automatically become your fathers. You start to destroy what you loved in your girlfriend: her beauty, power and strength, by wanting to domesticate and define her. You forget the dreams and fairy tales which fired your own youth.

Find your warrior power in a higher goal now. You do not own the dreams and longings of your lover, and you will never own them. They are as changeable and flexible as the Goddess Herself and cannot be tied down. Use your power and your own development to understand the cosmic dreams of the other gender, the dreams of the Goddess, and then to fulfil them with the help of the Goddess. All contact, sexual and also geistig, is dependent on whether or not we know and accept.

You will reach healing faster if you actively seek out new love-communities which provide conditions under which this traumatic situation of the child no longer has to arise. You will not make it without looking for forms of community in which you have a chance to solve your love issue. These forms of community do not arise naturally without your efforts. You will need your full commitment and a strong decision to create them. Things will become more sober on your new path, but also more fulfilling. You will take care that love is no longer a private matter. Instead you will become a lover for all women who take part in the destiny of the world and the destiny of the Goddess. The friends you need and who need you will come to you on this path. Rediscover that your destiny is full of such gifts. Your heart will come to peace when you have rediscovered Me in all women.

Some Remarks about Names, Places and Symbols

Some of the names and symbols in the messages I received, I later found in similar forms in the literature. I give some of the information from these sources in this chapter. The main references I used are indicated. The various temples and sacred sites are described under the heading 'Temple Sites'.

Names

Eve and Lilith

The Hebrew name 'Eve' means 'Mother of all that lives'. Originally she was the goddess from whom everything was born. But the writers of biblical history wanted to suppress this myth and its influence, and therefore made Eve into a creation of God in their story. The societal conditions in Israel, in which the woman was subjugated to the man, are legitimised through the concept of original sin.

Internal contradictions arise in this creation myth because there is not only the story of Adam and Eve in the first book of the Bible, but also a second, in which God creates man and woman in his own image. This discrepancy is solved in the Talmud, through a Jewish myth which says that the woman of the first creation myth is identified as Lilith. Lilith is Adam's first wife, long before he had Eve. This first woman, according to this story, refused to take the position beneath Adam during the sexual act. Her argument was that she had been created in the same way as him and was therefore no less worthy than him. She was not willing to submit to the man. Three angels of the lord, responding to Adam's complaint, were not able to make her return. So God created a better wife for Adam, Eve.[12]

Nammu

Sumerian Creator-Goddess, before the introduction of male gods. In numerous creation myths of ancient times, we find Nammu described as the Goddess, Mother and Source. In the Americas, she wears a skirt of snakes, which is interesting as the snake is also a manifestation of the Goddess in Europe, Asia and the Middle-East. In a cuneiform text from the second millennium before Christ, she is mentioned as a Sumerian Goddess who gives birth to heaven and Earth, in the ideogram with the meaning 'ocean'.[5]

Manu

The motive of the ark appears in Indian mythology. Manu is the first human being. He saves a little fish from being eaten by a bigger fish. To thank him, the fish – who has now become very large – warns him of an imminent cosmic flood and shows him how to build a ship and fill it with the 'seeds of all things'. The giant fish then steers the loaded ship to safety. This is how new life was able to develop after the great flood.

Paul

In the parish church of Rabat, built 1741–43, there is a golden relic in the form of an arm. It is said to enclose an arm of Paul the Apostle. An accompanying illustration shows Paul throwing a snake into the sea, liberating Malta from these reptiles (snake as representation of the female!) To the right of the entrance to the church, stairs lead down to the Cave of Saint Paul, in which the apostle is said to have lived during his time on Malta.[26]

Paul was supposedly shipwrecked off the coast of Malta in 56 AD (Acts, 28.1), was rescued and then founded a Christian community on Malta.[11]

Most of the temple sites were built between the middle of the fourth millennium and the middle of the third millennium before Christ. Different books give different dates. The oldest temple ruins, close to Mgarr and Zebbieh, seem to originate from the Skorba era around 4000 BC. The youngest seems to be Tarxien, which already shows signs of cultural change and decline. It was built between 3000 and 2500 BC. "One could see in the Maltese sanctuaries, sites of a prehistoric mystery cult which, like the later sites of antiquity, promised immortality, sacred places of hope and belonging."[18] Many small female goddess-figurines have been found, including the famous Sleeping Priestess found in the Hypogeum. The frequent appearance of phallic stone pillars leads to the assumption that the male principle was also venerated in addition to the Great Mother. These pillars are often interpreted as a symbol of a procreating male god, partner of the Great Mother. There are absolutely no images of male figures. Only when Tarxien was built do the first images reminiscent of the Mesopotamian praying figures start to appear. One can hardly determine their gender, but they are often interpreted as priest figures.

The end of the Maltese culture remains as mysterious as its beginning. Around the middle of the third millennium BC, the islands were suddenly abandoned. The temple-culture on Malta ceased to exist. There are only conjectures about the cause. Were the inhabitants forced to leave the island by a famine? An epidemic? Or did they escape from an attack from the sea? It is clear that there are no signs of fighting. It is also clear that the archipelago remained uninhabited for centuries. New settlers of unknown origin appeared around 2000 BC, bringing weapons made of bronze to Malta for the first time. The temples of Malta may have been part of a highly developed, possibly globally connected, archaic culture. Malta was probably one centre in a wide spiritual network. Lines seem to spread from the Maltese archipelago in all directions, connected with a cult that honoured the Great Goddess, and connected with a corresponding matriarchal society.

Now some remarks about individual temples:

Ggantija

The era of the giant Maltese temples started around 3600 BC with the southern temple of the double temple site Ggantija on the high plateau of Gozo. It is clearly visible that it was planned from the very beginning as a colossal construction, as the focal point of an area encompassing at least three smaller temples and the mysterious Brochtorff stone circle.[18]

Hagar Qim and Mnajdra

The first temple of Ggantija had already been erected on Gozo when a new religious centre was created on the steep southern coast of Malta. It was a sacred area within which several important sacred sites developed within a few centuries.

In a dip in the land at the edge of rocky cliffs lie the ruins of the three temples of Mnajdra. A little higher up is Hagar Qim.

Opinions vary on their date of erection. It is said that the oldest part of Mnajdra originates from the second half of the fourth millennium BC. But assumptions on these dates are continually being revised deeper into the past. It is generally assumed that the temples were used as oracle sites. "The appearance of Hagar Qim, whose name means 'Stones of Prayer', is still breathtaking today. In front of the altar lay five female figurines. Only the right apse remains from the second transept, which probably served as a place to consult the oracle. A ring of small tablets changed the room into the inner – or magic – circle in which one awaited the messages of the deities..."[18]

Mnajdra, whose fissured walls rise from the empty hard stony landscape against the infinite background of ocean and sky, has maintained its aura of a location of ancient mystic experience more than any of the other overground sacred sites. The lower temple was definitely the most important.[18]

The Hypogeum – Sanatorium in the Lap of the Earth
The subterranean Hypogeum on Malta is unique in megalithic culture. The round cupola halls, with their apsides, are carved into stone underground. Its layout is reminiscent, like the overground temples, of the female body. The ceiling and the walls of the cupola halls are covered with patterns of spiral and circular forms, in ritual red. Votive offerings in the wide round rooms, and the figurines in unusual positions, indicate that the Hypogeum was a sanctuary inside the earth. The famous sleeping lady, probably a priestess in sacred oracle-sleep, was found here. At this time it was usual that all images and figures of gods and humans were very small. The sleeping priestess is, despite her voluminous body, only 14 cm high. In the Hypogeum we also find signs of the tree of life as a mural.[21]

Mgarr
The temple close to Mgarr is called Ta' Hagrat. It was excavated between 1925 and 1927. Mgarr lies about 15 kilometres west of Valletta. The ruins consist of two groups of buildings, the larger of which has a trefoil form. Ta' Hagrat and the nearby Zebbieh temple are the oldest on the island, and they must surely be connected with each other.[25]

Brochtorff Circle
Three hundred metres southwest of the ruins of Ggantija lies the recently rediscovered prehistoric Brochtorff Circle, a megalithic stone circle about 45 metres in diameter. It was drawn for the first time by Jean Houel in 1770. Today one can only find three megaliths, integrated into walls surrounding farmers' fields. It was excavated in 1820, at which time Charles de Brochtorff painted it in watercolours. Some time

263

later a farmer cleared the site, breaking most of the megaliths to build a farmhouse nearby. Only in 1965 was the Brochtorff Circle rediscovered.

Tarxien

The ruins of Tarxien are in better condition than many others. They were discovered and excavated between 1914 and 1920. The temples are amongst the youngest on Malta, erected between 3000 and 2500 BC. Signs at the site of Tarxien can be interpreted as indicative of a new movement of theocratic priests, which later came to dominate and ended the highly developed culture of Malta. Indistinct traces hint of a connection with the Middle-East.[18][25]

Zebbieh

Together with the ruins of Mgarr, one of the oldest temple sites, dating from around 4000 BC, the Skorba era. All that remains are a few standing megaliths. Evidence of three circular sites has been discovered. Zebbieh is not far from Mgarr.

ANIMAL SYMBOLISM

The Fish

The fish, as water-being and a symbol of the Great Unconscious and the female yoni, was a globally recognised symbol of the Great Mother. The symbol of the fish is found in many ancient cultures, including the Minoan culture on Crete, where it was frequently used. The Chinese Great Mother Kwan-Yin (Yoni of all yonis) has often been depicted as a fish-goddess. In ancient Greek, 'fish' and 'womb' were synonyms. Both were called *delphos*. The oracle of Delphi originally belonged to the fish-goddess.

The Celts believed that eating fish could plant new life in the womb of the mother. The fish symbol of the yonic goddess was revered throughout the Roman empire, and was therefore emphatically adopted by the Christian authorities, after a thorough revision of the traditional myths to completely remove the significance of the female gender. Some Christians say that the fish represents Christ as the Greek word for fish – *ichthys* – was an acronym for 'Jesus Christ, son of God, the saviour'.

The Snake

The ancient world honoured women and snakes above all. In Egypt, just as in India, the snake was a totem form of the Great Mother herself. Egypt's archaic Mother of Creation was a snake. The Egyptian uraeus snake was a hieroglyph for 'Goddess'. In Palestine the snake was worshipped long before the Yahweh cult appeared. In many Gnostic writings, the Snake of Paradise is praised, as she brought humankind the 'light' of knowledge against the wishes of a tyrannical god who wanted to keep humankind in ignorance. In one Gnostic gospel it is said that the female principle of spirituality came from the snake, the preceptor, who taught them, "You will not die. He only said it because of jealousy. On the contrary, your eyes will be opened and you will become like the gods able to distinguish between good and evil."[22]

FURTHER TERMS

Art in the Ancient Times

One significant difference from art in later eras is that art in the Neolithic Era did not show any images of armed power, cruelty or domination. There are no images of 'noble warriors' or battle scenes, no heroic conquerors putting prisoners in chains, or any other signs of slavery.[5]

The Labyrinth

The mystical significance behind the design of a labyrinth was a journey into the world beyond, and the return to this world, comparable with the cyclical journeys of the divine king into death and rebirth. Early pictures of the labyrinth, for example on coins or in caves and tombs, referred to the womb of the Earth. The classic labyrinth was not a maze. It was an intricate path which led through the whole labyrinth. Labyrinths almost always had some connection with a cave. [21]

The Cycle of the Moon, and Sacred Springs

The ancients knew that some springs and certain stones can regenerate and revitalise animals and people if one drinks from them or touches them in certain ways and at certain times. Sacred springs and sacred stones seem to contain and radiate a power which waxes and wanes periodically. The phases of the moon are part of a great cosmic dance, of which everything is part: the movement of the stars, the pulse of the tides, the circulation of blood. Observation of the night sky, the stars and particularly the moon was the origin of mathematics and the natural sciences.[22]

Spirals

Since the Ice Age, the spiral has been a symbol of eternal female life-creating power. It can be found on Neolithic clay vessels and on the sacred female figurines.

Spirals have a sacred place amongst sacred signs in the Neolithic culture in the temples of the Great Goddess. For example, the twin spirals on thresholds and corridors in Tarxien Temple on Malta which are often misinterpreted as punishing eyes of the Goddess. Clusters of spirals symbolise the eternal power of life even more impressively.[12]

In the magazine *Emotion* no. 10, 1992, I found some further interesting references to the spiral. According to Wilhelm Reich, the spiral is one of the most important forms of movement of orgone energy. The spiral is a fundamental form of nature and a basic form of movement for processes of materialisation (and I want to add, when reversed, for processes of dematerialisation). Research into ancient cultures indicates that the spiral had not only an aesthetic meaning, but was an expression of knowledge already reaching far into the past – knowledge of the cosmic energy of life. "So the possibility exists that in this ancient Stone-Age image of the double spiral, they meant the 'normally' imperceptible spiral movement which stands at the beginning of every creation process in the ocean of life energy."[27] In this context, the incised pattern of dots found on some temple walls on Malta becomes interesting. They are strikingly reminiscent of orgonotic particles in sunny air and can be interpreted as a picture of cosmic life energy. [27]

REFERENCES

1. Heide Göttner-Abendroth: *Societies of Peace: Matriarchies Past Present and Future.* Toronto 2009

2. Karl-Heinz Deschner: *Das Kreuz mit der Kirche. Eine Sexualgeschichte des Christentums.* Düsseldorf, Wien 1974

3. Dieter Duhm: *Eros Unredeemed.* Belzig 2010

4. Dieter Duhm: *The Sacred Matrix. From the Matrix of Violence to the Matrix of Life.* Wiesenburg 2005
(See page 349 for the *Tamera Manifesto*)

5. Riane Eisler: *The Chalice and the Blade: Our History, Our Future.* San Francisco 1988

6. Eluan Ghazal: *Schlangenkult und Tempelliebe. Sakrale Erotik in archaischen Gesellschaften.* Berlin 1995

7. Marija Gimbutas: *The Language of the Goddess.* San Francisco 1995

8. Marija Gimbutas: *The Civilization of the Goddess.* Berkeley 1982

9. Elisabeth Gould-Davis: *The First Sex.* London, 1972

10. Herbert Gottschalk: *Lexikon der Mythologie.* Berlin 1993

11. *Konstanzer Kleines Bibellexikon.* Konstanz 1962

12. Annette Kuhn (Hrsg.): *Die Chronik der Frauen.* Dortmund 1992

13. **Michael Ladwein.** *Chartres. Ein Führer durch die Kathedrale.* Stuttgart 1998

14. **Sabine Lichtenfels:** *Traumsteine. Reise in das Zeitalter der sinnlichen Erfüllung.* München 2000

15. **Sabine Lichtenfels:** *Weiche Macht. Perspektiven eines neuen Frauenbewusstsein und eine neue Liebe zu den Männern.* Belzig 1995

16. **Sabine Lichtenfels:** *The Story of Manu and Meret.* Study Text. Available from Verlag Meiga

17. **Norbert Muigg:** *Sprache des Herzens. Begegnungen mit Weisen der Maya.* Wien 1999

18. **Sigrid Neubert:** *Die Tempel von Malta. Das Mysterium der Megalithenbauten.* Bergisch Gladbach 1988

19. **G. Riemann (Hrsg.):** *I-Ging. Das Orakel und Weisheitsbuch Chinas.* München 1994

20. **Alfons Rosenberg:** *Christliche Bildmeditation.* München 1991

21. **Barbara G. Walker:** *The Woman's Encyclopedia of Myths and Secrets.* San Francisco 1983

22. **Monica Sjöö, Barbara Mohr:** *Wiederkehr der Göttin.* Braunschweig 1985

23. **Dhyani Ywahoo.** *Am Feuer der Weisheit. Lehren der Cherokee Indianer.* Zürich, München 1993

24. **Hans-Joachim Zillmer:** *Darwin's Mistake.* Kempton 2003

25. *Die prähistorischen Tempel von Malta und Gozo. Eine Beschreibung von Prof. Sir Themistocks Zammit.* 1995

26. *Malta. dtv Merian Reiseführer.* München 1997

27. *Zeitschriftenreihe Emotion. Beiträge zum Werk von Wilhelm Reich, Nr. 10.* Berlin 1992

PROJECTS OF SABINE LICHTENFELS

Tamera Peace Research Village, Portugal

Sabine Lichtenfels is co-founder of the Tamera Healing Biotope in Portugal. The aim of the project is to build a self-sufficient model of a future society where violence, fear, hatred and jealousy are structurally replaced by trust, solidarity and global compassion.

www.tamera.org

Spiritual Economy – Humanisation of Money

For many years Sabine Lichtenfels has stood for the "Humanisation of Money" under the motto of "A peace village instead of a tank". She founded the GRACE Foundation to attract money for projects such as the Global Campus, an initiative which supports and connects peace projects worldwide.

www.the-grace-foundation.org

Global GRACE Day

Each year on the 9th of November – the anniversary of the Nazi "Kristallnacht" pogrom against Jews (1938) and the fall of the Berlin Wall (1989) – Sabine Lichtenfels calls for joining worldwide actions in the name of GRACE.

www.global-grace-day.com

International Peace Pilgrimages

For some years Sabine Lichtenfels has been leading each year several-week-long peace pilgrimages with several hundred international participants.

www.grace-pilgrimage.org

Spiritual Research and Litho-Puncture Circle – the "Prehistoric Utopia"

In cooperation with the geomantists Marko Pogačnik and Peter Frank, Sabine Lichtenfels has been building a stone-circle in Tamera: a complex and complete artwork that brings together the forces of human beings, nature and the cosmic powers, an acupuncture point for healing the Earth.

GRACE – School of Life

Sabine Lichtenfels is a role model for women who begin to say *yes!* to their sexual nature and to take on responsibility. Her school for a new women's awareness and a new love for men serves the development of female knowledge, truth in love and Eros and overcoming the battle of the sexes.

Ring of Power

Regularly, by email in English and German, Sabine Lichtenfels sends a meditation text and a greeting addressed to the growing network of peace workers: the Ring of Power. Whoever would like to participate is invited to write an email to:

ring-of-power@sabine-lichtenfels.com

To contact Sabine Lichtenfels:
GRACE Office
Secretariat Saskia Breithardt
Monte do Cerro
P-7630 Colos, Portugal
Phone: +351 283 635 484
Fax: +351 283 635 374
www.sabine-lichtenfels.com

Books By Sabine Lichtenfels

GRACE - Pilgrimage for a Future Without War

The story of a pilgrimage from Germany to Israel-Palestine. The author covers long stretches on foot without money. Her driving force is the decision to uncover and change those internal structures which externally lead to war and violence. Through this she discovers a strength which begins to shine ever clearer and brighter: "GRACE", the connection with Creation, empowers her to follow her inner voice more precisely and more forcefully than ever before.

ISBN 978-3-927266-23-0

Sources of Love and Peace - Morning Prayers

This book – prayer book and revolutionary text in one – contains 52 morning prayers. They are greeting words for a new revolutionary spirituality with the definite aim of supporting the transformation of both the human being and society. *Sources of Love and Peace* offers a precise proposal for how we can connect with God or the Goddess or whatever we want to call this source within us and outside of us, and from there take a stand for life.

"We have the real possibility to make a decision for peace, here and now. It is a decision for trust and against fear, for solidarity and against hatred."

ISBN 978-3-927266-11-7

CPSIA information can be obtained
at www.ICGtesting.com
Printed in the USA
BVHW082350080620
581027BV00003B/90

9 783927 266445

273